The Group Psychotherapist's Handbook

Personality, Psychopathology, and Psychotherapy: Theoretical and Clinical Perspectives

Henry Kellerman, *Series Editor*

Psychopathology and Differential Diagnosis: A Primer by Henry Kellerman and Anthony Burry
Volume One: *History of Psychopathology*
Volume Two: *Diagnostic Primer*

The Transference–Countertransference Matrix: The Emotional–Cognitive Dialogue in Psychotherapy, Psychoanalysis, and Supervision by Robert J. Marshall and Simone V. Marshall

An Interpersonal Approach to Child Therapy: The Treatment of Children and Adolescents from an Interpersonal Point of View by Stanley Spiegel

Theories of Object Relations: Bridges to Self Psychology by Howard A. Bacal and Kenneth M. Newman

THE GROUP PSYCHOTHERAPIST'S HANDBOOK

Contemporary Theory and Technique

Irwin L. Kutash, Ph.D.
Alexander Wolf, M.D.
Editors

COLUMBIA UNIVERSITY PRESS
NEW YORK

Columbia University Press

New York   Oxford

Copyright © 1990 Columbia University Press

All rights reserved

Library of Congress Cataloging-in-Publication Data

The group psychotherapist's handbook:
contemporary theory and technique
Irwin L. Kutash, Alexander Wolf, editors.

p.   cm.

(Personality, psychopathology, and psychotherapy)

Includes bibliographical references.

Includes indexes.

ISBN 0-231-06840-9

1. Group psychotherapy—Handbooks, manuals, etc.

I. Kutash, Irwin L.

II. Wolf, Alexander, 1907–   .

III. Series: Personality, psychopathology, and psychotherapy
(New York, N.Y.)

[DNLM: l. Psychotherapy, Group.   WM 430 G8829]

RC488.G6924   1990

616.89'14—dc20

DNLM/DLC

for Library of Congress

90-1839

CIP

Casebound editions of Columbia University Press books are
Smyth-sewn and printed on permanent and durable acid-free paper

Printed in the United States of America

c 10 9 8 7 6 5 4 3 2 1

To Irving Goldberg

A leading voice for psychoanalysis in groups
and co-author of *Beyond the Couch*
He lives in our minds and our hearts through
his legacy as a practitioner, speaker, author
and dear friend

Contents

Contents

Foreword

Clifford J. Sager, M.D.

At the annual American Group Psychotherapy Conference in 1957, the esteemed psychoanalytic theoretician, clinician, and teacher Lawrence Kubie seriously questioned the effectiveness of group therapy as a modality capable of making a significant and lasting impact on neurotic behavior. Using a closed psychoanalytic model of individual analysis of transference to the analyst, he reasoned that transference in the group would be diluted and could not be worked through analytically. Foulkes and Grotjahn, two pioneering group therapists, who were also classically trained psychoanalysts, ably refuted Kubie, pointing out the fallacy of arguing from the closed system of theoretical presumption that Kubie utilized. This debate was published in the *International Journal of Group Psychotherapy*: Kubie (1958). Foulkes' and Grotjahn's responses were published in the same issue along with Kubie's article. This article and its discussion dealt a blow to the invincibility of individual psychoanalysis to be the only really effective method of psychotherapy. *The Group Psychotherapist's Handbook* reflects the fruit of that thinking and indicates that group therapy has earned its place as a valuable and necessary modality that may be used to treat the entire spectrum of mental health disorders.

When I was in psychoanalytic training, Alexander Wolf, co-editor of this volume, was one of my control analysts (circa 1948). Fortunately, he was not controlling but opened new vistas for me. At that early date he was already pointing out the transference that group members have toward one another as well as to the group therapist and how these can be used in the group to further change.

Slavson, Wolf, and Moreno, the pioneers of group therapy in the United States, persisted in their work despite resistance shown by some of their colleagues. They and their students launched a therapeutic movement that slowly but steadily has led to the evolution of a modality that is now recognized as a leading primary as well as adjunctive method of treatment. Group therapy is now practiced in all general and most specialized psychiatric hospitals, mental health clinics, and by mental health professionals in private practice. It has been used for the treatment of nearly all conditions listed in all diagnostic nomenclatures.

The Group Psychotherapist's Handbook is a modest title for this book. It is a compendium of case histories with discussion by each therapist of his/her operational theoretical approach to their case. The relationship of each author's work to that of others in the book becomes clear. We can see when and how significant theoretical differences truly influence technique. Some papers will resonate to different aspects of each reader's theoretical and technique preferences. Other parts will open the door to a new vision, a new integration for each reader to make independently.

Irwin L. Kutash and Alexander Wolf are to be congratulated for developing this work and selecting such an outstanding and diverse group of authors and techniques. They have succeeded in providing readers with the data and tools they need for their own research, clinical work and to be able to arrive at their own synthesis. This volume demonstrates the depth and breadth of group therapy as it is practiced today. This much needed addition to the literature with its array of viewpoints, promotion of cross-pollination of ideas and communication among group therapists truly presents the coming of age of group psychotherapy.

Preface

Theories and schools, like microbes and corpuscles, de-
vour one another, and by their warfare ensure the con-
tinuity of life.

> Marcel Proust, *Remembrance of Things Past.*
> *Cities of Plain*, 1921.

The Group Psychotherapists's Handbook is intended to be a guide
to the theories and techniques of group psychotherapy most representative of those in use today. The value of this volume is that
this vast array of group therapies is accessible in one place, to be
examined, compared and learned from. As with an earlier volume
we edited, the *Psychotherapist's Casebook*, we proceeded from our
observation that psychotherapy practitioners often hold doggedly to
their own orientations without at times even knowing about or comparing them with others. We feel this is equally true, if not more
so, for group psychotherapy. This book is an attempt toward broad-
ening the group psychotherapist's knowledge of what is being done
by respected group therapists from other as well as their own schools
of thought. To make this of particular value and relevance, we have
asked all of our authors to provide annotated case histories that will
demonstrate the major group therapy approaches as they are ac-

tually practiced in group therapy sessions. We hope this volume will show group psychotherapists a variety of approaches and how they work, thereby stimulating us all to expand constricted ways of working with a group, increase evaluation of our own and others' techniques, and open our minds to appraisal of what is or is not effective in group therapy practice.

We have asked the authors to follow a loosely prescribed format in presenting the group therapy approaches described in this book. Theory and practice are presented in terms of how they translate into actual group therapy work. We asked each author to devote approximately 50 percent of his or her chapter to theory and technique and 50 percent to its translation into practice with an actual group. Each author was asked to preserve group and group members' anonymity, but to capture the essence in their descriptions.

We hope this book will be useful to group psychotherapists of every orientation and school of thought, whether they are psychologists, psychiatrists, social workers, counselors, nurse-practitioners, students, or teachers of group therapy.

This text should raise questions about group work, such as "Should group patients be matched to particular types of groups?" "Should groups be homogeneous or heterogeneous?" "Should groups be open- or closed-ended?" "Should groups attend to the individual dynamics of their members or to group-as-a-whole issues?" "Are there common curative factors across groups?" We hope the readers will come up with many more questions and find their answers, as well as add to the conclusions found in this book. We hope research will be stimulated.

There are a multitude of theories and techniques of group psychotherapy. Many are adaptations of techniques first applied in individual psychotherapy, and others are based on clinical experience or empirical findings with groups themselves. Some are, of course, derivatives or variations of others. In the selection of the approaches included in this book, we tried to select the most widely accepted and applied of group therapies in use. Since all forms could not be included, we tried to include representative examples of different types. We divided group therapy into two broad categories: psychoanalytic and post-psychoanalytic. The former includes groups that are psychoanalytic, psychoanalytic-derivative and psychodynamic. The latter includes groups that are postanalytic humanistic and postanalytic behavioral and directive.

In the psychoanalytic section of the book, four variations on psychoanalysis are included: from the work of Alexander Wolf on psychoanalysis in groups; from the work of S. R. Slavson on psychoanalytic group psychotherapy; S. H. Foulkes in his group analytic psychotherapy; and W. R. Bion in basic assumption groups. Chapters derivative of psychoanalysis include object relational groups, ego psychology groups, self psychology groups, and groups that utilize a group dynamics approach. The postanalytic, humanistic psychology group techniques include existential psychoanalysis, gestalt therapy, psychodrama and encounter techniques, while the postanalytic behavioral and directive groups include behavioral psychotherapy groups, and rational-emotive therapy groups, a variation on cognitive behavioral therapy and transactional analysis. We also include some chapters that utilized couples groups and family networks to show the extensions of traditional group populations.

The contributors to the book were selected based on their being experts who either originated an approach, helped to develop it, or are closely associated with it. Among the innovators are Albert Ellis (rational-emotive therapy in groups) and Alexander Wolf (psychoanalysis in groups). All are practitioners with years of experience in the technique, who believe in what they do and have a zeal for it. Some of the newer techniques, such as the object relational groups, the ego psychology groups, the self psychology groups, or the cognitive behavioral groups are also presented by practitioners who have used those techniques for many years with individual patients and have now more recently adapted them to group use. All the authors believe that their approach represents the best approach. The reader is left to decide who is right, to make comparisons and draw conclusions as to who truly sees the light. The reader is also left to consider which approaches could be applied universally and which in some more limited way; which work and which don't; which could be integrated with others or more fully developed and which should be disbanded. We hope this book will inspire our readers to explore, not just one school, but the breadth of the field of group psychotherapy; and that they might contribute, through their broadened scope, to its growth.

By way of acknowledgment, we would like to commend the contributors for their courage and willingness to reveal not only what they believe, but what they actually do. We are inspired by their convictions, the efficacy of their work, and their zeal in presenting it. We also hope they, like we, will learn from one another.

As with earlier books one or both of us have edited (*Violence, Perspectives on Murder and Aggression, Handbook on Stress and Anxiety,* and *Psychotherapist's Casebook*), we endorse controversy over premature eclecticism. We hope that this text makes what is presently in practice clearer to readers as they form their own opinions, develop their own group methods, and do research to see whether their ideas work. Our ultimate hope is that the multitudes of people in group therapy benefit from the knowledge dispersed in this volume.

I. L. K.
A. W.

The Editors

IRWIN L. KUTASH is in the private practice of psychotherapy and psychoanalysis in Livingston, New Jersey. He is a clinical associate professor of mental health sciences at the New Jersey College of Medicine and Dentistry. He is a senior supervisor, training psychoanalyst, and faculty member of the New York Center for Psychoanalytic Training and the Institute for Psychoanalysis and Psychotherapy of New Jersey. He is also a field supervisor at the Graduate School of Applied and Professional Psychology of Rutgers University and a psychological consultant to the New Jersey Department of Institutions and Agencies. Dr. Kutash received his Ph.D. (1972) in clinical psychology from the Institute of Advanced Psychological Studies of Adelphi University and holds a postdoctoral certificate in psychotherapy and psychoanalysis from the postgraduate Center for Mental Health, where he received a ten-year service award (1982). He also holds a diplomate in clinical psychology from the American Board of Professional Psychology. Dr. Kutash is currently president of the section on Group Psychotherapy of the psychotherapy division of the American Psychological Association.

Kutash served as president of the Society of Psychologists in Private Practice in New Jersey, president of the New Jersey Academy of Psychology, and as a board member of the New Jersey Association for the Advancement of Psychology and of the New Jersey Psychological Association. He is past chairman of the Mental Health Advisory Council to the Regional Mental Health Board and was a member of a presidential task force on employee assistance programs under the Carter administration.

Dr. Kutash is the author of many chapters and articles on psychoanalysis in groups and on di-egophrenia, including the section on anxiety and victimology in the *Encyclopedia of Psychology*, edited by Raymond Corsini. Dr. Kutash is editor and contributing author of the books *Violence: Perspectives on Murder and Aggression*, with S. B. Kutash and L. B. Schlesinger; the *Handbook on Stress and Anxiety: Contemporary Knowledge, Theory and Treatment*, with L. B. Schlesinger; and the *Psychotherapist's Casebook*, with Alexander Wolf. Both the *Handbook on Stress and Anxiety* and the *Psychotherapist's Casebook* were main selections of the Behavioral Science Book Club. He was awarded the Distinguished Writers Award of the New York Center for Psychoanalytic Training in 1988.

ALEXANDER WOLF is in the private practice of psychotherapy and psychoanalysis in New York City. He is a senior supervisor, training psychoanalyst, and faculty member of the Postgraduate Center for Mental Health and the New York Center for Psychoanalytic Training. For twenty-five years he was an associate clinical professor of psychiatry at the New York Medical College and a training analyst, supervisor, and faculty member in the psychoanalytic division there. He received his M.D. degree (1932) from Cornell University Medical College. Wolf originated the practice of psychoanalysis in groups in 1938.

Dr. Wolf and E. K. Schwartz were awarded the First Annual Mildred Burgum Award by the Professional Association of the Postgraduate Center for Mental Health for their publication of "The Quest for Certainty" in 1956.

Dr. Wolf received the Adolph Meyer Award in 1957 from the Association for Improvement in Mental Health "for his contributions to psychoanalysis in groups" and in 1963, the first Wilfred C. Hulse Memorial Award for outstanding contributions to group therapy from the Eastern Group Psychotherapy Society. He delivered the 28th Annual Karen Horney Lecture in 1980 on di-egophrenia and genius, on behalf of the Association for the Advancement of Psychoanalysis. He was awarded the Distinguished Fellowship in the American Group Psychotherapy Association in 1983 and received the Distinguished Writers Award of the New York Center for Psychoanalytic Training in 1985.

In 1975, Dr. Wolf was honored by his professional colleagues in the publication *The Leader in the Group* (edited by Z. A. Liff) for his thirty-five years of teaching, supervising, writing, and clinical practice (a series of chapters containing selected writings of Wolf's on the leader of the group as well as contributions by distinguished psychoanalysts are included in the book).

Dr. Wolf has published 113 papers in neurology, psychiatry, psychoanalysis, and psychoanalysis in groups, and he is at present engaged in writing a volume on di-egophrenia with Irwin L. Kutash.

Dr. Wolf is the author of *Psychoanalysis in Groups*, with E. K. Schwartz; *Beyond the Couch*, with E. K. Schwartz, I. Goldberg, and G. McCarty; and is coeditor and contributing author to the *Psychotherapist's Casebook* with Irwin L. Kutash.

The Contributors

FREDERIC ARENSBERG, Ph.D. Faculty member, Training Analyst and Senior Supervisor, Group Therapy Department, Postgraduate Center for Mental Health and Training, Institute for Mental Health Practitioners, New York, New York.

GEORGE BARTZOKIS, M.D. Assistant Professor of Psychiatry at UCLA School of Medicine and a Research Career Development Fellow at the Brentwood VA Medical Center in Los Angeles; Fellow of the National Alliance of Research on Schizophrenia and Depression.

JOHN F. BORRIELLO, Ph.D. Chief, Group, Family and Organizational Consultation Branch, Office of Training and Standards, District of Columbia Commission on Mental Health Services, District of Columbia.

ALBERT ELLIS, Ph.D. Executive Director, Institute for Rational-Emotive Therapy, New York, New York.

HENRIETTE T. GLATZER, Ph.D. Training Analyst and Senior Supervisor, Postgraduate Center for Mental Health, New York, New York.

ROBERT HIERHOLZER, M.D. Assistant Professor of Psychiatry at University of California at San Francisco and Chief of the Psychiatric Outpatient Clinic at the Fresno (California) VA Medical Center.

HERBERT HOLT, M.D. Dean of Graduate Training, New York City Division, Westchester Institute for Training in Psychoanalysis and Psychotherapy, New York, New York.

ROBERT PAUL LIBERMAN, M.D. Professor of Psychiatry at UCLA, Chief of the Brentwood VA Rehabilitation Medicine Service, and Director of the Camarillo State Hospital Clinical Research Unit; Principal Investigator of the NIMH-funded Clinical Research Center for Schizophrenia and Psychiatric Rehabilitation.

MALCOLM J. MARKS, Ed.D. Faculty Member, Control Analyst and Training Analyst, New York Center for Psychoanalytic Training, New York, New York.

MARIO MARRONE, M.D. Coordinator of Group Psychotherapy, Basque Psychiatric Services, Basque, Spain.

MALCOLM PINES, D.P.M. Founder, Member, Institute of Group Analysis, London, England.

PHILLIP REICHLINE, M.S.S.W. Licensed Clinical Social Worker, Van Nuys, California.

URI RUEVINI, Ph.D. Professor of Psychology and Behavioral Sciences and Director, Institute of Family and Community Development, University of Houston, Houston, Texas.

JAMES M. SACKS, Ph.D. Director, Psychodrama Center of New York, New York, New York.

JEANETTE G. TARGOW, M.S.W. Licensed Clinical Social Worker, Los Angeles, California.

SAUL TUTTMAN, M.D., Ph.D. Training and Supervising Analyst, Psychoanalytic Division, New York Medical College, New York, New York.

GARY M. YONTEF, Ph.D. Faculty, Gestalt Therapy Institute of Los Angeles, Los Angeles, California.

The Group Psychotherapist's Handbook

PART I

**Psychoanalytic and Psychodynamic
Group Therapies**

Under the heading of psychoanalytic group therapy there are two major branches: those that emphasize the importance of the individual within the group and those that emphasize the group as a whole. The former are derivative of the work of Alexander Wolf (1949, 1950), Wolf and Schwartz (1962), Kutash and Wolf (1983), and Slavson (1950, 1964). The latter are derivative of Foulkes (1940), Foulkes and Anthony (1957), Foulkes (1965), and Bion (1961). Both branches emphasize such basic psychoanalytic principles as the use of transference and resistance, an emphasis on the importance of the past history in influencing present behavior, and the concept of intrapsychic factors such as the power of the unconscious (with the exception of Bion, who does not stress transference, regression, or the unconscious, but does believe in latent themes.) They diverge in their emphasis on the primacy of the individual in the group in the former and the group as an entity in the latter. In psychoanalysis in groups, for example, the interaction between each individual and every other individual, including the leader, is stressed. In group-as-a-whole approaches the interaction between the group and the therapist is often paramount. The activity level of the therapist also varies, as well as whom the interpretations are geared toward—the individual, the group as a whole, or both. Wolf and Kutash (see essay 1) interpret interactions in groups based on their transference derivative, unconscious motivations, and historical determinants. Pines and Marrone or, more emphatically, Borriello in essay 4, follow in the footsteps of the beliefs of Foulkes or of Bion in emphasis on interpretations of the behavior in groups based on underlying group themes and on the transference between the overall group and the therapist. Practitioners of either of these techniques need training in psychoanalysis, and their techniques provide benefits of a psychoanalytic nature.

Psychoanalysis in groups was developed by Alexander Wolf in the late 1930s. While Schilder, Wender, and Tregant Burrow made early attempts at psychoanalysis in the group setting, the psychoanalytic approach to groups has been said to have "come to fruition in the hands of Alexander Wolf" (Anthony 1971). In their paper, Alexander Wolf and Irwin L. Kutash present the approach of psychoanalysis in groups as it is practiced in the 1980s. The approach still emphasizes the primacy of individuals and their psychoanalysis in groups through the interpretation of transference, the analysis of dreams both from the point of view of the dreamer and the associators to the dream, and the relating of the past to the present, all with the aim of making the unconscious conscious. The authors hold that the multitude of transference possibilities in groups along with the group environment facilitate the process of each individual's self-understanding. They contend that depth analysis can take place in a group with more profound changes in character structure than by individual analysis alone.

S. R. Slavson was the originator of analytic group psychotherapy, which contrasts with psychoanalysis in groups on the one side and group analytic psychotherapy (developed by Foulkes) on the other. Slavson, like Wolf, concentrates on the individual rather than the group as a whole, but he believed that transference cannot be as intense in groups as in individual psychotherapy, and he made interpretations at a level appropriate to that belief.

Psychoanalytic group psychotherapy as it is presently practiced is presented in a paper by Henriette T. Glatzer (essay 2). Glatzer takes issue with the belief that the depth of repression in group psychotherapy has to be less intense than in individual treatment, although she sees the episodes of repression as shorter. In her paper she stresses the key role of working through and the importance of the therapeutic alliance.

Analytic group psychotherapy helps the working-through process by accelerating regression so there is quicker access to unconscious conflicts. It also helps by reinforcing the analysts' work with superego and unconscious ego resistances. Superego resistance is considered by the writer to be a major block to therapeutic progress. Transformation of the superego from a corrupt to an incorrupt state is one of the decisive points in psychotherapy. This, in turn, strengthens the ego. Other members in the group often help with this task and become reinforcers of the incorruptible superego. Examples have been given to show the variety of ways in which the narcissistic anxiety caused by effective interpretations from the analyst is lessened in the group. When unconscious resistances are manifested in the elaborate network of transferences and analyzed in the dynamic here-and-now, the repeated evidence of transference distortions adds emotional impact. There is an eventual mastery of painful affects and a dynamic restructuring.

A brief history of the treatment alliances and the recent delineation of them from the transferences proper is given, as well as theoretical discussions and a clinical example to demonstrate how the group process accelerates the working alliance of all its members and is especially useful to borderline, narcissistic, and impulse-ridden patients who have fragile ego resources with which to form the special kind of object relationships necessary to begin and continue a working alliance.

In essay 3 Malcolm Pines and Mario Marrone present material on group analysis as developed from the work of S. H. Foulkes. They conclude that "Foulkesian Group Analysis" represents a singular integration of Psychoanalysis and a social psychology that is informed by some of the principles of Gestalt therapy. They describe its originator, S. H. Foulkes, as integrating his psychoanalytical training together with his work with Kort Goldstein and his interest in the sociohistorical matrix of personality. They distinguish the Foulkesian approach from the other British "group as a whole" schools, those of Bion and Ezriel. They describe how the Foulkesian approach regards the group as a whole as the underlying background and context that is latent in all group formation (Foundation Matrix) upon which is built the interaction pattern of the individual members of the group (Dynamic Matrix). This, they believe, leaves the therapist free to move between background and foreground, between group as context and individuals and their own psychodynamics.

The therapeutic emphasis in group analysis is upon communication. Neurotic and psychotic dynamics affect the development of free communication between group members and these disturbances, they put forth, can be recognized and located in the communication patterns of the group. Analysis and interpretation of such blocks, they contend, help to free the members' healthier and more highly developed personality characteristics and enable the group, under proper conditions, to foster healthier aspects of the individuals. Neurotic reactions, they explain, are worn down and aggression is harnessed in the service of this activity.

They further hold that the object relations school, which was highly developed in Britain over the past four decades, is an important part of the theoretical equipment of the group analyst, who also sees the process of group formation and development as replicating some of the basic patterns of the structuring of early mental life. They find intrinsic to the group situation a dialogue sharing and reciprocity that are necessary contributors to the structuring of the normal personality. Bowlby's attachment theory is also utilized by this school as a basis for the theoretical and technical foundations of group analytic work.

In essay 4 the group-as-a-whole technique in group psychotherapy is discussed by John F. Borriello from the point of view of Bion's pioneer work. A review of W. R. Bion's group theories are presented. This paper stresses the fact that Bion was not interested in applying psychoanalysis to groups, but rather his major interest was in finding concepts that would help him understand the material that emerged in psychotherapy groups. Borriello presents the point of view that one does not have to have allegiance to any particular theory in order to incorporate the group-as-a-whole technique into their practices.

As can be seen in the first four chapters of this book, even the pioneering techniques in group psychotherapy have incorporated new developments. For example, while the ideas of Wolf, Slavson, Bion, and Foulkes are still alive and well and actively evolving, psychoanalysis and the group theories derived from it have led to later developments.

Major developments in psychoanalytic theory and practice in recent years include the focus on object relations, the ego, and the concept of the self. These developments have been driving forces in group psychotherapy as well. It is not surprising that a therapy based on the interaction of individuals should lead to many of its practitioners deemphasizing or even rejecting Freudian instinct theory for more relationally derived formulations.

In their paper, Irwin L. Kutash and Alexander Wolf describe "Object Relational Groups," an approach based on the integration by Kutash of object relations theory with psychoanalysis in groups as orginated by Wolf. (See essay 1.) A system for diagnosing ego states is presented, as well as a classification of prospective group members in terms of their communication output and input. Three types of group climates are described: equilibrium, disequilibrium, and malequilibrium, with the first being the ideal. In the object relational model it is put forth that the group provides the new transferential arena for old introjects to be dispersed and a new presentation of the self and others to grow.

The focus of the paper by Malcolm Marks is the use of concurrent individual and group psychotherapy with a patient whose fear of engulfment and loss of boundaries kept him on the periphery of any central relationship. The author contends that the knowledge of psychoanalytic developmental psychology (or ego psychology) applied to group psychotherapy enables the psychotherapist to treat the patient at a distance in a group while enabling the therapist to bring the patient slowly and safely into the object world.

In essay 7 Frederic Arensberg describes self psychology as an approach utilizing empathy as its technique in the working through of selfobject transferences. The paper presents the application of the theories and techniques of self psychology to group therapy. The first part provides the reader with basic self psychology concepts and a broad historical perspective. Next, the application of the theory to psychoanalytic group therapy is presented. Some techniques and types of interpretations from this point of view are discussed. The paper concludes with material illustrating different transferences in group therapy from a self psychological perspective. The cases illustrate mirroring, idealization, twinship, and show how the analysis of empathic failures lead to transmuting internalizations.

In his paper Saul Tuttman provides guidelines and examples related to the application of group dynamic theories to conducting group psychotherapy. Following a brief historical review of relevant group theory and treatment, recent trends in applying group dynamics are described. The combined application of individual and group dynamics is examined. It must be explained that Tuttman is applying group dynamics from the point of view of applying group process principles and principles derived from the psychoanalytic psychotherapies already featured to group therapy as a healing art, as opposed to the group dynamics of Cartwright and Zander (1968), for example, who are concerned with advancing the knowledge about the nature of groups and their influence on individuals, stemming from a more purely social or industrial psychology origin. This is group dynamics as applied to therapy groups and derivative of theories in this section, and is therefore applicable to a treatment handbook.

Section 1

Psychoanalytic and Psychodynamic

1

Psychoanalysis in Groups

Alexander Wolf, M.D.
and Irwin L. Kutash, Ph.D.

Claims are occasionally made that the beginnings of psychoanalytic group therapy were undertaken by one therapist or another.
Perhaps one could demonstrate that group therapy began at meetings of young philosophers around Socrates and Plato or among the
Apostles and Jesus. Ernest Jones suggests that psychoanalysis in
groups began aboard ship in 1909 when Freud, Jung, and Ferenczi
analyzed one another's dreams on the way to the United States. If
any priority needs to be respected, it should perhaps be rendered
to Freud and his shipboard companions.

Group psychotherapy began in the first decade of this century.
Psychoanalytically oriented group psychotherapy began in the thirties, years that were especially conducive to the development of all
sorts of collective activity for a variety of ends. The leadership of
Roosevelt and the concerted social need helped to lay the groundwork for the flowering of group therapy. It was a time of protest

against failures in the establishment, a protest that took various social forms. Today this rebelliousness takes the form of withdrawal, isolation, and retreats into fantasy. This is done even in groups, where experiencing one's feelings in acting out inappropriate affect is being promoted as therapeutic when it is, in fact, regressive.

It is of some interest to speculate why there was in the thirties such readiness to seek therapy in a group, when generally there is reticence about exposing subjectible disorder. This was the time of the great economic depression. It was a time of restlessness, when people sought one another out in collective endeavor. Most people were short of money and tried to find solutions in common struggle, whether in attempts to deal with their impoverishment or their anxiety. Most patients could not pay the cost of an individual analysis. There were needs that were met by the opportunity to undertake analysis in a group: the availability of reconstructive therapy; treatment at a very reasonable fee; a sustaining and collaborative membership under the leadership of a clinician in a joint effort against an outer threat, an impoverishing social structure, and an inner threat, neurosis.

In the mid-thirties, Wolf became interested in the possibility of doing psychoanalytic therapy in a group setting. He read the papers of Trigant Burrow, Paul Schilder and Louis Wender, visited J. L. Moreno and participated as an actor in one of his psychodramas.

Moved by the success of these clinicians, he suggested to several of his patients that they forego their individual analytic work and continue their further treatment with him in a group setting. With little obvious resistance they evidenced an eagerness to pursue his proposal. In 1938, his first group had its initial meeting. The patients were stimulated and moved by the experience. Their enthusiasm spread so that by 1940 five groups of patients were in treatment with him, one of them made up of five married couples.

It is not possible in this space to provide a history of the development of psychoanalysis in groups, (see Wolf 1949/1950; Wolf and Schwartz 1962; Kutash and Wolf 1983). What follows, then, is a brief statement of our present concepts of its underlying theory and clinical practice.

Psychoanalysis in groups is the use of analytic means—free association, the analysis of dreams and fantasies, and the working through of resistance and transference—in the treatment of eight to ten patients in a group setting. Psychoanalysis in groups entails an understanding of unconscious processes and motivation. It seeks out the historical basis for current behavior in order to resolve its persistence in the present. It requires the working out and working through of repetitive and compulsive psychopathologic maneuvers. Psychoanalysis in groups pursues the latent as well as the manifest in patient interaction and function. The search for unconscious processes is achieved by the promotion of the freedom to express thought, fantasy, and feeling. The pursuit of unconscious motives moves patients away from attending only to the present and toward an understanding of intrapsychic processes, historical determinants, and the working through of transference distortions.

Individual Analysis

The traditional psychoanalyst tends to reject the group as a therapeutic milieu. He is more anonymous and less interactive with the patient than are group members or the analyst in groups. The individual analysand is thereby rendered more passive, regressed, introspective, isolated, and concentrates on the intrapsychic rather than on the interpersonal. He pursues his early history, and the focus of attention is largely upon himself, his associations, and reactions. The individual analyst is inclined to reject the idea that his values, his individual characteristics, and predilections provoke particular responses in the patient. The group analyst, however, becomes increasingly aware from his observation of group interaction that his commitments, his personal qualities, choices, and preferences elicit special reactions in his analysands.

The individual analyst is denied in the dyadic relationship a multifaceted view of his patient. He does not see the analysand in the multiplicity of reactions stimulated by other group members. He is not witness to the patient's responses to his projected nuclear or current family, his boss, his friends, to authorities and peers. He does not actually observe the multiple transferences that a group evokes. He is also less aware of the patient's positive resources in the healthy ways he deals with people. The individual analyst is inclined to regard the patient as more helpless than he is, because the therapist is in the vertical position of helping a dependent person. In the group, however, every member occasionally offers support and insight to a copatient. This is a new role for an analysand, one that exposes a previously unseen side of his character, the strength and perceptivity to encourage and offer insight to another patient, which is mutually ego-building. The presence of other patients provides new kinds of activity and responsive feelings induced less readily in individual analysis. The group analysand experiences peer interaction that is not available in dyadic therapy.

In individual analysis, the patient has more difficulty in asserting himself. Copatients in a group support each other in dealing with the authority-invested analyst in groups. The individual analyst is more easily able to govern one patient than he is several of them assembled. They encourage one another to express attitudes toward the leader less readily ventilated in isolation with the therapist.

Group Therapy and Psychoanalysis in Groups

There are some differences between nonanalytic group psychotherapy and psychoanalysis in groups. These differences are relative, not absolute, so that in the following list of distinctions between them there is some overlapping. The group therapist tends to treat the group as a whole and to use group process interpretations. The group analyst is more attentive to individuals in the group and their particular unconscious motivation. The group therapist is inclined to organize his membership more homogeneously and to treat the homogenized group as one with a bipersonal psychology. The group analyst tends to organize groups more heterogeneously and to treat patients with a multipersonal psychology. The group therapist looks for similarities in the membership, so that adjustment and conformity are therapeutic outcomes. The group analyst values differences among his patients, so that insight, individual uniqueness, and freedom are therapeutic derivatives. The group therapist focuses on the manifest behavior made evident by interaction and interpersonal processes. The group analyst scrutinizes the latent content, the intrapsychic processes, the unconscious material, and promotes self-examination to this end. As a result, there is less anxiety in nonanalytic group therapy and more anxiety in psychoanalysis in groups.

In group therapy that is not analytic, the patient may repeat his submission to the original familial expectation that he yield to parental dictates. This resistance to differentiation repeats the earlier ego-repressive experience. In group analysis, the examination of unconscious processes helps the patient to grasp in detail the character of his yielding up his own ego to his parents in the past and to group members in the present. He is emboldened to search for a way out, to repossess his own ego. The analytic group supports his distinguishing attributes, his difference, the emergence of his repressed ego.

Six Primary Parameters

The analyst in groups has in mind the existence of six primary parameters, which in part differentiate group from individual analysis.

The first of these is the presence of hierarchical and peer vectors in the group. They become apparent in the interplay of vertical and horizontal reactions that characterize parental and sibling transferences. Copatients in a group provide a peer vector and peer relatedness. The analyst provides a hierarchical vector, a responsible authority, and projected parental figure. The presence of leadership in the person of the analyst and of peers in the patient members makes for a setting in which vertical and horizontal interaction can take place that promotes parental and sibling transferences.

Second, there are multiple reactivities in the group in which each patient utilizes other members and the leader in healthy and neurotic ways. Some of the distortions are in terms of multiple transferences, identifications, abuse of another patient seen as oneself, etc. This multiple interaction engages group members with one another and the therapist in their feelings, thoughts and behavior. Multiple interaction tends to impel the more uncommunicative patient to participate. Reserved or silent members find it difficult to maintain their detachment. They are reacted to for their nonverbal attitudes until they are able to speak. In the course of multiple interaction, group members are sometimes inclined to gratify each other's archaic demands, until the members themselves are able to undertake this mutual analysis. Some masochistic patients manage to provoke the members into scapegoating them. This, too, requires analytic intervention.

Third is the dimension of interpersonal and intrapsychic communication. The intrapsychic process stresses self-knowledge leading to personal integration. The interpersonal process emphasizes knowledge of the self and others leading to personal and social integration. Individual analysis often tends to be more of an intrapsychic experience. Group analysis tends to be more of an interpsychic experience, but properly conducted can be equally intrapsychic. In dyadic analysis the analytic process usually proceeds from the intrapsychic to the interpersonal; in group analysis, from the interpersonal to the intrapsychic.

Fourth is the principle of forced interaction. Some patients are reluctant to reveal themselves in the group setting. There is, however, pressure on the less participant to become engaged. It is difficult to hold oneself apart in the face of the general push for collaborative interaction.

Fifth is the principle of shifting attention, which helps to resolve the expectation of the patient who was an only child that he receive all the attention. Group analysis confronts the monopolistic only child with the reality that there are others beside the self who need to be heard and attended. Sometimes it is the originally favored or unfavored child who tries in the group to exclude his siblings. Such a maneuver is less apparent in dyadic analysis where there is little if any necessity to compete for the therapist's attention.

In a group, the focus of attention shifts from one patient to another. No one has exclusive possession of therapeutic scrutiny. The analyst and the patients do not give any one member their exclusive regard. This shifting attention gives each member an opportunity to digest the insight that has been offered him. Others use the relaxation from examination as a breathing spell from what may be experienced as a somewhat threatening exploration. Still others may resistively seek avoidance of such attention in order to maintain their psychopathology.

Sixth is the principle of alternating roles. The group structure necessarily gives rise to the phenomenon of alternating roles. Every member is obligated or at least inclined to listen, to try to understand the other. Novel kinds of feelings, of reactions, of activity are evoked. Each patient talks, gives advice, tries to comprehend, responds, feels sympathetic, irritated, bored, and evokes appropriate and inappropriate reactions. He wants help and extends help. He is giver and taker, helper and helped. His roles are enlarged by new kinds of activity. He feels frustrated, angry, flattered, pleased. Now he is trying to understand the others. Later, they are trying to understand him. At one moment he is interacting spontaneously. The next, he is thoughtfully contemplating what has just been said to him about himself.

Group Organization and Goals

The group analyst tries to organize a diversified membership. Although he recognizes similarities among his patients, he tries to be awake to each member's novelty and originality. He is alert to every patient's right to be distinctive. For there is unhealth in the cohesion of a homogeneous group that too often excludes the new member as an alien foreigner. The group analyst sees health in the reciprocity and interdependence of unlikeness, in men and women working creatively together just because of their complementarity, in parents and children acknowledging their reciprocal need of one another. He views homogeneity as separating and isolating.

It is not possible to form a group heterogeneous in every respect. Patients are alike in many ways and their similarities make for some homogeneity. The leader does not assemble children, adolescents, and adults in groups. He treats these different patients in groups homogeneously organized with respect to their age. He does not mix the intelligent with the mentally retarded or the sociopath with the responsible citizen. While he is obliged to make some concessions to the need for homogeneity, as analytic treatment progresses, the members become more diversified.

If the leader promotes homogeneity, he limits the intensity of analytic investigation. Patients who make advances in treatment begin to ask for differentiated and complementary others in the group. This kind of request is some indication that the group leader is practicing analytic therapy. The more the analyst and analysands search for the latent beneath the manifest, uncover repressed past history, and seek out psychic determinants, the more individual differences, heterogeneity and diversity emerge among the members. The analytic approach to group members sponsors their individuality and makes the group heterogeneous. Each patient emerges as a distinct person with a singular past, evolution, and current psychodynamics. The members become more responsive to one another in their differentiation in pathology and the health. A struggle develops to understand and accept the stranger in the other.

Confidentiality

Occasional patients claim they cannot join a group because there is too much anxiety or danger in exposure to strangers whose commitment to confidentiality cannot be trusted. Such patients can usually be induced to join a group in time as their anxiety and resistance are analyzed. Confidentiality among members needs to be maintained. If a patient reveals to an outsider what goes on in his group, he arouses a good deal of fear and anger among the members. The therapist needs to analyze the resistive gossip. Such a breach of mutual trust is a resistive leak that threatens the secure existence of a group unless the problem can be quickly resolved. If not, the tattler may have to return to individual analysis until this difficulty is overcome.

The Alternate Meeting

The alternate session is a scheduled meeting of patients without the presence of the analyst. It alternates with regular meetings at which the analyst is present. Regular sessions take place once a week for about one and a half hours. Alternate meetings take place once or twice a week and last two or three hours.

There are a number of reasons for organizing alternate sessions. For one thing such a regimen says to the patient in effect: "One of our objectives in treatment is to resolve your need of me. I believe you can function effectively with your peers. I will be available to you at regular sessions or in individual consultations should they prove to be necessary but I believe it is in your interest to try to use and develop your own resources. You can do this, I am certain, at the alternate meeting." These sessions then are an attempt even at the very beginning of analysis to work through pathologically dependent transferential ties to the parental surrogate in the analyst, to move the patient toward autonomy. It is a movement toward ending at the beginning. It is a trial for the child-self in the patient—a trial without the parental figure. The good analyst, like the good parent, believes in paying judicious attention and judicious inattention to the child in the patient.

The alternate session provides the opportunity to compare thought, feeling, and behavior in the two climates, the regular and the alternate. For patients to a certain extent think, feel, and act differently in the presence and absence of the authority figure. And these differences become the basis for defining, elucidating, and working through parental transferences to the group leader. Many patients interact more freely in the absence of the analyst when authority transferences are experienced as less oppressive. As a result, often a good deal of material is expressed that is withheld in the analyst's presence. This material frequently is concerned with feelings about the therapist. With the support, encouragement, and sometimes the "betrayal" by other members, the attitudes and feelings expressed at alternate meetings are brought into regular sessions.

The parental transferences patients make to one another at the alternate session tend to be somewhat attenuated by an awareness that they are, in fact, among their peers. The absence of the helping analyst at alternate sessions forces the peers to help one another and promote their sharing and their equality at the same time that it reduces their child-like dependency on the analyst.

A by-product of psychoanalysis in groups, more particularly when alternate sessions are provided, is socialization. Socialization is usually looked upon as resistance, and in some instances this may be so. However, this is not necessarily true, if socialization is explored analytically for its resistive elements. Socialization has a reparative and humanizing function. Socializing may, however, limit the pursuit of unconscious processes. As a result, the group leader needs to examine the way patients use or misuse the alternate session, their participation in extragroup cliques or subgroups.

The therapeutic use of the alternate session provides further advantages. One of these is the clinical experience of spontaneous mutual support. There may be concern that the patients left to their

own inexperienced devices may do wild analysis and psychically, if
not physically, damage each other. But patients do not at alternate
meetings become decorticate and barbaric. If some of the insight
they extend is premature, poorly timed, too penetrating, or widely
off the mark, the member who is the target for analysis usually
discounts or resists it on the ground that the proffered help is coming from an inexpert peer. However, as patients become more experienced, sophisticated, and familiar with one another's psychological and pathological maneuvers, they often make very astute
clinical observations that tend also to be carefully considered. If
these insights fit, they are gradually accepted and worked with. For
certain patients who have extreme difficulty in accepting insight when
offered by the authority figure of the analyst, these same observations coming from peers appear to be more readily acceptable.

Resistance

Resistance is dealt with quickly in group analysis. Patients question
the appropriateness of each other's resistive operations. They will
not let a member sleep. They urge the silent patient to speak. They
energetically press for an end to resistive maneuvers. They incite
one another to change. They ask for new activity, demand interaction, protest against withdrawal or monopoly, and object to compulsive intrapsychic self-absorption or to inappropriate ways of relating. They induce participation until there is freely expressed and
examined interaction.

Resistance manifests itself in the myriad forms encountered in
individual analysis, but the group setting provides a special environment that lends itself to the elaboration of resistive forms peculiar to group analysis.

For Carol, a patient "in love with" the analyst, being in the group
was enlightening. She was soon as emotionally attached to another
group member as she was to the analyst. Her "unfaithfulness," the
rapidity and completeness with which she moved from one man to
another confronted her with the irrational and compulsive character
of her behavior. In time the nature of her activity became obvious
to her as transference. Carol was rigidly blocked in neurotic interest
in the analyst and insisted that she was truly in love with him and

that she would be neurosis-free if only the therapist would return her genuine feeling; the group experience dispelled the illusion. In the group, if such a patient does not transfer her affective claim to another patient, she is led to examine her feelings more deeply in the face of similar resistance and transference to other members. Their falsification of reality makes its impression on her. In most cases, she is brought face to face with the "infidelity" that impels her to exchange the analyst for a patient and is obliged to plumb earlier emotional attachments. She then discovers the neurotic resistance implicit in every such episode.

Another manifestation of resistance is the compulsive missionary spirit. One group member, George, persisted in looking after other members in a supportive, parental way, using this device subtly to dominate and attack the other members and to repress more basic personal psychodynamics. The group resented this false charity and demanded and evoked more spontaneous participation by rewarding the messianic for unguarded slips of feeling and by rejecting dogmatic helpfulness.

This does not imply, of course, that warm and spontaneous offers of assistance are rejected. On the contrary, as long as supportiveness is not compulsive but is thoughtfully sympathetic, it is welcomed as a sign of good health.

An interesting example of this kind of resistance is provided in the following case. In one group a professional teacher, Harry, habitually preached to his fellow analysands until their hostility bordered on the explosive. Later he reported that during coitus sometimes an hour passed before his sexual partner had an orgasm. To him, the sexual act, like his compulsive stewardship in the group, was a gesture of generosity. The other patients encouraged him to be less providing and to strive to enjoy his wife's allure with more spontaneity and pleasure for himself. At the next session he reported an ejaculation within three minutes and a corresponding simultaneous orgasm from his partner. The group conjectured that his earlier largesse concealed unconscious hostility, to which his wife had been responding with equal frigidity. They also suggested that his benevolent preachments and ostensible advice contained the same kind of irritating and unprovoked aggression. He was urged in this situation as well to abandon his compulsive role for one that was

more spontaneous and acceptable. After some time he became aware
that this specious charity was a form of resistance preventing the
development of real feeling. Variants of this theme appear in the
self-appointed do-gooder, in the overprotective, typical "mom" in
the group. It is also eminently displayed in the "mother is always
right" dogma.

Voyeurism is resistance that is more general in group analysis.
Robert tried to escape personal examination and engagement by
taking a "grandstand seat," which gave him a gratifying view of what
might have been the equivalent of the primal scene or its lesser
familial counterparts. He seemed willing and even eager to allow
others full interaction, while he assigned to himself a tremulous
watchfulness. Instead of engaging in interpersonal exchange, he
peered at it from a distance. But looking can be a prelude to participation. The group had little tolerance for a nonparticipant. It
engaged Robert by its welcoming self-exposure. It moved him by
inviting and provoking him to become involved in the warm emotional life of the new family. His resistance began to melt when the
sideshow to which he was drawn by dubious surreptitious motives
became a wholesome drama in which he was impelled to take a
legitimate part. Projected aggression gave way to a recognition of
reality, and he became prepared to act more appropriately in this
unforbidding environment. In this fashion, voyeuristic resistance
developed from an end in itself to a first step toward a normal relationship.

Hiding oneself behind the watchful analysis of others is a common form of resistance in psychoanalysis in groups. The group may
provide a convenient setting for the exercise of this kind of resistance. Abe concentrated on the neurotic behavior of other patients
while evading analysis directed toward himself. He cleverly shifted
attention from himself to the associator in order to defend against
disturbing examination. He was adept, when threatened by an observation that might become alarmingly penetrating, at neatly par-
rying the proffered insight. He managed to redirect the group's attention to any individual who dared to analyze him. He handled
what was said of him, for example, by remarking that his critic had
an interesting overtone in speech that he ought to examine. By
endless devices he deflected what might add up to deeper insight

into himself and tackled his examiner. Sometimes he produced brilliant, if compulsive, analyses in his own defense. Usually his techniques were so able as not to be easily broken down under critical examination. However, the group gradually dissolved his resistance by expressing its gratitude for his incisiveness and simultaneously demonstrating to him that behind his emphatic lecturing he made himself inaccessible, in terror of humiliation, to the helping hands of the group. It was pointed out that fear of castration or its equivalent by the parental substitutes in the group was forcing him into this compulsive role. To the extent that the members understood the frantic insecurity that underlay his bravado, they extended a reassuring friendliness that enabled him to relinquish his insistent critical study of others for self-examination. The maintenance of a compulsive complacency that regarded the other patients as neurotic inferiors could not withstand such an approach from the associated members. Their understanding enabled them to become friendly enough to help him, in time, give up his program of evasion.

The use of history as resistance deserves special comment. There is probably nothing in individual treatment more uselessly time-consuming and basically harmful to both patient and analyst than the practice of rehearsing the patient's past. Long, irrelevant biographies, usually distorted by the narrator, were Ted's form of continual evasion. He even used a recital of yesterday's events for this purpose. In a most unsatisfactory form the relationship between patient and group members was reduced to a day-to-day report of frustation that demanded nonanalytic advice on ways of circumventing it. This insistence on guidance instead of therapeutically valuable transactions was also used as resistance. Refusal to face the present with one's own reactive emotional and mental processes withstands only in extreme cases the impact of other patients' stimulation. Talk of what happened in childhood and even accounts of last night's dream became vicarious and pallid when compared with the dynamic interpersonal reactions produced by a suddenly articulate contact. Such dramatic provocation cannot be resisted by escape into the day before yesterday.

Of course, we do not mean that we regard history as unimportant. On the contrary, it is of the utmost importance. History has

the greatest significance when evoked and recalled by the discovery
and analysis of resistance and transference in the moment of their
occurrence—that is, when history has a bearing on the present that
is meaningful to both the patient, the analyst and the other members of the group. The present neurotic behavior is envisioned as
a multidimensional photograph of the significant past. Careful scrutiny of the immediate moment will recall pertinent traumatic events.
Personal flashback may be vividly illuminating, and the exploration
and understanding of the past in terms of its influence on the present are essential to creation of a wholesome present and future. But
allowing a patient to indulge these proclivities is encouraging him
in resistive subterfuge, his attempt to escape the resolution of similar conflict in the present.

Some patients, perhaps a majority of them during the early stages
of treatment, discuss sexual material with patent reluctance. This is
a kind of diffidence we try to dispel. Slighting or repressing sexual
data reproduces the prohibitive role of the original family. Unless
the patient frees his own sexuality, he cannot make an adequate
recovery. Access to sexual material is obtained partly by intuitive
free association. Once the initial resistances are broken down in this
process, there is usually little difficulty in getting patients to discuss
this fundamental matter.

An intimate relation exists between abnormal social behavior and
abnormal sexual behavior. Access to sexual material is obtained by
illustrating how a variety of interpersonal conduct that appears in
the group has its sexual counterpart, perhaps as yet unseen. Since
the average patient is wary, at first, of revealing his sexual predicament, and since he or she is hardly aware of either its extent or
its complexity, group members are urged, early in analysis, to examine the interplay of their personalities on the social level. Then
the analyst may begin to suggest that for each of the character traits
revealed by cross-examination there is a sexual analogue. The analyst's ease in taking the parallel for granted, without criticism, tends
to infect the group members with a like tolerance for otherwise
socially prohibited intimacy. The analyst might indicate that a manifestation of social impotence implies the existence of a corresponding sexual impotence, that they are both signs of a similar psychodynamic problem in the analysand. Similarly, for example, excessive

attitudes of male supremacy suggest a corresponding compulsive sexual excess, organized to conceal deep-rooted castration anxiety. A statuesque pose on the social level is probably accompanied by some form of sexual frigidity. When the therapist has thus schooled patients in the effort to uncover the usually concealed existence of these sexual correspondents of social forms, the members make numerous accurate guesses about hidden sexual data. By intuition, one after another uncovers sexual material. In the light of this relationship, nuances in curious social conduct are clarified in turn. One exposure excites release in others until, in a surprisingly short time, the cautious lose their caution and proceed to unburden themselves of the most intimate details.

A group afforded an illustration of an instance in which psychologically induced impotence was accompanied by social ineffectiveness. One of its preeminently male members, Dave, physically powerful and imposing, exhibited evidence of extreme shyness. His emotional reactions were, to say the least, deficient. References to plays, art, and literature both annoyed and embarrassed him, and when pressed for an explanation, he characterized them as effeminate manifestations of weakness. He secretly regarded any display of feeling as soft and feared he might be seduced into affective response by any emotional stimulant. At an early age he had lost his domineering father and had been forced to go out on the streets to sell newspapers in order to support his mother, his sisters, and himself. Attacked repeatedly by anti-Semitic hoodlums, he spent years toughening himself until tenderness, sympathy, and, by extension, any emotional symbol that did not connote hard struggle were ruled out of his life. In group activity it was noted that he evaded those social responses that might betray any underlying emotional attitude. He was formally considerate, proper, and unreactive, except for a compulsive need to display his masculine excess. This latter consisted in exhibiting his masterful virility whenever possible, in missing no opportunity to engage in intellectual debate, at which he excelled, and in a general supportiveness simulating strength which invited the dependence of other members on him but which was unconsciously intended to dominate and exploit them.

During various sessions, the group speculated about the sexual counterpart of his deficiency in feeling and gradually led him to a not-too-painful admission of his impotence. He was moved so deeply by the friendly reception accorded his confession of weakness that he burst into tears, the first crack in his resistive armor. With this disruption of neurotic defense against emotional expression, he began dreaming, free-associating, and "going around" at deeper affective levels. This enabled the group, in time, to analyze his masculine conceit and striving for power as defenses against castration and passive homosexual submission. He was able to acquire insight into his compelling preoccupation with erotically tinged struggle between himself and other men that removed him from sexual engagements with women. He was able to trace his aggression toward men to his domineering father and his later and repeated compulsive strivings with them as the ambivalent expression of submissive and aggressive conflict. He learned, too, how the loss of his father removed a masculine image with whom he needed too identify, leaving him with three feminine figures who played their part in further emasculating him, partly out of their playing a phallic role and partly by providing him only with feminine examples. This was added to by their own ambivalent eroticism toward him. To all this conflict he reacted with repression, attempting ever to surmount unconscious affective claims that would not be denied until he was both impotent and apparently unfeeling. But the group members' action, a wedge into his formerly impenetrable facade, allowed him to relax restraints successively and steadily build up lively and cordial contact. The return of feeling allowed him to relate to others with intensity, to fall in love, and to consummate an erotic and wholesome heterosexual relationship with full potency.

One such confession has a catalytic effect in producing similar uninhibited discussion by others. With varying degrees of stubborn opposition, the members finally yield to the potentiating influence of self-revelation induced by the permissive aura pervading the group. Emboldened by avowals from all sides, each sees around him his counterpart in sexual embarrassment and exposes his particular variant of the sexual theme.

Not all varieties of resistance that appear in the group can be dealt with here, for they are as manifold and distinct as human beings, but we shall mention some other common ones. Some patients resist by trying to hide in the group, whether by attempting to escape into group analysis from individual treatment or by coming late and missing meetings. Some leave the room on various pretexts. Others cannot recall their dreams or fantasies. A few exploit their tears and other devious emotional or psychosomatic releases to evade more direct responses. Some maintain a compulsive complacency among patients whom they regard as neurotically inferior and hence not to be entrusted with important private matters. Their resistance takes the form of supercilious silence or contempt. Some try to overwhelm the group with endless outpourings of irrelevant talk that is neither self-revealing nor permissive of emergence of others, and some act out.

Dreams, Fantasies, and Free Association

Analysts are often skeptical about whether group members can associate freely in the group, where there are so many interruptions of spontaneous expression. But even in individual analysis, free association must to an extent be limited, restrained, and bounded. It needs, in any case, to be used selectively. The leader's concern with interruptions of free association may be looked upon as his wish to do individual analysis in the group. The discontinuity in free association may clarify the fantasy or dream of a given patient but may also be used to analyze the interruptive associations of other members in multilateral interpretations. The leader's view of co-members' communications as discordant prevents the group from engaging in multilateral analysis. It demands individual analysis in the group and supports a competition to interrupt each other, a rivalry to win the attention of the therapist.

Supporting the right of the members to join in with their associations gives all the patients the right to be in treatment rather than just one person at a time. The therapist must, therefore, deal with presentations as reciprocal and interdependent, so that patient mutuality is improved. By this means, all patient free associations are increased rather than limited. In a group, a patient in his free associations is obliged to function with some awareness of others. This expectation of consciousness of the other is health-facilitating.

Unlimited free association without such awareness may lead to more serious pathology.

Free association may be interrupted or facilitated by comembers. If a patient in a group is searching in his associations for previously unexamined unconscious material, he generally excites and holds the attention of his peers and is, as a result, encouraged to continue. If he reproduces the same pathology, the members become bored with the repetition and usually try to stop him and plead for a more mutually gratifying alternative—like a fresh dream or fantasy. If his free association discloses more realistic or less compulsive imaginings, the other patients become more receptive in the hope that he will continue to make freer choices. If his associations take the cause of an isolating autism the members object to his masochistic and detached free association.

The presentation of a dream is followed by the dreamer's associations, then the other members associate in relation to the dream. Following this, the patients try to interpret the dream as well as the latent meaning of each member's subjective associations. In this way, the dreamer is prevented from monopolizing a group session, for every patient's unconscious contribution to the original dream is made conscious and insightful.

Dreams may lead to insight, provoke elaborate free association, and cut through resistance. But in the clarification of transference, dreams are also valuable therapeutic adjuncts (Wolf and Schwartz 1962).

Since a patient in a group tends to take up a large part of group time when he tells a dream and his associations to it, it is useful to ask the other members to free-associate to the dream so they do not feel bored or excluded and can also benefit. Then the members can explore not only the dreamer's but the nondreamers' associations for insightful psychodynamics and psychopathological material. Using this method rather than encouraging the exploration of the meaning of the dream to the dreamer alone welcomes this intrapsychic participation of all the participants. More is gained for each member than if the nondreamers simply offer their interpretations of the dream—often a resistance on their part to self-exposure and self-exploration.

A member, Bill, projected an associated woman patient in a dream in a dual role: both as a menacing figure and as a lovable one. He did this before free association or biographical acknowledgment had given us any indication of his mother's ambivalent attitude toward him. Interpretation of the dream enabled him and the group to discover the castrating mother image with which he compulsively invested the woman. As he recognized the transference features of his vision of her and saw her as in fact a friendly associate, he was able to divest her of her threatening aspect, and she became more lovable. As he progressively analyzed the compulsive character of his attachment to her, he dispelled even this maternal hold, and she became simply an engaging friend, stripped of maternal qualities but with an attractiveness of her own. In these instances, reality proved much richer and more rewarding to the patient than his illusion.

In psychoanalysis in a group, if a copatient is aggressive toward the dreamer, his dream, or his associations, it is good practice to explore the provocation for the attack in the dreamer and in the aggressor. In this way we attempt to arrive at some understanding of the encounter, so that the dreamer may be encouraged rather than discouraged to report further dream material. Generally, some members of the group see the positive in the dream. If, as an occasion happens, there are only negative reactions, the analyst ought to explore with each member this homogeneous manifest response and search for latent material. At the same time the analyst may wish to emphasize what is constructive in the dream.

Patients may use a dream to break through or support resistance. Dreams may also be used as resistance by a patient. One patient, Irene, came to each session with a dream. Although these dreams were revealing of her psychodynamics and the group worked with them, resistance took the form of not expressing personal reactions to the analyst. This dynamic was acted out in her life in two ways. First, Irene maintained great distance from her father, really wanting him all the time but isolating herself in a remote part of the house and hoping he would come to her. Second, she never really related to a man. While in treatment, she finally began to build a relationship with a man. She had not yet reached orgasm in intercourse. That some part of her problem still exists is expressed by her putting the dream in the way of her relationship to the analyst. The fact that she tells her dreams, however, is in itself positive.

Activity and Acting Out

Acting out is more readily discovered and revealed in the group than in the therapeutic dyad and can, therefore, be more easily examined for resolution. Patients who reveal "secrets" to one another in private dyads outside of group meetings engage in a form of cliquing, a resistive leakage that subverts the analytic process. It is an acting out, a resistance to treatment. Members are, therefore, encouraged to expose one another in the group setting. They are urged to "betray" one another's secrets to the whole group.

In any therapeutic group there is a good deal more activity than in the therapeutic dyad. The activity may be appropriate or an acting out or both. Much of the activity is not acting out but a wholesome consequence of vigorous group interaction. There is lively expression of good will, friendliness, and support as well as anger and aggression. When acting out occurs, it is partly a consequence of the strong emotional multilateral excitement. If the analyst pursues an interpretive role with respect to acting out, it can commonly be checked. When analytic confrontation fails to limit acting out, the therapist may, all else failing, be obliged to forbid it. Such imposition of restraint generally provides so much relief from anxiety that patients usually appreciate the superimposed control.

Even if the analyst does not limit acting out, the patients themselves before long put an end to it. If they seem unable to do so they plead with the therapist to help them exercise control. There is finally such frustration among acting out patients that they turn to the group and the leader for restraint and insight.

Clinical experience has demonstrated that there need be little concern about acting out. If patients can function twenty-three hours a day without the analyst, they can be relied upon as a rule to exercise reasonable restraint. Factors supporting control over acting out are the wholesome realistic goals patients set for themselves and the preservative influences in various healthy ego functions. Other sources of restraint are the projection of reasonable authority, regard for the analyst as an appropriately controlling influence, the wish to be guided by conventionality and tradition, by what is fit and unfit, by rules of conscience. A deterrent to acting out is that it will in time be exposed. All acting out ends in such frustration that self-corrective needs and leadership in the group move the members to set their own curbs on the pathological activity.

We must ask whether the group setting provokes more acting out and what values we are applying to patients in a group. Some analysts believe that any sexual behavior during analysis is acting out. There are probably some who feel that having sex seven, seventeen, or twenty-seven times a week is acting out. Others may think that not having sex is acting out. At what point is the particular sexual activity acting out—that is, contrary to the best interests of the patient's growing development, to the resolution of neurotic conflicts, and the discovery of new, more fulfilling, and healthier ways of behaving and living?

When is masturbation a forward movement, and when is it acting out? Let us consider two cases.

A young man, Gary, had never masturbated and had never had a conscious experience of sexual feeling or fantasy or a sexual relationship with another person. The exploration of his sexuality led to the beginnings of masturbatory activity. The expression of himself in masturbating may, at that moment, be considered forward-moving. It would become resistance if, for example, he refused to continue to struggle to develop a heterosexual relationship or, after establishing one, returned to masturbation.

Another young man, Jeff, had a large number of girlfriends. His sexual activity was pathological. He was a Don Juan who would have a one-time contact with each woman and end up in bed with her. After entering treatment, he separated himself from women and concentrated on masturbation as his only source of sexual gratification. This was, in part, a healthy development. There came a time when to continue to do this was resistive to forward movement to constructive change. It was an attempt to maintain the status quo. He had used masturbation to overcome the repetitive seduction of one woman after another and to avoid early confrontation of his fear of the father. It became clear that he was now using masturbation to resist having a sexual relationship with a woman and resolving his problems. His isolation from women was a form of resistance. He feared facing the anticipated violence for being sexual, in a transference with the analyst as the forbidding father. Rather than come to grips with his own felt and projected violence regarding the castrating father and resolving the conflict, he sought to avoid it. The persistent masturbation had to be approached by the careful analysis of these two factors, the resistive element and the transference element, and the relation between the two.

Working Through

It becomes apparent in any therapeutic group that the analyst's advocacy of freedom to express associations, fantasies, dreams, thought, and feelings leads to a good many highly charged responses. These interactions are both appropriate and inappropriate. Group members become increasingly aware of the typical distortions that characterize each one of them. As time goes on, these transference reactions are traced to specific familial antecedents. The process of working through entails a conscious struggle to choose more reasonable and realistic alternatives to the persistent transference maneuvers.

There is more reality-boundness in group than in individual analysis. In the group, even while the patient reveals what he thinks and feels, he is obliged to be regardful of the thoughts and feelings of his peers. This consideration for others prevents pathological retreats into loss of realistic bounds. It enables each member to become aware of his own provocative behavior. Not only is self-understanding meaningful but consciousness of one's effect on others is equally relevant.

Patients and therapist offer different kinds of help. Patient help is offered more spontaneously, more impulsively, and more compulsively. The therapist's helpfulness has more purpose, more usefulness, and is suggested with more discrimination.

A concern of some therapists is that a patient may inappropriately offer another insight with which he is not yet ready to cope. The impression is that a poorly timed proffer of insight may be damaging to a member as yet unable to deal with the anxiety evoked by the penetration of his defenses. Patients, however, seem able to deal with insights from their peers either by rejecting them or by gradually assimilating them. When the analyst poorly times his interpretation, the patient becomes more upset, because the insight comes in the authority vector.

A patient does not have the knowledge and skill in timing interpretations that the therapist has. Patients nevertheless often make useful comments about one another with good intuition and considerable acuteness. They are not by nature experts in psychoanalytic theory and practice but their unpremeditation, plain matter-of-factness, liveliness, naivete, free of the technical language of psychoanalysis, and the manifest wish to be helpful enables them to be constructive with one another. The emotional intensity associated with their observations is also an element in their influence on each other.

Understanding and confrontation among copatients are both more easily resisted and invited because they emanate from peers. The group analyst can more often than not simply permit the patients to interact, for they generate less anxiety than he does. He may then selectively interpose his own impressions when they are most useful. Interaction and interpretation among patients generally invigorates, supports, and intensifies the improvement of the members.

Perhaps the citation of a few examples of the transference process as it occurs in the group will be illuminating.

In prior individual treatment Helen evidenced erotic interest in her analyst that was associated with some fear and anxiety, mixed unconscious feelings originally directed toward her father in childhood. These were never conscious nor expressed. During an early group meeting, the analyst complemented James on his brilliant intuitive appraisal of her. She felt, at once, that he was being favored, and she reacted with jealousy, feeling that he was more highly regarded for his intellectual talent than she. Immediately anxious, she challenged his statement and reacted with marked hostility toward both him and the analyst throughout the duration of the meeting. Despite her competition with him for the analyst's esteem, she felt that James would inevitably do better than she and that the therapist would just as certainly always promote him because he was a man. The compulsive nature of her conduct, together with its interesting sequel, came out at the next session. Helen said that on leaving the previous meeting she had gone automatically to a florist to order an elaborate bouquet for her mother. Suddenly confounded in the flower shop, she stopped and tried to realize what she was doing. There was really no occasion for sending her mother a bouquet, for the mother was not ill, nor was it a holiday or an anniversary. Understanding followed directly. She knew then that in the group the analyst had changed from a father to a mother figure; James, the man the therapist had complemented, had become a substitute for her brother, with whom she had been in perpetual rivalry for her mother's attention. Praise of him elicited the projection of the mother figure onto the analyst. It also aroused a keen hostility toward James and especially toward the analyst. The gift of flowers was to propitiate a mother who was annoyed by her conduct, to conceal her welling resentment, and to appease her conscience for coming so close to fully expressing her anger against her mother. Of striking interest was her abandonment of the father image in the therapist as soon as the group provided a situation in which the analyst could reward a man, who was at once invested with a brother quality. Apparently Helen was able to recreate the father image as long as the analyst was alone with her. As soon as the original family was reanimated by the group setting and more particularly by the authority figure's approval of a man, a particular familial constellation was revived that necessitated a revision in her earlier investment in the analyst. A high estimate of a man unconsciously recalled greater admiration of her brother and disapprobation for herself. Her mother had been the prime agent in the construction of this historical configuration.

Later meetings brought out her mother's actual preference for Helen's brother because he was a boy. Helen's compulsive penis envy, her disregard for her feelings, and her excessive regard for excelling intellectuality, in the company of which she always felt doomed to come off second best, reproduced her relationship to mother and brother. By attention to the aspects of her shifting transferences to the analyst and to James, we were at last able to help Helen relinquish familial claims on her and to react in her own and other's right.

Another example likewise shows how transference on change when the patient enters a group. In thirty preliminary sessions, Joe and the analyst got on famously. Joe was brilliant, serene, and exceptionally friendly. There was good rapport on both sides; they liked each other. He made rapid progress. There seemed to be no resistance. He interpreted a dream, and the analyst would add an additional point. Joe accepted it, usually with a modification that seemed appropriate. There were no stumbling blocks—it all seemed too unneurotic. The analyst proposed that he join a group, where certain areas of his personality might reveal themselves more adequately. It took the first group meeting to provoke the only indication of negative transference that could be discovered. He was a changed man. The harmonious relationship, his appreciation of what the analyst had done for him, and his willingness to act on insights vanished. He challenged substantially everything the analyst said, and his keen intuition, though extremely helpful in analyzing other patients, was unconsciously intended to forestall and belittle the analyst's contribution.

Whereas in prior sessions there had been easy exchange, in the group Joe would hardly allow the analyst to speak. He interrupted, he anticipated and predicted (often accurately enough) what the analyst was about to say. The analyst held his tongue for the time being. But very soon the group noticed Joe's compulsive behavior and began discussing it. When the analyst called to his attention the contrast between his former complacent demeanor during individual analysis and his subsequent truculent attitude toward him in the group, Joe expressed surprise and embarrassment at having been guilty of such behavior. But even as he spoke, he was struck with a flash of historical insight: he recalled with what pontifical dignity and Victorian strictness his father had held court at the dining table when Joe was a child; how one had to tiptoe about the house when his father was napping on Sunday afternoons; how he was not allowed to speak in his father's presence unless spoken to. And he remembered other indignities, extending to his not being allowed to enter the bathroom as a very little child when his mother was bathing—a privilege, however, that his father permitted himself. At subsequent meetings he explained how all his life he could talk freely and easily with one person, just as he used to do with his mother. But in the presence of a group he felt driven to excel, to be the genius in the drawing room. In every social gathering, he habitually recreated the family milieu and automatically strove to become its guiding intellect. The group suggested, and Joe acknowledged, that he might now be playing an assumed paternal role in the new family. Then he remembered how as a child he had been almost irrestibly impelled to challenge his father in everything the latter did or said, but he had never quite dared to carry it off.

The reproduction of his relationship to his mother when alone with the analyst and to his father and family when in the group led to deeper insight into his oedipal conflict, his attachment to his mother, his repressed rivalry with his father, and his compulsive replacement of the father in every regenerated family. Certainly, Joe's transfer to a group revived old family ghosts that could not have been so easily discovered or dispelled without reproducing the household unit.

Helen's and Joe's stories raise at least three salient points. The first is the sudden appearance of occasionally unforeseen bursts of transference toward the therapist or another member after a patient has been introduced to a group. The second is the inevitable appearance of previously latent facets of personality, new and multiple transferences in the recreation of the old family, so that movement into a group changes behavior. The third is the recall of significant incidents in early life by the flashback method in relation to the analysis of immediate transference.

Analyst's Transference and Countertransferences

Countertransference is thought by many to be the analyst's transference. The distortion is perceiving the patient or patients in a group as if he, she, or they were members of the analyst's original family. We consider the analyst's transference distinct from countertransference but nonetheless of great importance. Kutash (Kutash and Wolf 1983) coined the following terminology to cover some important types of analyst's transferences: *direct transference, projected identification transference,* and *introjected transference.* In direct transference, the analyst or group therapist reacts to patients or group members as if they were members of his or her original family. In projected identification transference, the analyst or group therapist identifies with the patient or patients and projects his own early feelings from his own family onto the patient. In introjected transference, the therapist takes on the role of his own parents in the way he ministers to the patient or group, who become original family members; influenced by introjection, the therapist acts as his or her own parent might as leader of a recreated family. The analyst who finds himself thinking, "How could he, she, or they have done this to me after all I did for them?" might find he is the victim of an introjected transference reaction.

The following is an example of transference in a patient in a group, met by transference as well as countertransference in the therapist. Bob, on the death of his sister, spent the next group session projecting the group as a family that, unlike his own, would comfort and be with him, to the point that he invited all the members to his house while he sat shiva. He called on the group leader to take the role of his long-dead father, who had shown him some affection, phoning him to ask him to call group members to let them know he was sitting shiva at his home. The group leader, under supervision with one of us, described how he identified with this neglected patient, now without the father from whom he had got some sustenance. He found himself encouraging group members to attend, and only when one gentleman said, "I'm confused—are we supposed to be a group or a family?" Did the therapist catch his transference and countertransference and say "A group. But you may, of course, have your alternate session at Bob's."

The following situation exemplifies the transference/countertransference cycle in a group setting. It is possible to illustrate this effect because we know the patients' transferences and their implicit expectations, as well as the analyst's psychodynamics. Mary lent Fred, a copatient, some recordings, which Mary claimed Fred scratched and Fred claimed were already damaged and hurt his hi-fi needle. These patients were both music lovers. Their transferences were similar in that both patients projected "bad mother" images on the other and turned to the analyst as the "good mother" who would side with each against the bad mother projected onto the other patient. The transference of the analyst was having to settle arguments between the symbolic mother and father, which always gave him some anxiety, but his countertransference was immediately to fulfill the passionful, irrational demand of Fred and Mary by trying to settle their argument. The chances are that the analyst could avoid countertransference if he were not also in transference. Most parents want the child to side with either father or mother. There is much opportunity and pressure in the group for the analyst to become an omnipotent judge as a way of handling his anxiety and helplessness.

Our transferences and countertransferences may account for many failures because they elicit copatient transference and countergratification and encourage patients to try to meet our transference and countertransference needs. Countertransference may be concealed in what the therapist chooses to emphasize or analyze in the contestants when she is, in fact, favoring one or rejecting the other. Often, by some technical or theoretical device, she rationalizes the taking of sides or an irrational, inappropriate action in a contretemps between patients. Sometimes the analyst has a pressing need to solve a conflict immediately and thereby to cut off any interaction between patients. This is true of patients' expressions not only of anger but also of positive feelings, which may give rise to anxiety in the analyst and a need to interpret quickly.

Role of the Group Analyst

The primary ingredient of psychoanalysis in groups is attention to unconscious material, the study of intrapsychic processes. The therapist sets the tone of group meetings by his lead in the pursuit of unconscious material, free association, and the analysis of dreams, resistance, and transference. The search for unconscious processes and motivations leads the patients to their suppressed history, awareness of its compulsive repetition in the present and speculation about the conscious choice of more realistic alternatives.

As multiple interaction develops in the group, the therapist leads the patients into the exploration of unconscious motivations and their genetic determinants. If the leader permits the group simply to interact without analysis, he supports resistive and defensive behavior.

Analytic intervention needs to be made in such a way that the interactive participants are given insight multilaterally. One member should not long be the exclusive focus of analytic attention. If he is so scrutinized by the whole group, the therapist should examine the contribution of the observing copatients and confront them with their resistance. In so doing, the analyst does not permit any one member to stand alone under critical analysis. A single patient subjected to group scrutiny often has the support of certain other members. If he does not have any allies and needs one, it is the function of the therapist to afford him whatever support is needed.

In the advanced stages of treatment a central problem is that of working through vestiges of pathology. Here, too, a discriminating estimate of the uniqueness of each patient's disturbed psychodynamics and therefore the particular devices to be used to move him or her toward a more reasonable adjustment have to be studied, planned for, and employed.

Let us, for illustrative purposes, considered one member, John, who is extremely impulsive in expressing his feelings but who considers thinking things through as unspontaneous and controlling and regards planned activity as too frustrating compared with immediate yielding to affect. Working through this problem for John entailed a discriminative review of the kind of emotion he indulged. When this emotion was irrational, our struggle with him was to bring him, in time, to the expression of more appropriate feelings. But having progressed so far, he has not yet reached the optimal therapeutic experience. It is necessary, further, that we help him see the value not only of relevant affect but of thinking things through and of planned activity.

Let us now consider a second member, Susan, who withheld feelingful responses but exulted in her intellectual and interpretive productions. Here an adequate resolution of the problem called for an analysis of the patient's resistance to her own emotion in order to liberate it and a corresponding demonstration to her of how her compulsive intellectuality was equally defensive.

Reference has often been made in the literature of group psychotherapy to the emergence of group leaders and auxiliary therapists among patients, particularly later in therapy. A note of warning is in order to caution the analyst against the patient's exploiting such a role in resistance to participating affectively. By engaging as a leader and interpreter of other members' difficulties, the patient may well conceal his own affective detachment, his underlying compulsive seniority, or his competition with the therapist. The latter, in his ready appreciation of help from all resources in the group, may be too readily inclined to condone whatever analystic aid he can get in the group and accordingly be misled into tolerating what may at times be a resistive maneuver. This is not to say that analytic observations coming from patients may not sometimes be evidence as well of their budding resourcefulness, in which case their interpretations can be welcomed as therapeutic for both the donor and the recipient; but it would seem reasonable to say that only the analyst is the leader in terms of expertness, that although patients can certainly play reparative roles, they have neither the knowledge nor the training to be considered auxiliary therapists. If they are so regarded by the group or so regard themselves, their activity may well be examined for its disordered significance. And if the analyst looks on a patient as an auxiliary therapist, he may well explore his perception for countertransferential content.

A third member defied impromptu activity to the neglect of thought and feeling. He was accordingly very active physically in the group—he couldn't stop moving. Where another patient was verbally tender, this patient embraced; where one member spoke in anger, he was ready to throw something or strike; and where one man wept, he, rather, tore his hair. Here, working through involved the exercise of control over such undeliberate activity, the quest for more planned operations, and the pursuit of the uses of reason and affect.

A fourth member was compulsively devoted only to those activities that were, in essence, defenses against repressed material, rationalized as strategically reasonable. Here the resolution of the problem lay in the analysis of his behavior as defensive and compulsively repetitive, lacking in the sensible planning that might lead to fulfillment of his real potentials.

In all these instances, we are interested in each of the three dimensions of thought, feeling, and behavior, in the kind of intellectuality, affect, and activity, and in which form of these is pursued to the neglect of the others.

The same discriminatory emphasis is required in the study of what temporal accent the patient gives to his productions. If he is enmired in an exclusive preoccupation with his past, we are interested in his present and his future. If he is engrossed primarily in here-and-now experiences of the moment, we would lead him to an exploration of his history and a consideration of eventualities. If he is wrapped up with his future, we want to know more of his background and current necessities. If the patient is absorbed in sexual matters, we would direct his attention to his interpersonal relations apart from his sexual obsession. If he excludes sexual content from his revelations and seems exclusively consumed with social relationships, we would attempt to analyze the resistances that exclude consideration of his sexual needs.

One member, prepsychotic or psychopathic, may need stronger superego controls. A second, overconscientious and bound by rigid inner monitors, may need some release from an incorporated sense of duty. A third, a borderline whose ego has been weakened by schizophrenic parents, may require ego strenthening as the primary therapeutic intervention.

Another member, too readily given to value only his unconscious production, may have to be led to lay store by conscious activity. Still another, inattentive to unconscious material, should be guided to a more serious contemplation of underlying motivation. One patient, preoccupied with dreams, may have to be induced to explore other dimensions of his life in waking experience. Another, who never reports dreams, should be induced to pay attention to this voice of his unconscious.

One member, too involved with the other patients, would be directed to develop and explore his extragroup contacts. Another, detached from the group but seemingly involved with people outside the group needs to be induced to extend his interaction in the group.

One patient, haunted by his parents, may not be able to let others intrude on his continuous involvement with his forbears and may require a weaning toward admission of nonparental associates into his limited circle of experience. Another, divorced from her family and in reeling flight toward nonfamilial figures, may need a careful review of the real and projected defenses that keep her from a wholesome acceptance of her parents.

These examples are sufficient to illustrate the importance of the analyst's maintaining a discriminating view of the particular pathological dynamics of each patient, so that she can keep in mind the specially indicated means of working through. In doing so, she also makes group members aware of their uniqueness in terms of their needs as well as their potentials, so that they are not so commonly impelled to demand from the therapist that she treat them all the same way. Even in the most homogeneously organized group, there are always enough differences in character structure, psychopathology, and resources to call for such differentiated study and treatment. Moreover, when the analyst is thoroughly aware of these distinctions and the need to treat them differently, she no longer feels threatened by the patient's complaint that "you don't treat me the way you treat him." But if the therapist persists in making discriminating estimates of each member, she finds before too long that group members soon follow her lead, cease demanding undifferentiated responses from her, and, in their own interest, recognize the value of differences and complementation.

According to some group therapists, the leader is somewhat more active during the end phase than during the middle phase of group psychotherapy. Here again, we believe a discriminating view of the therapist's activity, passivity, or neutrality must be taken, and consideration should be given to the timing of his interventions as well as to the kind of engagement he chooses to serve the patient's positive evolution at this moment or in the future. With a member who is initially silent, the analyst may choose to be active or passive, depending on which maneuver he believes will best call forth a response. With an initially verbally monopolistic member, the therapist may have at first to intervene very actively in analyzing his narcissism and, in a terminal phase, just as actively in esteeming his allocentrism. With a shy, withdrawn patient, the analyst may in the beginning be quite active in encouraging him to participate, in a middle phase be just as energetic in appreciating his more vigorous communication, and, nearing termination, be more passive as the patient appears to be doing well enough on his own. These differences in patient requirements point up once more why a nondiscriminating, stereotyped prescription for the therapist's role at so-called group phases can no more be appropriate to the needs of

all than to the needs of one patient in different periods of his progress.

The analyst's or a patient's comment to member A may apply as
well to patients B and C. But even D and E may get something
out of it by virtue of comparison, learning to appreciate their differences from A, B, and C gaining insight by contrast. Understanding here occurs, then, not only out of identification but out of difference. The analyst is careful when he generalizes from one patient
to the next. A collective interpretation tends to obscure specific differences that may vary with each patient. A generalization may enable a member to resist deeper and more refined insight into his
unique dynamics. Still, the therapist seizes the opportunity, when
a recollection or dream brings insight to one patient, to encourage
exploratory reactions of other members to the same recollection or
dream.

Termination

The end of treatment for any given patient stirs the remaining
members. Their being witness to one patient's recovery is encouraging to them. By departing member impels the others to try harder
to attain a similar state of well-being. He may animate them in a
time of relative despondency. He may make them more introspective in order to learn how he attained his goals. He may induce in
them a competition to succeed as well. Occasionally, the success of
a "graduate" may induce a contentious resistance in which another
member may insist on his readiness for discharge when he is hardly,
in fact, ready to do so.

Conclusion

Psychoanalysis in groups can be effective because patients become
aware of one another's appropriate needs and develop increasing
ability to understand and cope with their transferential distortions.
Patients achieve in groups a remarkable ability for mutual exploration and understanding and for multilaterally reparative behavior.
In the group, interaction is examined as it occurs, not just between
patient and analyst but among copatients as well.

The psychoanalyst in groups has been up to now the student, the pupil of the individual analyst. Developments in group analysis over the last thirty-five years may now improve and intensify individual analytic treatment. If individual analysts would acquaint themselves with the value of group interaction, of socialization, of engagement with personalities other than the analyst, of solving hierarchical and horizontal vector difficulties, of working though compulsive preoccupations with rank and status, of multiple interaction in attaining intrapsychic gains, these phenomena would receive the attention they deserve—even in the course of individual analysis.

It is of some interest to set down some of the integral characteristics that determine the content and process of group as compared with individual analysis. The numbers of patients in the group provide for the simultaneous presence of vertical and horizontal dimensions. The analyst is experienced as more distant and copatients as more accessible. Transference reactions are aimed at both the leader and at fellow patients. Transferences in the group are less uniform and less entrenched than in the dyad. The number of provocative peers in a group makes it more difficult at the outset to detect what is a reasonable response from what is irrational in the course of the manifold interactions. Despite this, the excitation of feeling, whether positive or negative, healthy or sick, provides each patient many opportunities for experiencing assurance and insight. In the group, there are both more securities in reality and hazards in unreality than in the analytic dyad. Still, the leader's distortions are more acutely examined by his assembled patients. And the possibility of the therapist's acting out is generally excluded in a group setting.

The multilateral character of transference becomes more obvious in a group. The affective intensity of transferences among patients is more easily tolerated than is one-to-one transference because its power is lessened when aimed at a fellow patient. Occasionally, lateral transferences bind patients together and become a force that keeps patients in treatment. Such intense feeling for an individual analyst might induce an analysand to flee therapy or to feel helpless or terrified. In the group, interaction is engaged in by the patients, and the therapist can maintain a somewhat detached but active observing role. It is not easy for a patient to isolate himself in a group because others push for activity, reactivity, and mutual responses. As a result, relationships become transferentially intensified. The occasion for more provocation of pathology as well as analytic therapy coexist because of the interactive intensity in the group. Following such interpersonal interaction, analytic examination of unconscious processes provides insight.

No one patient monopolizes analytic attention. Examination of intrapsychic material follows the interaction of dyads, triads, etc. No member is expected to play only one kind of role, to subscribe to a group process or to be homogeneous with his group. The patient is so encouraged to engage in noncompulsive and liberating activities that he is finally free to leave the group.

2

Psychoanalytic Group Psychotherapy

Henriette T. Glatzer, Ph.D.

The *working-through* process is the warp and woof of analytic group therapy. Those who practice both individual and group analytic psychotherapy recognize that working through is as essential in the latter as it is in the former and requires the same laborious going over of detailed material, with repetition and elaboration of interpretations of defenses so that the defenses become less rigid and mechanical. The working-through process, briefly defined, is the continuous attempt to transform intellectual insight into affective understanding by resolving those resistances (Greenson 1965) that impede insight from leading to significant and lasting changes. Since affect makes insight more believable and therefore more subject to reality testing, it is, in short, what produces the therapeutic results.

Much of this material is adapted from Glatzer 1969 and 1978.

How is the transition effected between intellectual insight and genuine change in feeling and action? Why is it so difficult to achieve even in the best regulated analytic treatment? This is so (Freud 1914) because the three unconscious areas of the id, ego, and superego involved in the reactions to the working-through process are not only in resistance to this process but are in conflict with each other and within themselves.

Resistances of Id, Ego, and Superego

The Id

The id contributes to the working-through process by projecting its archaic wishes in the transference and by striving continuously to accomplish them through the unconscious repetition compulsion; in bringing them to the surface, the id is involuntarily helpful in our efforts to analyze these infantile drives. The tenacity of the id in resisting change, however, creates great difficulties in therapy. Well known is the entrenched masochistic pattern of repetitive, passive, self-defeating behavior in patients. The individual analytic session was once considered the most effective arena for the production of regression, but experience over the past thirty or forty years with analytic psychotherapy groups has disclosed that the group milieu, by its special effects such as emotional contagion, splitting of the transference to the therapist, target multiplicity, peer identification, mutual support, and universalization (Slavson 1950) is also effective in inducing regression, and fears, guilt, and chronic infantile behavior patterns are revealed relatively early.

Although there is a general agreement that there is regression in group psychotherapy, there is a disagreement as to its depth. The presence of fellow members makes therapeutic regression in analytic group psychotherapy different because of the quicker check with reality; but I question whether this difference is so basic. Although the repeated transference regressions with different members in the group make the episodes of regression shorter by the undeniable evidence to the patient that he is projecting similar distortions on dissimilar people in the group, this does not mean that the regression is necessarily less intense. The reliving of old hurts and traumas in the group can be extremely vivid even though the duration of such reliving may be briefer. It is as if the group patient receives short, irregular shocks instead of long, equally spaced ones.

The Superego

Superego resistance stems from unconscious feelings of guilt and the unconscious need for punishment and operates against the success and recovery of the patient in analysis, although at first the superego inadvertently helps the analysis by tormenting the patient to remember and confess repressed material. In the group, there is the added masochistic element of exhibiting one's self negatively to others. Later on the superego uses the working-through process as proof that the patient is a hopeless case. Negative therapeutic reactions are evidence of the superego's misuse of interpretations for purposes of torture. Alexander (1929) noted this, and Bergler (1949) elaborated upon it. Alexander found that the superego was corruptible and could be bribed with pain and depression to accept disguised id wishes. Bergler showed that in a successful working through the superego does not become benign but changes its methods of torture. While the superego still remains cruel and antilibidinous, the aggression is now directed against the id and much less against the ego. The transformation of the superego from a corrupt to an incorrupt state is one of the decisive points in therapy, but constant work is required before the bribing and appeasing of the superego with pain, unhappiness, and depression can be brought to an end and the superego enabled to assume its "normal" punitive functions. If the therapist stresses this aspect of analysis and uses it in the group, he will find that group psychotherapy can be of inestimable value in the long, uphill job of working through of masochism, guilt, and depression. In the group, the other members often reinforce the therapist's interpretations of the patient's masochism. They point out his compulsive need to blame himself for what is unavoidable or not his responsibility. They show him also that if he makes a mistake or falls into a trap, he need not endlessly atone for it. The group can assume the functions of the incorruptible superego and not accept suffering and guilt as the price for the patient's unconscious enjoyment of his miseries. They can help the patient to say no and to avoid neurotic interacting or acting out so that he will not later have to repay the superego with depression.

The Ego

The resistances of the unconscious ego to the working-through process are varied and subtle. The unconscious ego, having arranged a compromise between the id and superego at the price of symptoms, anxiety, and character problems, tries to preserve the neurotic balance and uses every means to defeat and offset any effective interpretations. Learning something new, especially something painful, upsets the basic narcissism of patients and they react with anger. It also revives their fear of passivity, with its unconscious meaning of being pushed into a passive position and overwhelmed or wiped out. The patient is in conflict between the pleasure and reality principles. Removing the resistance of the unconscious ego enables the patient to accept the limitations of reality. The infantile ego wants to cling to the fantasy of megalomania and, resenting any imposition of reality by effective interpretations, it defends rigorously against them. The long, tiresome, and repetitious task of working through further infuriates the unconscious ego, which reacts with anger, boredom, and pessimism.

In several papers (Glatzer 1959, 1965, 1967) on group treatment of orally regressed characters, it was shown that interpretation to fellow group members of similar chronic character problems lessens the narcissistic hurt for these patients. It is also less anxiety-producing for them to accept such interpretations from peers who are not as invested with the archaic witch fantasy, especially for those patients who have an inordinate amount of unconscious fear and hatred of the pre-oedipal mother. But there is another kind of group interaction that has come to my attention, that of repairing the narcissistic wound sustained by having had to accept an interpretation by the therapist in individual treatment. In order to obliterate the insult, the patient represses the interpretation and then uses it on another member as if it were his original discovery. When this is called to the patient's attention in the proper setting, it becomes subject to reality testing and helps to promote genuine insight. The following is an illustration of this.

> Among her other problems, Gloria, an intellectual college graduate, had enormous difficulty in reading. This created great tension on her job, and it was only her phenomenal memory that carried her through. In individual treatment we had connected this reading inhibition with her early guilt about using reading as a way of indulging in incestuous fantasies. Not being able to read easily was a reaction formation against the wish to peep and the price she paid her superego for her childhood voyeurism. We had also related her inhibition to her rebellion against her mother's urging to read and be intelligent. Her resentments of her mother were numerous, but one of the principal hurts was her mother's preference for her brother. These interpretations, which were partially understood and accepted, helped to improve her relationship with her mother but did not substantially lessen her reading block. At one group session, when another member talked about his difficulties in studying and reading, Gloria began to question him. She eventually made the "electrifying discovery," first for him and then for herself, of the link between the reading block and the voyeuristic inhibition and the rebellion against the mother. She could accept these interpretations only when her narcissism was placated, only when she believed she had actively discovered these interpretations for herself and did not feel pushed into the passive position and thus rendered vulnerable to the power of the dreaded preoedipal mother. She could also repair any narcissistic injury by identifying with the powerful mother and actively giving to another member (younger brother). At a later session, when another group patient also made a "new" discovery, the group reminded him that they had heard it before. I called to their attention this general unwillingness to give the therapist credit and explained it as a defense against fear of passivity, applying its particular application to each of them.

A survey of all analytic therapies indicates that all too often results fail to meet expectations, especially with severe psychoneurotic, borderline, and character disorder patients. Analysts have found that the ideal aspect of working through does not materialize, no matter how well conducted the analysis. Brodsky (1967), in an article on working through, discusses this problem. Although he agrees that transforming insight into affective experience leads to changes in character and behavior, he feels that the aspect of this that is central to working through is the mastery of painful affects, particularly anxiety, and refers to working through as suffering through. In my examples, I hope I show the dynamic quality of reliving painful affects as it takes place in the "here and now" group setting, where multiple crosstransferences, identifications, and defenses are enacted in an elaborate network that produces striking insight. Karush (1967), writes that an impediment to working through is often introduced by the analyst's countertransference, which is compounded by the theoretical concepts of proper passive techniques. He advocates that the analyst be more active as a teacher and an idealized object who influences by example. In another paper (Glatzer, 1962), it was described how the role of group analyst makes one more flexible, active, and responsive than the individual analyst, and how together with other group members one can more easily convey reality. The greater activity of the group therapist makes one a more available object for constructive identification, and he can ultimately become the representative of the stronger ego and less corruptible superego.

The feeling of impatience on the part of the analyst almost inevitably associated with the working-through process is intensified when working with orally regressed, long-suffering, masochistic patients. The therapist often becomes involves in countertransference with these difficult patients and may respond with anger, boredom, pessimism, or passive masochism himself. In the group, transferences to peers provide the patient with opportunities to break up the transference neurosis impasse with the analyst. The other group members often take over for the analyst and insist that the patient face his transference distortions, thus giving the therapist enough of a respite to regain his objectivity. Kubie (1968) has stated his pessimistic opinion that resolution of the transference phenomenon is limited even under the best of conditions and urges that it is essential to explore the effect of introducing extraanalytic contacts between patient and analyst and/or changing therapists. In an almost apologetic way, he also suggests that the therapist consider placing the patient in group analysis toward the end of an analysis.

As Fried noted (1961), there is greater productivity and action in analytic group therapy than in individual treatment because the patient is likely to express his feelings directly in reactions and actions rather than just reporting them. We who have been doing combined individual and group analysis know the tremendous impetus group therapy gives to an analysis and how much it contributes to resolution of the transference neurosis. Even the most passive patients can resolve their sticky dependence on the analyst and are able eventually to give up individual and later group therapy and be on their own. The summation effect of other members' observations, the repeated evidence of the distortions in the interconnecting transferences, and the continuous exposure of the defensive structures reinforce reality for the patient and help him to break through to affective and lasting understanding. This does not mean that the working-through process in group psychotherapy is not long, laborious, and tedious, and sometimes it is particularly unwieldy because of the greater opportunities for acting out. But the splitting of the transference to the therapist and the projections onto others in the group make it more bearable for the analyst.

Clinical Illustration

In individual analysis, Andy, a young lawyer, had made many gains, but his rivalry with his peers suggested that group therapy might be of benefit. His keen competition with others undermined his strong potential in his profession and seriously affected his social life. He was also still locked in a symbiotic relationship with his wife, with whom he acted out the part of the deprived child of a niggardly mother. His wife was baffled by his strong dependency needs, his infantile rages and hypochondriacal worries. Although their relationship had improved so that they were no longer contemplating divorce, there was still a large residue of neurotic acting out between them. (She was in treatment too.)

When Andy entered the group, he expected to be not only the therapist's favorite but the group's. His years of analysis, his intelligence, good looks, and appealing ways made him anticipate an easy victory. To his dismay, he found himself with a group who saw readily through his defenses and began to resist his attempts at a "snow" job. This had the effect of making Andy try harder to be more charming, sincere, and concerned about everyone, but he only succeeded in exposing this brittle defense.

Andy's rivalry in the group centered on Richard whom he envied and wished to show up. This negative transference was reinforced by the fact that Richard came from the right side of the tracks and possessed all the social and intellectual attainments which Andy felt were his prerogatives. Richard was well liked and admired in the group because he had moved a long way from his former schizoid detachment and caustic provocations, and the group members appreciated the witticisms and goodwill he was now able to express. Having the group prefer Richard to him repeated earlier traumatic experiences in which Andy had felt that his father, and later his stepfather, had taken his mother's attention away from him. In his youth he had worked at undoing this by trying to get friends to love him and win them away from the favorite. When he could not, he would go to his mother for consolation. He repeated this in the group and again became the little pygmy who tried to fight the big giants by being smarter and more endearing. His constant efforts to turn the group and the therapist from Richard only resulted in exposing his blandishments and pushing Richard into the role of the "wise" elder who either ignored Andy or explained him.

Simultaneously, Richard, on his part, was unknowingly working through with Andy his relationship with his dead younger brother who had been "better looking," more social, preferred by their mother, and sought after by the girls. This transference to Andy was not clear until the day Andy brought in a dream in which his mother, father, and grandmother (who had adored him) were alive. Associations revealed that Andy's dream was a defense against the group's insistence the week before that Andy face up to his mother's death and stop reliving the fantasy that she was still alive and a bulwark against his dying. The group was also united in their insistence that he give up playing the role of the charming little boy and be himself. The group now became the incorruptible superego who would not let him get away with exhibiting himself masochistically. The superego was still exacting and antilibidinous but in a more constructive direction. He was being forced to grow up and face the unpleasant task of relating and dealing directly with people.

Richard's unconscious jealousy of Andy was touched off when the group devoted a great deal of time to Andy's dream and connected his fear of death with his rage against the omnipotent mother who abandoned him to mortality by dying herself. This jealousy of Andy plus the death theme reactivated Richard's anxiety, which he expressed in two brief dreams. In the first, he heard that his cousin, mother, and sister were dead. In the second, he had to complete his unfinished fourth year at a state university (not the Ivy League college from which he had graduated). It was a breeze for him, but when he had to give a talk on De Soto in front of an audience, he found he had not prepared it and woke up in a panic with perspiration rolling down his face. Richard's associations indicated that the cousin was his brother and that the previous week's discussion about Andy's fear of dying had revived his anxiety about his brother's death. A woman member suggested that Richard's going like a breeze through his fourth year at the state university represented his fourth year in the group, where he had earned a position of respect and admiration for his therapeutic changes. Another member observed that there might be a connection between Richard's brother and Andy. Some of the more recent members in the group had not heard details about the brother's death and asked about them. They were told by Richard that his brother was killed while asleep in his girl friend's De Soto convertible, which she was driving. Richard stopped and gasped, "Oh, my God, the talk on De Soto and the De Soto car. I never recalled the make before. I had completely forgotten it." Chuck, another member, said with deep emotion that Richard's fear of women as killers was strengthened by his brother's death and that he connected falling asleep, orgasm, and being killed. This was one of Chuck's anxieties too. Although it had been gone over many times in Richard's individual treatment that he felt guilty for his brother's death and that he experienced women as killers, these two ideas had never been linked together. Through the unique byways of the group process—the discussion of anxiety-producing topics, such as fear of dying and omnipotent mothers, as well as the reliving of intense rivalry feelings plus the spontaneous reactions, involvements, and interpretations by group members—there was enough of an impact in all of this to produce the dreams that revealed Richard's still unresolved guilt for unconsciously wishing and accomplishing the death of his popular brother by the dreaded all-powerful female and the great anxiety that he would be punished for this by being killed himself by her. The basic superego accusations were finally exposed, and we could begin to grapple with the heretofore almost inaccessible core of repressed fear and guilt.

The Working Alliance

Until recently, the treatment alliances have not been accorded the same importance in analysis as have transference and transference neurosis, the prime interactional processes (Glatzer 1978).

The term "working alliance" as used in this paper is similar to Greenson's (1965), and refers to the healthy, realistic collaboration between the patient and the therapist and between patient and patient. The contention of this paper is that the group process stimulates the unfolding of the working alliance in all patients. The appropriate use of therapeutic interpretations, which constitutes the working alliance, is accelerated in a group in several ways. The group therapist can limit himself to appropriate interpretations because (1) the other members provide the means to effect a working alliance when he is in countertransference or makes mistakes with a patient, and (2) they also maintain the working alliance by helping the patient to regress to fantasy material and then assisting him in examining and analyzing his regressed behavior.

The group process is also useful in developing enough motivation to establish and continue the alliance in borderline, narcissistic, and impulse-ridden patients whose ego resources are usually too fragile to form the special kinds of object relations necessary to weather the stresses and frustrations of treatment.

The Group Process

Patients with poor ego functioning who are able to regress in treatment but have difficulty in observing and synthesizing reality test-

ing often respond to the inherently natural atmosphere of a group
with its more realistic, straightforward, and direct procedures. The
reassuring presence of other group members decreases dependence
on the therapist and reduces initial anxiety about passive submission to an omnipotent figure, which, in turn, makes the analyst
seem more human and less frightening. It is easier for a more regressed patient to identify with his peers than with his therapist
because the other members are not as enmeshed as the analyst in
the patient's archaic transferences. The patient is, therefore, better
able to accept reasonable observations from them. Challenges by
them of his characterological defenses become less threatening to
his narcissism as he sees others responding to the same challenges
with self-scrutiny instead of hurt feelings and defensive anger as is
his wont. It is not only the analyst but the other members and the
group as a whole who act as an auxiliary reasonable ego. Fellow
members may verbalize for a patient when he finds it difficult to
find words. They may free-associate, introspect, and help an inhib-
ited patient to regress to fantasy material; at the same time they
also reinforce reality by stopping the regression as they press him
to examine and analyze his behavior with them. An ongoing, cohesive group has learned from the therapist to find meaning behind
behavior and words and so can conceptualize for the patient the
underlying connections between what he feels and how he acts.
They effectively and caringly take on the therapist's analyzing role.
The patient's self-esteem is raised by their friendly interest in, and
speculations about, his interactions with them, and he is eventually
stimulated to search for his own deeper motivations. His sense of
being an active adult is reinforced when he finds that he can contribute to everyone's intrapsychic understanding by disclosures of
his own irrational feelings and conflicts and the other members are
able to use his unconscious material for their own benefit. As the
group moves from the beginning to the middle stages it becomes
more task-oriented and the analyst's interventions become less necessary and less frequent. The more regressed patient now finds it
easier to identify with his peers and to participate in the working
alliance. His self-respect improves as he joins them in their explorations and evaluations of all material, including the giving and associating to dreams.

The true sign of the working alliance is when the patient actively uses the interpretation and applies it meaningfully. If he does not make use of the interpretation, he is at the mercy of his neurosis and is not identified with the therapeutic process. When he has the insight, he has to deliberately decide whether or not he is going to continue with a piece of neurotic behavior. In a well-functioning group, the members help him make the choice. They search for signs of change, and if he keeps on repeating the same neurotic pattern, they become impatient and accuse him of wasting the time of the group. The group expects a patient to become an adult working member and does not hesitate to put pressure on him to grow up and use his insights to change his behavior.

The patient's ability to identify with the therapist's reasonable ego can strengthen both the horizontal (between members) and verticle (patient to therapist) working alliances in a group. The impact on the group member who is helping another is ego-reinforcing. He is able to perceive in others what they cannot perceive and his valid insights are accepted by the other patients and/or the therapist. When piecing together interlocking transference behavior in the group, it is best to refer back by name to the members who have made insightful and productive observations and agree with them before the leader adds any additional interpretations of his own, if they are necessary. This is not done as an artifice but as a natural reaction and respect for the accurate perceptions that members contribute to the developing insight. This interaction is probably similar to the "real relationship" which Greenson describes as "genuine and real." The group also acts as a restraining influence on the therapist when he becomes therapeutically overzealous. They become realistically jealous or angry if he becomes countertransferentially involved. When the group analyst realizes this, it is imperative that he admit it, as this acknowledgment reinforces the working alliance or "task relatedness" (Bion 1961) of the entire group. By acknowledgment it is not meant burdening the group with self-revelations, which is an error and a caricature of being authentic. On the other hand, if his expressed human appreciation and respect for other patients' appraisals of the situation is transferentially distorted, some group members will support the analyst. They reinforce reality for the jealous or angry patient when they remind him that his contributions have also been acknowledged by the group therapist in that session or in the past and put pressure on him to question the ego-syntonic quality of his character defenses.

A group analyst does not have to take extra measures at nurturing the nontransference reactions between the resistive patient and himself. The other members and the group as a whole share with the therapist the role of becoming a "new object" for the patient. The group members have the means to effect this as they intuitively provide the please-specific types of support the patient needs. It is natural for them to suggest, confront, disclose, clarify, educate, reassure, or whatever with relative ease. The group analyst, therefore, can more easily restrain his "proprietary zeal" (Freud 1921) and restrict himself to the therapeutic task of interpreting transference and resistance. He can limit his noninterpretative efforts to maintaining a working alliance to the basic human influences his personality will have on the patient as he manifests qualities of courtesy, friendliness, human understanding, empathetic neutrality and warm but not intrusive interest.

Clinical Illustration

Perhaps the following material will illustrates some of these points. As expressed earlier, the group analyst does not have to work so hard at fostering the working alliance in a well-functioning, interacting group. Even when he does get caught in countertransference, anxiety, or therapeutic overzealousness, other patients will extricate him. In this illustration, sibling rivalry with one patient, Noel, was an added incentive to another patient, Melinda, to work harder at being more successful than he in expediting the analytic progress. This happened when I got bogged down by my own overappreciation of Noel's catalytic role. He was an extremely bright, articulate man who was the most open in the group about revealing feelings and primitive fantasies. Melinda was a borderline woman who could sense relatively easily the underlying crosscurrents in the group. Recognition of this ability by me and the group had increased her self-esteem measurably. Competition with Noel acted as a further impetus for her to use her fine intuitive ability to unearth the repressed intragroup tension which had been stirred up the week before.

Noel came in thanking the group for having helped him so much last week with some disturbing aspects of his new affair and said he was eager to pursue it further. It was unusual for anyone in the group to try to dominate the session after he or she had had a productive hour and was not in a state of anxiety. When some man said Noel was trying again to hog the time, I commented that maybe Noel had stirred up some anxiety in the men last week and encouraged them to stay with his problem. This was so, but they were not ready to probe this area. Noel had touched on his archaic fear of women, and I thought he might stimulate some of the men to examine their similar repressed fears if he continued on this topic. They went on, but, of course, the discussion grew flat and dull and went nowhere. Patty, another member apparently jealous of my attention to Noel and apparently unconsciously encouraged by my permission to rehash, stiffened her resistance and described her "new" old problem with her boyfriend and her "now" old insights about him. Since these were variations of similar superficial insights with which the group had worked many, many hours with her, I began to wonder to myself why the group was still trying to struggle with the same deeply entrenched defenses instead of picking up her resistance. But I did not interpret. In retrospect, I felt that I must have felt guilty about encouraging the group to continue with Noel's problem and wanted to be "fair" to Patty and give her equal time, so I let them persist in telling her what they had always told her and what she never seemed to synthesize—that she was still expecting more from him than he was capable of giving. This went on for a while until Melinda interrupted to say that the group was avoiding something and was going along with the camouflage problems of Noel and Patty. She added that they both had gotten a lot of help from the group the week before but wanted special attention from me and kept looking to get my okay. The group was letting this happen, she said, to avoid some embarrassing kinds of feelings that were going on in the group. She was right. Although some people, like Patty, accused Melinda of being jealous of the attention paid to Patty and Noel, most of the others realized and agreed that the group had become boring and repetitious. Bolstered by the majority of the group, Melinda turned to Alex, a married man with strait-laced and puritanical ideas, and said, "You and Rhoda were flirting with each other last week." Alex turned crimson but poo-pooed the notion by saying that of course he liked Rhoda but only as a father since she was as young and pretty as his daughter and was so sincere about trying to work out her problems. I now recalled the subtle sexual repartee between them. Someone else remembered that Tom, another member, got upset last week when someone "joked" that Tom's always backing up Noel had homosexual overtones. Tom had indeed transferred his homosexual anxiety about his brother onto Noel and, like Alex and Rhoda, was content to let the group stay with safe material. The others were probably reacting to my seeming overinterest in Noel, and, in unconscious protest, they stopped working analytically. The group, spurred on by Melinda, now began to dig in and talk about their repressed feelings to one another and to me. The tenor of the group changed dynamically as the working alliance was restored and the deeper layers and anxiety masked by more superficial concerns were released and their transference meanings investigated.

3

Group Analysis

**Malcolm Pines, D.P.M.
and Mario Marrone, M.D.**

S. H. Foulkes' group analytic psychotherapy is a distinctive British contribution to psychodynamic group psychotherapy. There is a widespread belief that there is a unified British approach to psychoanalytical group psychotherapy, often termed "the Tavistock Approach" or "the group as a whole." We shall try to explain that there are considerable and significant differences both in theory and practice between group analysis and other British developments in group psychotherapy.

Historical Context

S. H. Foulkes, who already was a well-trained and experienced psychiatrist and psychoanalyst, came to the United Kingdom in 1933 as a refugee from Frankfurt, where he was Director of the clinic of the Psychoanalytic Institute. He began to work with therapeutic

groups in 1939, when he was again in exile, this time from London
and the confines of the British Psychoanalytical Society. He was
now free to try out ideas that he had been developing for the previous decade, in which the influences of social psychology, sociol-
ogy, and history were combined with the dynamic forces of psychoanalytic psychology. World War II led to an explosion of group
work in the British Army and Foulkes took a prominent part in
this, largely through his work at Northfield Military Hospital. His
first book, *Group Analytic Psychotherapy* (1948),[1] (see 1983) was
based on these experiences and in it he lay down the first comprehensive theory of group analytic psychotherapy, successfully
combining both social and individual psychology.

The Sociocultural Context

The post–World War I years in Britain, 1920 to 1930, was an era
where the psychic sequels of warfare—grief, loss, mourning—and
the defenses against these experiences—imposed themselves on social consciousness, bringing about a recognition of the importance
of a dynamic social psychology that began to understand interpersonal bonding. This led to studies of separation and loss, to the
recognition of object relations as a fundamental aspect of personality
development and thus to the beginnings of the British Psychoanalytic School of Object Relations. The early work of Ian Suttie, John
Hadfield and John Bowlby, all connected with the Tavistock Clinic,
laid the foundation for a psychoanalytic psychology of interpersonal
relations that received a great impetus from the controversial work
of Melanie Klein in child analysis. Melanie Klein worked in London
from the mid-1920s onwards and had a great influence on British
psychoanalysis. The former workers began to explore the infant's
tie to the mother, the pre-oedipal period of personality development, which Klein expanded in dramatic detail through child analysis. Though Klein's work was based on psychoanalytic instinct theory, not on the study of the mother–child relationship, Bion later
added the crucial dimension of the mother's response to her child's
projections through his theory of the container and the contained.
This dimension is well complemented by Donald Winnicott's concept of "holding" and the "facilitating maternal environment." The

concepts of projective identification, of containment and holding are influential in group analytic theory and technique.

W. R. Bion's experience in World War II and the immediate postwar years at the Tavistock Clinic led to his Basic Assumptions theory, which was expanded with great force and considerable obscurity in his very influential book *Experiences in Groups*. He became the leader of the postwar Tavistock Clinic, which had then changed from its prewar eclecticism to a solely psychoanalytic approach to individual and social psychology. Many of his colleagues had shared in the experiences of military psychiatry and looked to Bion as their leader.

The Tavistock Clinic entered the National Health Service in 1947 and was an active center of group psychotherapy for the next twenty years. Bion himself quickly switched to individual psychoanalytic work, partly through the influence of Melanie Klein with whom he was in training analysis and who was strongly opposed to group psythotherapy, seeing it as a resistance to individual analysis. Bion's later work concentrated on the psychoanalysis of borderline and psychotic patients.

The Tavistock Institute of Human Relations was formed as an independent body outside the National Health Service in order to continue the exploration of psychoanalytic social psychology as applied to social institutions and industry. Much of the international reputation of the Tavistock School arises from the work of the Tavistock Institute of Human Relations. Foulkes was never on the staff of the Tavistock Clinic.

The differences between Foulkes' and Bion's approach to group analytic psychotherapy are significant. Bion subordinated work with the individual patient to his/her significance in the dynamics of the group. Foulkes viewed group psychotherapy as "the treatment of the individual in and by the group" and felt free to address both the individual as well as the dynamics of the group as a whole (see below). The passage of time has shown that Foulkes' approach is effective as a treatment mode whereas Bion is more effective as a demonstration of the power of group dynamics and is best used in a training situation. A numerous and effective group of colleagues gathered around Foulkes, forming the Group Analytic Society and Institute of Group Analysis, and the work is represented in the journal *Group Analysis,* which he founded. Bion dispersed his group of coworkers; he preferred to work alone.

The Development of Group Analysis

The Group Analytic Society (London) was created for the purpose of exchanging ideas and experiences about group analysis. The intention was to form a center for scientific meetings, to extend the training and teaching work carried out by Foulkes and some of his close associates at various teaching hospitals, and to stimulate research and publication. The work of the Society grew until it became too complex and extensive to be handled by a scientific society alone. In 1970 the Society delegated the specific tasks of training and qualification to the Institute of Group Analysis, which was formally organized in 1971. While the Group Analytic Society has grown into an international network with its administrative base in London, the Institute of Group Analysis is a teaching institution and has been responsible for the establishment of a widely recognized professional qualification in group analytic psychotherapy.

Throughout its development group analysis has defined and maintained its own theoretical and methodological identity. Yet, it has been characterized by a certain degree of eclecticism. Such eclecticism has been a blessing for the group analytic movement and is still necessary. While at one level we treat group analysis as a self-contained system of ideas and therapeutic strategies, at another level group analysis is regarded as a territory capable of accommodating and integrating an interplay of different perspectives and ideologies. So, within the British and European group-analytic movements we give ourselves permission to accept and welcome a plurality of tendencies and styles, coexisting and cooperating among ourselves while united by some *basic and important principles.*

The main basic characteristics of a group-analytic group are: (1) verbal communication is privileged, (2) the aim is clinical, (3) the number of group members is small, (4) the therapist acts more as a facilitator than as a director, and (5) the participants are out-patients. Nevertheless, group analytic principles have been applied to working with large groups, to in-patient group therapy, and to teaching in higher education.

The following are theoretical elements of group analytic psychotherapy.

1. The essence of man is social, not individual. Each one of us occupies a nodal point in a family network and in society. The great forces of conscious and unconscious psychological dynamics are transmitted through group and social networks and we are deeply imprinted by these great forces, through to our very core. In the healthily functioning group and society we play our part in the reception and transmission of psychological forces in ways that develop, accept, and respect the unique nature of the individual that are complementary to the nature of the group.

However, the inevitable conflicts between the developing individual and the primary family group can lead to neurosis. No longer a *nodal* point of the functioning network the individual becomes a *focal* point of unconscious conflict within the primary group. The neurotic position is abnormally individualistic, the result of individual and group incompatibilities. From this viewpoint therapy is the uncovering, alteration, and resolution of these early conflicts in the therapeutic group, which first repeats and then transcends the original neurotic process.

2. Symptoms are expressions of unconscious conflicts. They can be understood and translated into articulate language and thereby the symptom gains in communicative and social value. When heard and understood the patient can gain an effective nonneurotic place in the group process and enhance the growth and understanding of the other group members. Group analysis emphasizes communication as more or less equivalent to the therapeutic process. As the members of the group make themselves understood to each other at ever deepening levels they mature as persons and gain insight into a mastery of the neurotic process. There is an ever-present dynamic between the process of *insight* and of *adjustment*. Group pressures drive toward the necessity of understanding oneself in the context of understanding and being understood by others. There is a constant pressure *to adapt and to change*, to be part of the developing and maturing group. Neurotic behaviors become clearly revealed as interpersonal relationship problems within the therapeutic group and as disturbances in the communicative process. The group becomes concerned with the individual's presence and their

behavior within the group, more than with their symptoms and problems without the group. One aspect of the therapist's task is to establish and maintain the climate of exploration and of understanding by the group members. Much of the therapeutic work can be done by group members once this aim has been achieved.

Methods of communication in the group are conceptualized in terms of four levels.

1. *The current level.* On this horizontal level persons bring to the group their involvement in their current life situation. They engage in here-and-now responses to each other, which they explore in their roles as patients in a group. The group represents the community in miniature and the relationship to the conductor is seen on a manifest level as that involving a leader or authority figure.

2. *The transference level.* Here relationships and interactions are understood in the light of transference meanings. The members transfer to each other their earlier interpersonal experiences. Group members represent sibling and parental figures, and play out significant earlier relationships within the group. Therapeutic work at this level is to understand and clarify these processes and thereby to transcend them.

3. *The level of bodily and mental images or "projective level."* On this more primitive level other members may reflect unconscious elements of the individual self, as a "stand-in" for aspects of the self—thinking, feeling, reacting—that have been discarded and displaced onto or into an "external object" that then contains the projection (Projective Identification). The discarded aspects of self might be either valued or denigrated: "good" qualities may be recognized in others but not in the self if those good qualities are incompatible with a predominant negative self-representation, for example, of a worthless self. The "bad" aspects of self that threaten a rigidly defined "good" self will equally be invested in others. The group as a whole can symbolize and represent a maternal entity.

4. *The primordial level.* This is the mythic and archetypal level in which the group members come to recognize that they are engaged in a deep unconscious process of change that can be best understood through the concepts of Jung and the archetypal unconscious.

It is axiomatic in group analytic psychotherapy that the group as a whole develops a history over time. The processes of communication and of relationship are laid down in what is called a *group matrix*, the sum of all the interpersonal processes and networks of relationship and communication that have been established. It is the laying down of this matrix that contributes to the capacity of the group to contain, to hold and to integrate the individual members' inputs into the total psychic system. Primitive, aggressive and destructive affects imposed by individual members on the group situation can be responded to and understood at a higher level of psychological functioning. Each person can be helped to see their own experiences in wider perspective and to take back into their own understanding a modified, more comprehensive experience of themselves. The "group as a container" has replicated the task of the mother of infancy, as expounded by Bion. The "unmetabolized alpha elements," the elements of raw experience, are responded to by the group as a parental entity who can understand, contain, respond in the way that the capable parent cares for the distressed infant, and in Bion's terminology are transformed into beta elements, available to the mind. This is a very powerful and fundamental mechanism of group analytic psychotherapy that will carry the individual members through many a distressing experience. For the group to develop this capacity to behave at a more mature level than any one individual can, there has to be a proper selection and balance of group members and a proper therapeutic technique. These issues will be addressed later.

Object Relations Theory and Group Analysis

From the theoretical point of view, group analysis in Britain has been fertilized by contributions made by Jungian analysts and Object Relations oriented psychoanalysts. Although Foulkes himself was biased toward the ego-psychological point of view, as represented by Anna Freud and her coworkers, much of her formulations are congenial with the ideas of Object Relations theorists. In recent years, the work of Winnicott, Fairbairn and other Object Relations theorists has been influential as an important part of the reference framework for group analysis. Furthermore, the work of Bowlby and his associates on their Attachment Theory is of import to group analysis.

Because of its historical and conceptual roots, group analysis has always been more congenial with those schools of psychoanalytic thought that have moved from the study of the individual as a single entity to the study of the person as part of a relationship network. In this sense, Object Relations Theory and Attachment Theory—which we see as an offspring of the first—have been important sources of insight. In essence, what these points of view concern themselves with is the part that maternal behavior and early experiences of the child with his immediate environment play in the formation of personality structure. This line of thinking is often referred to as the "relational/structural model."

But even if group analysts have been very interested in using psychoanalytic insights and the far-reaching theory of the mind formulated by Freud and his followers, we must not forget that group analysis is not applied psychoanalysis. Traditionally, psychoanalytic ideas have derived from observations made in the dyadic and private setting of the therapeutic session. Yet, in recent years, some psychoanalysts have made conceptual formulations on the basis of data taken from sources other than the clinical situation, such as—for instance—baby observation. Account has been taken of information given by research done in the fields of family therapy, developmental psychology, ethology, and so forth. In any case, group analysis has direct access to an important source of information that cannot borrow from other disciplines and that other disciplines do not have, namely the interaction and communication in the small group.

Technical Issues

The first task of the group analyst is to work toward integration and cohesion of the group. The group has to become a secure base from which each individual member can explore unhappy and painful elements of his present and past life. The group cannot always be a secure base to an optimal degree because there will inevitably be interpersonal conflicts, members will leave and be replaced by new ones, some stages of the group process will be more favorable in fostering a sense of safety than others, and many times members will show failures of empathic responsiveness to one another. Yet, the group analyst, by means of being reliable, supportive, and facilitating can do a great deal in terms of achieving an optimal level of security.

The group analyst has gradually to help group members relinquish their false selves and get in contact with their true selves. He does that by helping patients freely to express their feelings and needs and by allowing them to break down emotionally in a holding environment. Very often, when a patient is able to express intense feelings of sadness, deprivation of grief, other patients—by means of a process that we call "resonance"—are able to get in contact with similar feelings and express them. When this occurs, the group feels a unique sense of togetherness, of being able to understand each other at a deep level. Repeated experiences of this kind induce a climate of group cohesiveness. The more secure the patients feel, the more they will be able to express themselves and make contact with their true selves. Conversely, the more they can express themselves and show their true selves, the more secure the group will become. When a group member leaves, it is important to explore all the implications of this departure. Among other things, this will put in perspective the fact that becoming a group member and separating from the group are important events that reflect the way a person forms relationships and deals with loss. Frequently, group members are wrapped up in themselves and find it difficult to listen genuinely and to respond to other group members. This failure of empathy can be ascribed to the probable situation of their not having had empathic parents in their years of immaturity, so that they have not internalized the capacity to respond to others in an empathic way, to see the other as a separate individual, to see the world through the other's eyes and to have concern about the other's problems and difficulties. However, in the group, most members gradually develop or increase their empathic responsiveness and understanding.

Frequently, group members talk about their social situations, their financial difficulties, their reactions to and interest in political events, etc. They can also—explicitly and implicitly—see the group as a representative of the community at large. One can say that on these occasions the group is functioning at the "current level" or that one can conceptualize what is going on in the group at this particular level. Provided that communication does not have the characteristic of "chit-chat," the group analyst may take these communications seriously, insofar as they may be serious attempts at exploring the sociocultural, economical, and political milieu in which we all live. To have a better understanding of the kind of society in which we live is very important and it is a task that group analysis can better afford than individual analysis. We all have many needs: to survive, to be protected, to have affectional bonds, to understand, to participate in social networks, to have leisure, to create, to have a sense of identity, to have freedom, to intervene in decision making, to find meaning in what we do. Many of these needs depend on social factors, not only on our internal or personal capacity to achieve what we want. However, when group members talk about social issues, these communications may contain transference aspects or reflect mechanisms of splitting, projection, and so forth; the group analyst should be able to think about this material also in terms of their unconscious meaning. For instance, while patients may be clearly justified in expressing their dissatisfaction with the world in which they live, they may also use external reality to reflect projected and split-off aspects of their selves.

Patients come to the group session with stories that often consist of accounts of their recent or present circumstances. Normally, these accounts are anxiety-ridden. In other words, the patient may show that he feels unduly anxious in the course of a particular event, or he may be very anxious in reporting such episodes. On the other hand, defenses against anxiety or anxiety-linked affects may be detected. The defense may take different forms (denial, projection, displacement and so on) and the group analyst should have no difficulty in detecting them. In watching out for signs of anxiety and defense, the group analyst can indeed formulate a hypothesis regarding (1) the nature of the anxiety, (2) the current life situation that reactivates the anxiety, and (3) the pattern of parent–child relationship that may have given rise to this type of reaction. Very often, the present or recent situation that the patient is describing does not objectively warrant such anxiety and this can be understood only as a reactivation of anxieties related with situations of childhood or adolescence. Free communication in the group is in itself a powerful way of dealing with defenses and resistance; all of which are basically a blockage against communicating memories, thoughts, ideas, emotions. Members can take one another, as well as the conductor, as transference figures. Transference can be analyzed as it occurs in the here-and-now. But it can also be interpreted in terms of what sort of transference reaction there seems to be in these relationships that the patient currently has with others outside the group. Transference is seen in terms of misattributions that the individual unconsciously makes under the influence of representational models of himself and others.

Working at the transference level, the group analyst encourages his patients to consider how his representational models of parents and self dictate their transference reactions and the way they engage in relationships in their current life. It is useful to trace the historical origins of representational models, to explore how the manner in which an individual assesses himself, perceives people, interprets events, shapes his social roles, responds with certain type of feelings, forecasts outcomes, organizes his behavioral reactions, selects persons with whom he hopes to make initimate relationships, and so on, can be related with episodes and scenes of his early past.

At the projective level, the group analyst tries to understand communications in the group as processes whereby each individual alone or several members conjointly project aspects of their selves into other members, into the therapist, or into the group as a whole. This normally has an effect on the interaction and when those people who are recipients of these interactions react, then we can conceptualize what is going on in terms of projective identification. Adequate containment and processing of these projections contribute to the integration of different aspects of the self.

A distinctive theoretical contribution of group analysis is the concept of mirroring. Foulkes coined the word to describe the way in which the patient can recognize aspects of his own self in others, the others acting as mirrors. What is not acceptable to the self or recognized in oneself can often clearly be seen in others. This process of recognition of the self in others can lead to a gradual enlargement of self-representation and the reownership of those aspects of self that have been discarded. An equally important aspect of mirroring is that we have to recognize how others see us and to work with their perceptions. At the neurotic "higher" levels of personality organization, mirroring processes are accepted and used, sometimes quickly, sometimes slowly. At the "lower" levels, particularly in narcissistic and borderline patients, mirroring is threatening. It is experienced as endangering the precariously maintained self and threatens its cohesion and coherence. Then mirroring will be denied and counterprojected. This has been termed "nondialogical mirroring" as contrasted to the "dialogical mirroring" that occurs when the mirroring processes are accepted.

Once the group analyst has been able to offer a model of therapeutic work, much of it can be performed by the members themselves. In this way they depend less on the conductor and rely more on their growing capacities to understand and respond with empathy and insight. Foulkes called this the "decrescendo" in the conductor's authority and the "crescendo" in the authority of the group. The aim of the conductor is primarily to create the setting for psychodynamic work that can be carried out by the group members themselves.

Beyond the Small Group

The incorporation into group analytic theory of concepts formulated by sociologists, social psychologists, and those developmental psychologists who are interested in the process of socialization have led to a growing awareness of the importance of social experiences in wider contexts, wider than the family group and other primary groups. These wider contexts are influential in the formation of those representational models that constitute the internal map that we have about our "being in the world."

The Large Group aspect of group analytic theory and practice has been the particular emphasis of Patrick de Mare. This work (de Mare 1972), which began with a therapeutic community aspect of group analysis based on the lessons of Northfield in World War II, has become the basis for de Mare's theory of large group processes.

Group analysts frequently work in hospital settings, conducting ward groups, and in community settings, such as day centers. The task of the group analyst in these settings is to understand the social dynamics of the institution, to create a space for group analytic work that may be with small or with large groups of patients or clients, or with the staff.

De Mare suggests that the large group can have the function of transforming the hate that inevitably arises in social life from restrictions on individual narcissism, into that form of love that contributes to the ability to share social life in citizenship and within the community. Clearly this can become a very important group analytic contribution to dealing with many troubling social issues.

We will now show the technique in practice with the following case example.

Clinical Example of Group Analysis

This group has been going on for years. It has eight members, whose names—for reasons of confidentiality—we change and call Stuart, Peter, David, Anthony, Clare, Susan, Anne, and Geraldine. Not all of them participate in the part of a group session we transcribe here. The group analyst is Tim.

David says that he is anxious about going to Canada to see his parents. He does not know how he is going to be treated. He gives some indication about the nature of his anxieties.

At this point Geraldine comes in, a bit late. It seems that all is not well with her. Nevertheless, the group is busy discussing David's feelings about his next trip to Canada. Furthermore, Geraldine quickly tunes in and says to David: "You look very unhappy, and although I know how anxious you may feel about going to Canada, it seems to me that something else is adding to your anxiety."

David, as if he were suddenly discovering something about himself, agrees. In fact, he has had a terrible row with Elaine, his girl friend, with whom he lives. The row was about money. Elaine wants to take a larger mortgage and move into a larger house, while he would like to spend less money on it and more on other things. David says that he is concerned with his own reactions, because when he gets angry he reacts in an explosive way. At the time he reacts in this manner, he feels fully justified in doing so, but later he regrets having done what he has, feeling embarrassed, guilty, sad and disconcerted with himself.

At this point, some group members say that there are several issues involved. One has to do with anger and explosiveness. Another has to do with money and what meanings might lie behind it. Susan says that she likes and hates money. Anthony, who is always interested in politics, says that the utilization of money in the capitalist society alienates people from one another. Stuart suggests that this discussion is partly related with the issue of borrowing, namely, taking a larger mortgage. He things it is quite in order to borrow money and he has done so, often, in the past. Geraldine does not like the idea of borrowing. She earns a very high income but she does not feel it is rightfully hers. So much so that she converts all the money she earns into material goods before anybody can claim it back. Peter says "We are talking about hoarding and I hoard money even when I am not earning very much. Also I don't like lending or borrowing. Perhaps, I cannot give or take very easily."

Now, David says that there is something more to it all. When Elaine moved into his flat, the house was in his name. If they take another mortgage, Elaine will want to share the ownership of the house.

Tim, the group analyst, says: "David, it seems to me that there is a connection between your anxieties about going to Canada to see your parents and your fears of making a firm commitment to Elaine. In both cases the anxiety is related to ambivalence: ambivalence toward your parents and ambivalence toward Elaine. At the same time, the whole group is taking up issues such as hoarding, borrowing, giving and taking. I wonder what you mean . . ."

Peter says: "What comes to my mind is something that may upset you, Geraldine, but I have to say it. Last week, in the warm weather, you wore light clothes and your breasts were sticking out. I realized that, sitting next to you, I would be able to see your nipple. And I saw it and I wanted to keep looking. I felt I was stealing something from you but also that you wanted me to do so and that there was a feeling of vindictive triumph in you. But I did not feel I was benevolent, I felt like an intruder but also I wanted to possess your body but without being discovered. I wanted to possess your beautiful breasts in my mind. I don't know if this has something to do with ambivalence, but the other day in the group I thought that my desires for access to my mother were not acceptable."

Geraldine responds: "I always feel very guarded about you, Peter."

The group analyst says: "It seems to me that we are moving on into the question of how we relate with each other. Do we relate with the other as a person, with interest and concern? Do we treat the other as an object to be used or exploited? Do we take and give as an act of mutuality and sharing? If not, what are the underlying anxieties and difficulties?"

Geraldine says: "Well, I came in feeling very upset but I did not feel I could talk about myself. I felt there was no time for myself, that I have no right to talk about my problems. Yet, deep down, I resented you all and especially Tim. You, Tim, knew I was upset, didn't you? Yet, you did nothing about it."

The group analyst says: "Geraldine, there are two issues here. One is that you have been upset for reasons we don't know yet. You may want to tell us now. But, the other issue is that you feel resentful for not being able to talk about yourself, assuming you don't have the right to do so, or—perhaps— that we are not interested. In the group you find it easier to talk about other people than about yourself."

Geraldine breaks into tears and says: "My father is divorcing again. He is depressed and wants to confide in me. I find him overwhelming." She cries. Anne becomes weepy too and explains that she identifies with Geraldine, as she has a very demanding mother who has never been in touch with her own needs.

Now, let's review this part of a session. David is a professional man in his late thirties. He has been in the group for four years. His parents live in Canada and they have been professionally and financially successful but emotionally unreliable and unpredictable. On account of his past experience with them, David feels consciously ambivalent and anxious about visiting them again.

Geraldine, a young, attractive, and intelligent woman, who has been in the group for two years, comes late and visibly upset. Very quickly, she becomes involved with David's problems and helps him to realize that he is not only ambivalent toward his parents but also toward his girl-friend. His ambivalence interferes with his conscious commitment to her. David also mentions his outbursts of anger which are ego-syntonic when they occur and become ego-dystonic later on. Momentarily, Geraldine finds relief to her anxieties by talking about David's anxieties.

Free-floating discussion in the group touches upon issues such as borrowing, giving, taking, hoarding. The group functions in a cooperative and productive way. At some point, the group analyst makes an interpretation about David's tendency to relate in an ambivalent way and leaves the question of borrowing, etc. as an open issue, inviting people—in this way— to make further explorations.

Peter, a young man who joined the group seven years ago and has had traits of polymorphous sexual perversion, talks about his excitement when he saw Geraldine's breasts. Previous work in the group enables him now to make a connection between his need to secretly possess women's bodies and his frustrated desires to gain access to his mother. He had told the group many times that when he was a child he was in the hospital for several months. At some point he was in an isolation cubicle and saw mother only through a glazed window. Peter had been able to recall childhood traumatic events with a great deal of emotion but this time his remark sounds somehow intellectual.

The group analyst takes the opportunity to define the discussion in terms of a preoccupation about the quality of relatedness in the group. Geraldine responds by admitting that, on the one hand she wants the group to perceive and respond to her needs, on the other hand she expects rejection and feels silently resentful. Geraldine's mother left home when Geraldine was ten and from then on she had to look after her father and younger siblings. Her behavior in the group is characterized by her tendency to nurse her needy bits in others. It is always difficult to differentiate her projections from her genuinely emphatic responses. The group analyst elicits the nature of her anxiety: she feels compelled to fulfill a maternal role at the expense of her own needs and fears that people around her—as it happened in her childhood—will make demands and yet, neglect her. This anxiety is reactivated both in the group situation and in her current life situation: her father is divorcing his second wife and turning again to her for support. The group analyst makes a transference interpretation that evokes strong emotion. Geraldine is able to give up her "false self" and show her "true self." This provokes resonance in the group and another group member, Anne, realizes with strong emotion that she, too, has been subjected to role-reversal in the parent–child relationship.

4

The Group as a Whole

John F. Borriello, Ph.D.

A review of the literature reveals a multitude of group psychotherapy techniques for use with patients/clients (Weiner 1984). All
techniques have therapist, patient, and group as components; what
varies from technique to technique is the role assigned to each
component. This variation is dictated by the technique's prescription of what is relevant in order to achieve therapeutic goals. Some
techniques place equal emphasis on the roles of therapist, patient,
and group. Some place greater emphasis on therapist role than patient and group roles. Others emphasize patient role more than
therapist and group roles, while still others emphasize group role
more than therapist and patient roles. All have the same primary
task: to deal with the psychologically troubled who present themselves for group psychotherapy.

The group-as-a-whole technique is used by many group psychotherapists in the world at large. If one were to observe sessions of

these practitioners, one would observe considerable diversity among them. Intervention language would differ; interpretation language would differ. Some would restrict their comments to "the group" and never make mention of individual members. Others would refer to themselves only in the third person. About the only common denominator would be the attention paid to group dynamics. This is the one dimension that distinguishes this technique from others.

Another crucial fact that confuses many is the relation between this technique and the study group of the Group Relations Conferences founded by the Tavistock Institute of Human Relations (Rice 1965). The tasks of each differs. The task of the group-as-a-whole psychotherapy technique is to provide the opportunity for psychologically troubled persons to affectively understand their psychological distress. The task of the study group is to provide the opportunity for members to learn about group dynamics. In the group as a whole, participant motivation for joining is that things are not going well in their everyday living. For the study group, participant motivation for joining is to learn about group dynamics through a study of the here-and-now of the group.

The group-as-a-whole technique as I practice it emphasizes the role of the group in group psychotherapy. Group dynamics are seen as the chief therapeutic agent. I adhere to the group theories as elucidated by Bion. Individuals in psychological distress compose the membership. The group is the medium through which their distress is encountered and dealt with. The task of the group as a whole is to deal with each and every member's psychological distress. It is not to treat the group, a commonly held erroneous myth.

This technique makes certain assumptions on which it bases its work.

1. There are no innocent bystanders in the here-and-now of the group. Said another way, whatever happens in the here-and-now of the group, happens because all members and the therapist in their unique individual ways sanction it.
2. The here-and-now of the group provides the opportunity for each member to study all facets of his or her behavior, especially the interpersonal and the relationship to authority. In other words, the group is a microcosm of the outside world for each member; the group provides each member the *in vivo* opportunity to in-

vestigate his or her behavior and to come to an understanding
of his or her psychological distress.
3. The emotional relationships established between and among the
members and to the therapist are related to the unique past developmental histories of each member and the therapist.

All observations and interventions are shaped from these perspectives. The therapist's ongoing assessment of the here-and-now
concerns:

1. What is happening in the here-and-now of the group (preoccupation of the group, group theme)
2. What is each member's contribution to the here-and-now of the
group
3. What is the relation of each member's contribution vis-à-vis every
other member to the here-and-now of the group (in psychoanalytic terminology, transference between and among patients)
4. What is the relation of each member's contribution vis-à-vis the
therapist to the here-and-now of the group (in psychoanalytic
terms, transference to the therapist)
5. What is the relation of each member's contribution vis-à-vis the
group to the here-and-now of the group (in the language of psychoanalysis, transference to the group)

The data collection and the interventions derived from the data
develop around these five foci. The interpretation language depends
on the therapist's theoretical persuasion. For example, if he or she
is a psychoanalyst and belongs to the Freudian or Kleinian school,
his or her language will logically cohere to that of these systems.
Most group-as-a-whole therapists do belong to these schools, and
their language is couched within these systems. The model, however, will accommodate other systems. The therapist could just as
easily make interpretations of parent, adult, and child interrelations
between himself, other group members, the group as a whole, and
the individual's contribution to the group as a whole.

What is crucial to remember is that the group-as-a-whole technique provides a framework, a way of looking at a group, to use
when conducting psychotherapy groups. It acts as a guideline or
yardstick of measurement for the therapist. It is not defined by any
particular theory. When practitioners want to define it based solely

on their particular theoretical orientations (e.g., psychoanalytic), widespread usage suffers, because then only believers in the theory tend to use it. Of importance is this technique's attention to the group dynamics that facilitate the psychotherapy task. It provides the opportunity for the therapist to use the group dynamics in his or her task of dealing with the psychologically troubled. This technique shapes the therapist's perceptions about the psychotherapy group. The technique acts as a framework within which the therapist can do his or her work. It provides patients the opportunity to confront directly their psychological problems. For patients, the group is a microcosm of what they experience in the outside world.

Theoretical Rationale

Winfred R. Bion is considered the pioneer in the development of the group-as-a-whole model. During World War II, while a psychiatrist in the British Army, he became fascinated by group dynamics, particularly the phenomena of leadership, followership, membership, and task accomplishment (Sutherland 1985).

Eric Trist (1985), a psychologist, was a colleague of Bion's. He worked closely with Bion during the ten years that Bion developed his theories about groups. According to Trist, Bion was not interested in applying psychoanalysis to groups. He was interested in developing concepts that would lead to an understanding of what emerged in a group. Bion spent about ten years developing his theories about groups, during and after World War II. Trist was invited by Bion to join him in one of his first therapy groups at the Tavistock Clinic. Bion wanted someone with whom he could converse about the group and he thought it was better to have this person in the room during the sessions. Trist's role was as an observer. This group met twice a week in hour-and-a-half sessions. Some very disturbed persons composed this group. Trist reports on Bion's style.

He was detached yet warm, utterly imperturable and inexhaustively patient. He gave rise to feelings of immense security—his Rock of Gibraltar quality. But the Rock of Gibraltar is also powerful and he exuded power (he was also a very large man). This did not make the patients afraid of him; rather it endowed him with a special kind of authority that gained him added attention. The patients became aware that they had secured a very exceptional person as their therapist. It represented an X factor of which I could not fathom.

His interventions were on the sparse side and tended to be terse. They could be kept so because he always waited until the evidence for what he would say was abundant. He then expressed himself in direct, concise language that everyone could understand. If a patient made an intervention before he did, so much the better; there was no need for him to make it. He seemed to want to make the group as self-interpretative as possible and to facilitate its learning to become so. (Trist 1985:30–31)

According to Trist, Bion was adamant in his insistence that his only contact with his group therapy patients be within the group. After sessions, Bion and he would go to a neighboring pub to discuss what had occurred. Before Bion would go, Trist would check to see if the coast was clear, that is, if any of the patients were there. The patients in this group had outside contact such as giving parties at each other's homes. Bion was invited to these but he never went. Trist went instead and reported that the norm of not talking about group matters outside of the group was so highly entrenched that it prevailed. He never heard them discuss group matters. He doubted that they did even when he was not present. Trist speculated that these outside-of-the-group parties served a developmental function for these patients. Up until they joined the group, their field of social relations was restrictive and impoverished. These parties provided the opportunity for them to put in practice what they were learning about themselves in the group sessions. Before he was able to discuss this with Bion, he took another assignment to deal with a relatives' group at a mental hospital and resigned as observer of this group.

Trist regrets that not more of Bion's colleagues from his World War II days participated as he did with Bion in his therapy groups at Tavistock. These persons had first-hand experience with what Bion did during the war but not after. As a result, a lot of mystery remains about what Bion did or did not do in small groups as well as in larger organizational settings. Trist observes that today "most people have either repeated parrot-like what he did (baD) or ignored it (baF)" (Trist 1985:2). For the reader, baD in Bion's system refers to basic assumption dependency. An expert/dummy paradigm prevails. The practitioner behaves as if he or she were the dummy (empty-headed) and Bion the expert. Said another way, the practitioner behaves as a clone of what he or she believes that Bion does in groups. BaF refers to basic assumption fight-flight. In this basic assumption, the practitioner behaves as if Bion's theories about groups are the enemy that has to be fought or fled from. Bion concentrated on the group's attitude to himself and his interventions dealt with this.

In 1942, Bion was placed in charge of the training wing of a military psychiatric hospital. The administrative necessity of organizing 300 to 400 psychologically troubled soldiers into some kind of manageable therapeutic enterprise led him to develop a sophisticated therapeutic community. The success of this enterprise brought an invitation from the Professional Committee of the Tavistock Clinic to continue his work there.

While at Tavistock he established one of the first study groups. It was composed of staff and interested colleagues from other institutions. Bion was interested in exploring the phenomena of the here-and-now when people meet in a group to study what is happening in the group. The group began with ten members, but within six weeks there were only five. Bion defined his role as that of observer and commentator on that which he saw occurring within the group. He believed in intervening only when what was happening was being left unsaid. He observed that the group had its own boundaries and that his function, to observe and comment on what was going on within its boundaries, facilitated its study. Defining his role as he did, he became the designated leader and focal point of interest. This role definition is consonant with that of the psychotherapeutic model. He also used the study-group format with patient groups. His first civilian therapy group met twice a week with ninety-minute sessions.

From his experience with these groups, he inferred and postulated the existence of certain phenomena (Bion 1955, 1961). These phenomena, which he labels as basic assumptions, he postulates are operative in all types of groups, whether they be psychotherapy groups, study groups, political groups, or even such large and diverse groups as the army or the church. The basic assumptions are: (1) fight-flight, (2) pairing, and (3) dependency.

For Bion, a group is defined by a task or function. Without a task or function, there is not a group but a collection of individuals. With a task or function, this collection of individuals becomes a group. Bion observes that a group works when it demonstrates consciously motivated behavior directed toward task implementation on the basis of reality. He observes further that basic assumption mentality is forever impeding work-group function. According to him, basic assumption mentality stems from an unconscious assumption on the part of members that the group has met for some purpose other than accomplishment of its task. However, he observes, in specialized groups such as the army or church, basic assumption mentality must be used in the interest of work-group function and survival of the group. The army, for instance, must mobilize the basic assumption of fight-flight in order to accomplish its work. Likewise, the church must tap into and harness the basic assumption of dependency for implementation of its primary task.

The basic assumption of fight-flight operates when the group behaves as if it had met to fight somebody or something or when it behaves as if it had met to run away from somebody or something. Action and panic are essential ingredients of this basic assumption. Fight is evident when:

1. The group decides to battle the therapist because of its fantasy not related to reality that he or she is persecuting it.
2. The group challenges the authority of the therapist when he or she "doesn't do anything."

Flight is evident when:

1. The psychotherapy group decides to invite friends for a party during its session.
2. The psychotherapy group avoids the self-investigative task because of its fantasy not related to reality that a disaster will occur if it is pursued.

Bion notes that the most severely paranoid member will most likely emerge as leader when fight-flight is operative.

The basic assumption of pairing operates when the group behaves as if it had met for the purpose of reproduction, to bring forth a messiah through a pair in the group. An essential ingredient

of this basic assumption is an air of hope and expectation not related to reality considerations. It is as if by a pair getting together
for the group bigger and better things are sure to come. Optimism
reigns.

However, in this basic assumption, the messianic hope must never
be realized since hope exists only when there is something to be
hoped for. Pairing is evident when:

1. Two members of the group predict how much they will have
   improved come next year because they are in the group.
2. Group psychotherapy will cure all ills when its fruits become
   widely known and implemented.

The basic assumption of dependency operates when the group
behaves as if it had met in order to be sustained by a leader on
whom it depends for nurturance, protection, and so forth. Greed
is often of primary concern. Dependency is evident when:

1. In the beginning psychotherapy group, the group members behave as if the therapist were the repository of all knowledge,
   adequacy, and maturity and that all they need to do is worship
   that authority and their problems will go away.
2. The group casts the therapist in the image of a mechanic who
   has hung out a sign reading "Lives fixed while-u-wait."

In this process the group members collectively give to the therapist their individual capacities to do, think, and feel for themselves, or to be curious about themselves, the group, or the therapist. In short, they render unto Caesar what they believe to be
Caesar's.

At this point the term "projective identification" needs to be introduced. It is a term used by, among others, Bion (1962) and named
by Melanie Klein (Segal 1973) who strongly influenced Bion and
with whom he underwent analysis (Bion 1955). Projective identification describes what the author calls "putting in process."

In group, members fit each other and the therapist into unconsciously needed roles. Between and among themselves and the
therapist, they form relationships that are ongoing and that become
the potential objects of repressed needs. In projective identification, members project these repressed needs (part of themselves)
onto each other and onto the therapist. For this to occur, a mem-

bers must be prone to and be perceived by the other members as being capable of realizing their repressed need. Projective identification can be seen when:

1. A need in several members combines around one member. For example, an extremely aggressive member unwittingly may be prompted or coerced to express to the therapist the hostility belonging to all.
2. A very dependent patient may be unconsciously established by the group as the "sick one," "needful one," "one with the most pain," in short, the identified patient to be taken care of by the therapist as a means of vicariously satisfying the dependency needs of all.

Sometimes, the expression of the need arouses too much anxiety or guilt and then the patient being used for its expression is attacked (fight) or rejected (flight). Obviously, this phenomenon can be destructive unless interpreted by the therapist.

1. The patient with the highest dependency need may become established by the members of the group as the repository for their collective dependency. As this process is continued and reinforced, this patient will probably become crippled under the staggering weight of the others' projections of dependency with their accompanying unconscious identifications. When the therapist frustrates this dependency need by refusing to meet the combined need in the other member, the group may behave aggressively toward him (the therapist) through another member.

2. The patient with the greatest propensity to act on and express the aggression of the group may become fixed in this role. The result is that he becomes the constant recipient of the aggressive projections of others as well as of their accompanying unconscious identifications. Eventually he may be pushed into feelings that are very powerful and that, because of their combined strength, are experienced as bizarre and surreal.

If the therapist is ignorant of the projective identification phenomenon, such behavior may prompt him to consider hospitalizing the member or the member may terminate, to the relief of both the therapist and the other members. Either of these eventualities will likely result in the projective identification of the dependency or the aggression in the group onto the next most appropriate member. I believe that this can be avoided by interpretation of the phenomenon to the group.

Bion notes that all individuals have the propensity for combining with the group to become the active server and/or expresser of the different basic assumptions operative at any given moment. He calls this propensity "valency." Valency operates to determine that the individual chosen to meet a particular need is the individual with the highest need to perform the function. For example, the group will unconsciously select for the leadership function the individual with the highest valency to take care of and place others in a dependent position to himself when it is in basic assumption dependency mentality.

The logical implication of this concept is that every dependent leader basically will not believe that an individual can do for himself provided he is given the opportunity. This implication is manifest in the history of institutional care. In earlier years staff and patients colluded to demonstrate that most of the patients' potential for growth and health was gone and existed only in the staff. In recent years, however, some institutional care is focusing on the effort to help patients to realize their own potential. This necessitates working with staff to understand the dependency of the long-term institutionalized patient and to understand what they can do to eliminate this dependency on them. It also necessitates patients working through what they feel as staff exploitation of them. This feeling is the price that the members of any group eventually pay if they continually insist that they do not know how to do for themselves even though presented with the opportunity. The leader who takes over and does for the group is eventually blamed for the group's dependency and is experienced as exploitative. In such situations most leaders eventually feel despair and martydom.

Bion emphatically states that the group psychotherapist must be in touch with his own emotional reactions in the group if his interventions are to be useful. He must distinguish between feelings due to countertransference, which are not to be interpreted to the group, and feelings due to projective identification, which are to be interpreted to the group. Although difficult, a rule of thumb is that when the therapist feels manipulated to behave or feel in a certain

way, projective identification rather than countertransference is operative. Bion respects the traditional analytic position that interpretations based on the emotional reactions of the therapist reflect
his psychopathology rather than the dynamics of the group. However, this did not deter him from making such interpretations. Dicks
(1970) comments that to this day many traditional British analysts
consider Bion a "deviant" in the psychoanalytic group.

Application of the Technique

Some of my typical interventions might be:

Each of you (patients) behave as if I (therapist) am supposed
to answer all questions.

None of you seems to have any curiosity about what is happening in the group.

Each of you behaves as if only Mr. Jones is angry with the
therapist.

There seems to be no curiosity about what's in it for each of
you to have Ms. Smith be so angry with the therapist.

Is there a similarity between what you are experiencing in the
group today and what you have experienced before?

Today each of you behave as if I (therapist) am the only one
who can make sense out of what is happening between and
among you.

Does what is happening in the group today relate to the last
session?

What thoughts are each of you having about the discussion
between Joe and Jill? What do these have to do with me?

Each of you have spoken of feeling down today because of the
unexpected death of Mark. Put into words what it's like to
feel down.

The experience that Joan talks about today, how is it similar
to what the rest of you have been talking about, and what
does it have to do with me?

In the group today each of you are behaving as if your problems will go away if I (therapist) would just say something.

Each of you behave as if Joan is the only one who has experienced hate toward the therapist. What do you suppose
this is all about?

The therapist attempts to demonstrate through his interventions that what brought the patient to seek help is clearly manifest in his or her behavior in the group. He communicates that a serious analysis of the patient's group behavior illuminates his everyday problems. The therapist's behavior reflects a commitment to the belief that investigation and simultaneous cognitive and affective understanding of the emotionality of the moment in the group results in personality change.

Initial Interview

When a patient calls requesting an appointment, I first obtain necessary identifying information and referral source. Next I inquire about why an appointment is wanted. When I actually see the patient, I get a developmental history, give a mental status examination and question in detail about the chief complaint. If not referred by the family physician or internist, I also inquire about whether the patient has a family doctor or internist and when was the last time he or she had a physical. If they do not have one, I will encourage them to get one and will suggest several names if asked. Since my practice is in a large metropolitan area, I cannot recall any not having had one.

Because of my bias and the type of patients referred, I generally recommend all patients for group psychotherapy unless:

1. Patient is experiencing a severe crisis that dictates the need to talk it out. I have found that these patients can be very disruptive to the work of an ongoing group if admitted prematurely.

2. Patient is acutely psychotic, which necessitates admission to a hospital. Once the decision for group psychotherapy has been mutually agreed upon, I interview regarding what the patient expects to achieve in psychotherapy and any resistances to joining the group. Following this, I educate about group psychotherapy. I explain that the patient is the single most important person in the group. He or she will experience feelings toward the therapist, the group and others, both inside and outside the group. Although difficult, he or she is to put these feelings into words.

There are three tasks focused: patient, therapist, and group.

Patient task is to be self-investigative; to be aware of cognitive
and affective internal and external behavior moment-by-moment, to be aware of affective responses to the therapist,
to the group and to other members and to verbalize the
recall of past events that arise while in the group.
Therapist task is to listen and to comment on what is happening in the group moment-by-moment vis-à-vis the therapist, the members, and the group when such gets left unsaid. Interpretations are rarely given; I prefer that the patient
arrive at these. This is based on the belief that the patient
can do this for himself or herself better than any therapist
or analyst as long as the therapist provides the opportunity.
Group psychotherapy task is to provide the opportunity for
each and every member to investigate his or her cognitive
and affective behavior moment-by-moment vis-à-vis the
therapist, the members, and the group.

In terms of group composition, the traditional guides are followed. Heterogeneity with an avoidance of extremes and minorities
is the rule. Heterogeneity revolves around race, age, sex, ethnicity,
marital status, socioeconomic level, educational achievement, intellectual endowment, and ability to tolerate anxiety.

Case Example I

This example comes from a group that is open-ended, meets
twice a week with two-hour sessions (intensive) and is long-
term (extensive). Except for an initial interview and a session
to educate about the group, no members have had individual
sessions; I do not see patients in combined individual and group
therapy.

During the forty-sixth session of an ongoing group of five—
two women and three men—in their twenties and all gainfully
employed, Bill blurted out that he has been thinking about
the group and the only image that he has had was of his father. He said that as he was telling this to the group, the
image of his father reappeared. When he was asked what this
was all about, he responded that he was puzzled. He expected
to have an image of all the group members, as he had been
having until this week. Jim questioned if something had oc-

curred during the last session that may relate to this. He responded that he could not remember what had happened during the last session and asked Susan to fill him in. As she was telling Bill, his facial muscles tightened and he glared at her. Tom and Jim asked what was wrong. Bill said that Susan really irritates him. She reminds him so much of his mother who used to fuss over him and give him very little breathing space. Jack said that that was the spitting image of his mom but not his dad whom he rarely saw. Mary said her father fussed over her, not her mother. Bill said that as a child, he spent little time with his father because he worked the late afternoon–early evening shift. Jack said his father was overseas and came to visit only for birthdays and holidays. Bill related that he yearned to spend time alone with him. He remembers that his dad would always say that if it was all right with his mother he could go with him to the carwash, auto store, and so forth. But his mother always vetoed these trips saying that Bill really did not want to do this, that he really preferred to stay home and play with his friends. He experienced Susan like this, especially when she would tell him what he should do or how he should feel. Also she irritated him when she would put down the group and especially his praise of it. He could not stand her put-down of his oft-repeated statement that he would be ready to leave the group if he could figure out what it was all about for him. Susan said that she was only trying to be helpful and that Bill should have told her early on in the sessions that it irritated him. Bill said that he was not aware of what his irritation was about until today. Susan thanked him for being so honest and asked if it was really irritation that he was experiencing. Bill said "here we go again." At this point, Bill became very angry and Jack joined in. Jack related that he always felt his father worked overseas because he did not like him. When he was in eighth grade he learned that his mom did not want to go overseas because there was no job for her there. He stated he is angry at both his mom and dad: his mom, because she never told him that they were not with his father because she did not want to live overseas, and his father because he never insisted that they live overseas. Jack said that his father acceded to his mom and asked Bill if his dad did the same. Bill agreed. Mary offered that maybe if his dad had insisted, that his mom and dad would have gotten divorced. Jack did not agree and instead repeated over and over that his father acceded to his mom. Mary reported that as she was listening she began to reminisce about her childhood. She saw herself with her mom swinging in the backyard and her dad coming out the back door, shouting to be careful and not swing too high. She reported that her dad would take her to school every morning and instruct her mom to pick her up. Mary said that she hated this but did not tell her parents. One day she told a teacher who told her mom. Her mom questioned her about this. She told her mom that she was afraid to tell. When her mom told her dad, he responded that they were going to continue to take her to and from school and explained to her that it was because it was much safer than the bus. At this point, Jim said that he lost his dad during the war and does not remember him. He left when he was one month old. He had been sitting, listening, and feeling down because he never had a dad with whom to do things. Susan asked if he had a stepfather. He said yes, but he has never lived with him. After his dad died, he and his mom lived with his grandparents. His mother remarried when he was in eighth grade. He continued to live with his grandparents since he wanted to continue with his friends in the same school. His mom moved out of state and he stayed with his grandparents until he went to college. At this point Bill asked Susan what about her parents. Susan responded that her parents and she got along very well when she was a child. Her childhood was a good time for her. This infuriated Bill and he blurted out that he was wondering what her thoughts were. She responded that she was thinking about what she does that infuriates Bill. Bill said he got some idea today. She reminds him so much of his mom. Bill asked her if he reminded her of anyone. She said a fine young man who gets upset very easily when someone tries to help him. Bill asked about her past and she said no-one. Bill said I give up on you today but thank you for helping me get a handle on what went on with me and my parents. He continued that his girlfriend was very similar to Susan and his mom and that maybe this accounts for his ambivalence about the relationship. He laughed and said his mom does not like his girlfriend. He imagined it was because she saw in his girlfriend what she did not like about herself, like we find out about outselves here in the group.

Bill stated that it was as if today the group had become his dad with whom he had wanted to share so much more when a child. Jack said that was similar for him. Jim said for him also. Mary said that it was the opposite for her. She wanted to share more with her mom. She said initially she was feeling very angry at the group but now this feeling is toward her father who was so bossy and controlling. At this point time was called.

This case example demonstrates how members work in the group-as-a-whole technique as I practice it. We have an example of the emotional reactions of the members (Bill, Jim, Jack, and Mary) to the group and the relationship of these reactions to each member's unique developmental past. We also have a demonstration of the emotional reactions of members to each other. The interaction between Susan and Bill is an example of this. We also are provided with the opportunity to witness the patient (Susan) who uses denial as her major defense to avoid working in the group. Subsequent sessions revealed that she had a choatic living situation growing up wracked by violence and deprivation.

This session also reveals to the reader something of my working style. In groups that are new, my interventions prompt for and acknowledge any behavior that supports the group-as-a-whole technique. Once the technique has been shaped, patients work according to the technique. Subsequently, there is less need to prompt and acknowledge for the technique. In this example, each member was working for affective and cognitive understanding. In Case Example II there is greater need to intervene, since it is the first session and each member has not mastered what he or she is supposed to do in order to achieve affective and cognitive understanding. This is relevant since many who observe my groups remark that I say very little or nothing. The rule for me is keep my mouth shut when the group is working.

Case Example II

This is the first session of this group. It is composed of eight members. Seven are gainfully employed, one is a full-time student and three are part-time students. One woman is working part-time in the evenings on an MBA; one goes to law school in the evenings; another is a psychiatric resident; another is a social-work student. One man is working part-time in the evenings on an MS in engineering; another in the evenings on an MS in computer science; another is working on an MD; another who teaches in the evenings is working on a Ph.D in physical education.

This group meets in the evening for two hours once a week. This group is similar to Case Example I except for the meeting frequency. This group is composed of those who have work and class schedules that fit in with the once-a-week group.

The group convenes at the appointed hour. Dr. B (therapist) summons the members from the waiting room to the group room. They all sit down and look at Dr. B. There is silence. Kathy breaks the ice and introduces herself and the others follow suit. Questions are asked about what they did. Silence follows. Next Victoria volunteers why she is in the group.

All follow suit. Members ask each other questions and offer advice to each other. Then all look at Dr. B. Frank asks Dr. B what they are supposed to do. Following this, silence prevails. Dr. B comments that through Frank the members of the group are behaving as if they had not been prepared for what to do in the group. This comment results in members comparing what preparation for the group each had had. Then there was silence again. Next Joseph spoke of his anxiety. Lenora says that it is scary for her since she does not know what is going to happen. Several others nodded agreement. Lenora said she did not know how being in this group was going to help her with her problems. She demanded that Dr. B tell them what to do. Sam said it is evident that he is not going to tell us what to do. Next Alan turned to Michelle and said since she is a psychiatric resident she should know what to do. Michelle said she knows that psychotherapy helps most if the patient works on solving his or her problems. If the therapist does it, the psychotherapy does not work.

Next, Alan speaks of an encounter that he had last week with his boss. He had to have a six-month evaluation. He was shocked when his boss told him that he do his own. Afterwards they would go over it together. He had been anxious for weeks anticipating the worst and he was amazed that his boss wanted him to do his own evaluation. He related to the group that he told his supervisor he did not think he would be able to do it. This was his first job after graduation from college and his first evaluation. He was not familiar with the procedure and he did not want to mess up. The boss retorted that he had faith in him, that he could do it. In fact he could do it better than he, since he is the one who has been doing his job, not him. Alan said he started his evaluation and initially had difficulty understanding what the questions meant. Next he had difficulty thinking of work examples that the questions asked for. He put the evaluation aside, and worried and ruminated about it all day. During the night, he awoke and thought about it again. He broke out into a sweat and then fell asleep. The next morning he met his boss on the elevator and he asked how the evaluation was coming. Alan retorted "I am doing my best but I don't know if it is going to be all right." His boss responded that his best is all that he wants, and that he would not have been hired if he felt he could not do the job. This alleviated some of Alan's concern but not all. He wondered what kind of a boss does he have. He entered his office with the resolve that he was going to finish his evaluation today, which he did before he left for home. At home that evening he reviewed his work, made several changes and decided he would seek an appointment to discuss it with his boss. The next day he saw his boss at three. They discussed the evaluation and the boss made some suggestions and told him to think about them and see if he wanted to incorporate them in his evaluation. This blew his mind. When in his office and at home he reviewed the suggestions, took some and rejected others. He turned in his evaluation the next day and his boss asked what he would suggest for a final evaluation rating. Alan suggested excellent, which his boss agreed with. Following this Alan left and said to himself that he was going to make it in this job and he would gladly work as hard as needed.

While Alan was talking, the other members listened intently. Dr. B commented that he wondered if Alan, for each member in the group, was talking in camouflage about what was happening in the group today. Silence came over the group and then Victoria smiled and said she agreed. Lenora asked her to elaborate. Before she could Frank explained that for him it meant that Dr. B was going to let each member work to understand his or her problems with help from him when needed. Joseph said that what it suggested to him was what Dr. B told him when he prepared him for the group. In effect Joseph said that what Dr. B said is that he was going to behave in the group like Alan's boss did with Alan. At the mention of preparation for the group, others joined in. With a sense of relief the others said they are beginning to understand what is going to happen in the group and what they are supposed to do in order to work on their problems. Dr. B commented that what he was now hearing is that Dr. B believes that each patient has what it takes to understand what brought him or her to the group. At this point time was up. Dr. B got up, opened the door and walked out.

This case illustrates how the interventions of the therapist shape the therapy behavior of the patients.

1. Each member is involved in what happens in the group (Dr. B commented that through Frank each member of the group behaves as if he or she had not been prepared for the group).
2. The therapist is not going to answer questions if the information (answer) is known to all (Dr. B did not answer Lenora's request to tell them what to do).
3. The therapist believes that each member has what it takes to come to an affective and cognitive understanding of what brought them to the group (Dr. B commented that what he was now hearing is that Dr. B believes that each patient has what it takes to understand what brought him or her to the group).

Section 2

Psychoanalytic Derivative and Group Dynamic

5

Object Relational Groups

Irwin L. Kutash, Ph.D.
and Alexander Wolf, M.D.

Object relations can be defined in terms of intrapsychic structures which are mental representations of the self and the external objects or others. They have a maximal bearing on an individual's mode of interacting with the external world and in a person's relationships with people in particular. What forms this inner object relations constellation is the internal effects of the person's critical relationships with early parental figures. The internal self representation and object representation formed through relating with the primary parenting figures during the first years of life endure throughout the lifetime and in the healthy ego are further developed by ongoing later experiences in positive growth. In unhealthy development these early formations may remain static or evolve in a pathological manner having been distorted by early experiences during their formation.

Differences in development in terms of the type of interaction as well as the onset of the aversive interaction create different kinds of pathologies with regard to self representations in individuals and consequently different kinds of disorders which feature interpersonal difficulties. In an object relations framework, the interaction between an individual's emerging developmental needs and the ability of the environment to meet them is a key factor to personality development and the formation of self and object representations ultimately displaying itself in object relatedness. Faulty object relations as a pathological feature occurs under several varying circumstances encountered by a person during the years of ego emergence. One of the most potent of these is how the person's emerging ego was greeted by the primary parental figures.

By age two or earlier the child's ego begins to emerge from the mother's ego as the symbiotic stage ends and as the child's mental and nervous systems develop. The ongoing climate around which this emergence occurs will help determine the self and object representations, personality traits and enduring patterns of perceiving, engaging with environment and the self remotely or closely, and contemplating the environment and the self. In some individuals these personality traits are rigid or maladaptive and result in unhealthy social or occupational adjustment or in psychological disorders, i.e., personality disorders.

These disorders have as their etiology the environment prior to ego emergence, the climate at ego emergence, and the climate as the ego further develops. These conditions are the behavioral results of various ego conditions that come about due to pathogenic ongoing climates which had effected self and object representations.

To apply this to personality disorders in *DSM III-R* (1987) the personality disorders have been grouped into three clusters. Those that appear "odd or eccentric" include paranoid, schizoid, and schizotypal. The second group are those that appear dramatic, emotional, or erratic, histrionic, narcissistic, antisocial, and borderline. The third group are those that appear anxious or fearful, avoidant, dependent, compulsive, and passive aggressive. These are all based on descriptions of symptoms of behaviors. It is proposed (Kutash 1986) that these disorders be classified based on object relatedness issues based on developmental predisposing factors.

The personality disorders are divided into four clusters based on the ego-development conditions; those with heavily armored egos, paranoid and compulsive; those with split egos, schizotypal and borderline; those with weak egos, schizoid, histrionic, and narcissistic; and those with submerged egos, dependent, avoidant, passive-aggressive, antisocial, and di-egophrenic. Kutash (1986) has labeled the first cluster armored ego disorders, the second split-ego disorders, the third weak ego disorders, and the last submerged ego disorders.

DSM-III-R describes the essential features of borderline personality disorder as "instability in a variety of areas, including interpersonal behavior, mood and self image." *DSM-III* describes the essential features of a narcissistic personality disorder as "a grandiose sense of self-importance or uniqueness; preoccupation with fantasies of unlimited success; exhibitionistic need for constant attention and admiration; characteristic responses to blows to self-esteem; and characteristic disturbances in interpersonal exploitativeness, relationships that alternate between the extremes of overidealization and devaluation, and lack of empathy." *DSM-III-R* describes the essential features of a passive aggressive personality disorder as "a resistance to demands for adequate performance in both occupational and social functioning; the resistance is expressed indirectly rather than directly." Finally, *DSM-III-R* describes the essential features of a dependent personality disorder as "passively allowing others to assume responsibility for major areas of his or her life because of a lack of self confidence and an inability to function independently:" the individual subordinates his or her own needs to those of others on whom he or she is dependent in order to avoid any possibility of having to be self reliant. For the borderline personality and the narcissistic personality *DSM-III-R* lists for predisposing factors and familial pattern "no information." For the passive-aggressive they describe as the predisposing factors "oppositional disorder in childhood or adolescence" and for the dependent personality "chronic physical illness" and that "some believe that separation anxiety disorder and avoidant disorder of childhood or adolescence predispose to the development to dependent personality disorder. No information on familial pattern is provided for either.

The various types of personality disorders described above may be better understood in terms of concepts of self-object theory and the concepts originated by Kutash (Kutash and Greenberg 1986, 1989): ego emergence climate, and the resultant ego emergence condition.

The ego emergence conditions and ongoing climate that lead to each of the personality disorder clusters that feature object relations deficits as a central symptom will now be described. If those whose ego emergence is met with a lack of basic trust in others (either because they couldn't trust their parents or their parents couldn't trust the world at large), they begin to develop pervasive and unwarranted suspiciousness and distrust of others. Their attitude of suspiciousness becomes their armor in a world that seems unsafe. The paranoid personality may then feature remoteness as a defense against aversive contact. Those whose emerging ego is met with regimented parenting lacking warmth and tenderness, but fraught with rules and hierarchies of family power, develop restricted ability to express their own feelings. They become perfectionistic and insist others submit to their own way of doing things and can be compulsively productive. Their driven cold perfectionism is their armor in a world where their only safety and rights seem to come from rules and not from others' warm regard, and where the security of a superior position is attainable if the rules are subjective. The obsessive compulsive personality as part of their armor remains remote as a result of their lack of experience with the benefits of closer, warmer relationships.

Those whose ego emergence is met with very inconsistent reactions from parental figures develop a split in the ego itself. These individuals had parents whose behavior was guided by internal stimuli rather than external events. The child of such parents can receive unpredictable reactions for the same behavior based on the internal state of the parent on the day or moment of the action. The ego cannot intactly deal with mediation between these individuals and an external world where the ego's mediation seems only intermittently to have an effect. The ego becomes split into two parts, one of which functions according to the pleasure principle, the other according to the reality principle. An intact ego cannot develop to deal with reality since reality is not fixed, and in such an environment following id impulses is no less effective than ego control.

When the fragments of the child's personality interact with the parenting person, with an inconsistent and unpredictable other in the early years the child's experiences of life cannot help him or her form a cohesive self-representation. Such persons may also be remote since the result of interactions for them has been so unpredictable and uncontrollable.

Those whose ego emergence and ongoing development is met with apathy or neglect develop a very weak ego. Such children assume that others like the parenting figures will not find them worthy of notice. Not having experienced warm satisfying relationships as the ego emerged, there are three possible pathological outcomes. Individuals may become schizoid, lacking the capacity to form social relationships. They may become histrionic looking to overreactions to get some external reaction from a world they unconsciously expect to be apathetic like mother. Third, they become narcissistic as a reaction formation with a fragile facade of grandiosity or self-importance. Narcissism, however, is most complex since in addition to narcissists who got too little warmth at ego emergence and thereafter function in a narcissistic manner as a reaction formation, others got too much. They were initially the apple of mother's eye when they were extensions of mother, and they try to function as the center of everybody's attention ever after. The former is classified as a weak ego narcissism and the latter submerged ego narcissism, and they are placed in clusters accordingly. Those who adopt the schizoid defense will then present themselves as the epitome of the remote patient.

Those whose ego emergence and ongoing growth is met by affirmation when the resultant behavior conforms to parentally endorsed patterns and a lack of affirmation or rejection when it does not develop submerged egos. Simultaneously there is an introjection of a parental ego, which the child repeatedly and compulsively rebels against with an equally protesting pseudo-ego derived from the submerged ego. The rebellious psuedo-ego is a kind of antibody response to the parentally introjected derived pseudo-ego. Those with submerged egos are labeled dependent personalities if they primarily comply, as avoidant personalities if they shirk relationships to escape compliance; as passive aggressive personalities if they outwardly comply and inwardly rebel, as antisocial personalities if they compulsively rebel and as di-egophrenic (see Kutash 1984; Kutash and Greenberg 1986; Wolf and Kutash 1984, 1985) if they alternate between complying and rebelling.

All of these later disorders can be labeled as pseudo-egoality, a term coined by Kutash in Wolf and Kutash (1985). The avoidant personality will appear as the most remote.

Although the model presented dichotomizes the intrapsychic structures into four separate diagnostic groupings, these categories are not mutually exclusive. A patient's psychopathology can be accounted for by more than one type of ego structure dependent on parent-child issues dating from the time of ego emergence and development and their resultant self and other representation structure. Such is the case where one had to comply to insure parental love and approval, but if compliance was not elicited, the parental response was harsh. One would expect then to see a personality structure that was both di-egophrenic and amored.

As can be seen with regard to personality formation, the central aspect that must be considered is the development of object relatedness. Specifically, it appears that internal self and object representation derived from the interaction between child and parent is the form of positive emotional availability that becomes a foundation of the structure taken by the developing self. It can be said that the selfobject is derived from the affective states that initially comprised the interaction of child and parent.

Bringing these concepts into a person's present-day interactions, he interacts in his present relationships partially according to his notions of the others that are based on his introjects. A successful external relational adjustment is therefore largely due to one's intrapsychic object relations. Therapy of the individual within the group is therefore designed to alter intrapsychic object relations through object relational groups and corrective experiences within external relationships provided by the group setting.

In the object relational model the group provides the new transferential arena for old introjects to be dispersed and a new internal representation of the self and other to grow.

It is helpful in understanding people and particularly in forming groups to see which of these four general categories coined by Kutash in 1968 (Kutash 1968) best describes the qualities of a person's self-awareness and the accompanying ability to relate feelings to others or the quality of their self-representations, self-awareness, and communication output.

First, there are some people who are predominantly *consciously open*. These are the people who are in touch with their self representation and express their true feelings openly.

Second, there are some people who are predominantly *consciously closed*. These are the people who are in touch with their self representation but will not express their feelings to others (e.g., weak egos).

Third, there are some people who are predominently *unconsciously open*. These are the people who are not in touch with their selves but their feelings are obvious to all those around them. The patient who would be characteristically saying, "I'm not angry" and believing it even when they are.

Fourth, there are some people who are predominantly *unconsciously closed*. These are the people who are not in touch with themselves and their feelings and they are a mystery to those around them as well.

A group should not be weighted with people from any of the last three categories if it is to be effective. Consciously open people can be most helpful to each other.

Communication is, of course, a two-way street, and people must understand others and their feelings as well as being self-aware. These four categories describe the quality of a person's awareness of others' feelings or the quality of their object relations and communication input.

First, there is the type of person who is predominantly *consciously receptive*. These are people who can understand and respond to all levels of communication.

Second, there is the type of person who is predominantly *consciously rejective*. These are the people who can understand but refuse to respond to others (e.g.: armored egos).

Third, there is the type of person who is predominantly *unconsciously receptive*. These are the people who may intently respond to the feelings of others who, for example, respond to the distress of others without consciously even being aware that anything is wrong.

Fourth, there is the type of person who is predominantly *unconsciously rejective*. These are the people who do not understand or respond to others since they are not even aware of what is being communicated. They, for example, at best understand the face value of what is said having had very minimal early relationships and consequently limited external object representations.

Here again a group should not be weighted with people from category two or four if it is to be effective. Receptive people have the most potential to help others.

The picture sketched so far is, of course, a vast simplification. To size up potential group members and put together effective groups, the communication output categories and communication input categories must be combined in all their sixteen combinations to do some justice to the complexity of possible personality types and interpersonal vectors. Now, if you combine the quality of a person's self-awareness with the quality of his understanding of others, you have a handy way of sizing up a potential group member and some of his strengths and shortcomings. Here then are the combinations and a few examples of the personality types they include:

The *consciously open, consciously receptive person* is one who is both in touch with his own feelings and willing to express them and is in touch with those expressed by others. This is the ideal model for a group leader and describes a well-adjusted person. Someone who is consciously open may express his feelings but be inappropriate or inaccurate, for example, the hysteric, in expressing them. However, also being consciously receptive provides the feedback necessary to make expression of feelings appropriate and accurate.

The *consciously open, consciously rejective person* is one who is in touch with his feelings and willing to express them but refuses to receive the real communications of others. An example would be the narcissist who only talks about himself and chooses not to listen.

The *consciously open, unconsciously receptive person* is one who is in touch with and willing to express his feelings and is intuitively in touch with the feelings of others. He is the type who may outwardly disagree with what you say but what you tell him is actually sinking in. This is the person who may suddenly show therapeutic gain, and people may falsely think he had a "spontaneous recovery."

The *consciously open, unconsciously rejective person* is one who is in touch with his own feelings and willing to express them but is incapable of understanding the feelings of others. An example would be the person who thinks he is the only sensitive person in the world who suffers because he cannot recognize feelings in others.

The *consciously closed, consciously receptive person* is one who is in touch with his feelings, is unwilling to express them to others but can understand the feelings of others. An example would be the patient who sits there quietly but you can tell understands all that is happening. This can range from an introvert to a catatonic schizophrenic. The receptive aspect makes improvement likely.

The *consciously closed, consciously rejective person* is one who is in touch with his feelings but will not pass them on to others and at the same time will not listen to or accept as factual what others express. If such a person does this out of wariness or suspicion of others, he may be paranoid-schizophrenic.

The *consciously closed, unconsciously receptive person* is one who is in touch with his feelings and won't pass them on to others and outside of his awareness receives the communicated feelings of others. In a group he may open up since he can be reached unconsciously initially.

The *consciously closed, unconsciously rejective person* is one who is in touch with his feelings, won't pass them on to others and is oblivious to what is going on in others or what they communicate. This combination invariably leads to distorted feelings and in the extreme would describe an individual out of touch with reality or psychotic.

The *unconsciously open, consciously receptive person* is one whom everyone can see right through, cannot understand himself while being able to understand others. An example would be the bright sensitive adolescent who is undergoing an identity crisis and is trying to find himself. Outwardly he rebels, but not inwardly.

The *unconsciously open, consciously rejective person* does not understand himself and chooses not to tune in on others. You can read this person like a book, but he can't understand himself and won't bother with you.

The *unconsciously open, unconsciously receptive person* is one who everyone understands but himself but with whom what you say, while outwardly appearing not to sink in is actually having an unconscious effect which can lead to change.

The *unconsciously open, unconsciously rejective person* is one whom everyone understands but himself and is incapable of tuning in on others.

The *unconsciously closed, consciously receptive person* is unaware of his feelings so he can't express them but is able to understand the expressions of feelings by others. He is open, therefore, to reeducation and can be helpful to others.

The *unconsciously closed, consciously rejective person* is unaware of his feelings and therefore can't express them, and he refuses to tune in on what others say or feel. He is cut off from his feelings and isolated himself. This could describe the schizoid personality or simple schizophrenic.

The *unconsciously closed, unconsciously receptive person* is unaware of his feelings but outside of his awareness is able to understand and profit from what others say.

The *unconsciously closed, unconsciously rejective person* is unaware of his feelings and cannot receive what others say or feel. He is a mystery to himself and others and the world is a mystery to him. An example would be a psychotic completely out of touch with reality.

With these character sketches in mind, the formation of a group and its interactions can be more readily understood. A good group needs a combination of people who can help each other, and a good group leader can serve as a catalyst for this to occur.

Different combinations of different individuals create very different group climates. In Object Relational Groups the interpersonal environment which includes early familial, social and cultural phenomenon that have been part of the individuals self object formation must be particularly considered. In the corrective experience of the group, the interpersonal environment of the group can fall into a generally destructive balance or pattern of interaction, a generally constructive balance of interaction of most insidious, a generally comfortable but stulifying balance or pattern of interaction. Kutash has termed these three group situations, group equilibrium, group disequilibrium and group malequilibrium (Kutash 1980, 1982; Kutash and Wolf 1984, 1986); Wolf and Kutash 1986). Group disequilibrium takes the form of a transferential pathogenic, uncomfortable recreated family, group equilibrium takes the form of a comfortable transferential family with a new look, and group malequilibrium takes the form of a pathogenic but comfortable family.

Group Disequilibrium

Disequilibrium for the individual in the interpersonal environment occurs when a person experiences too little intimacy (for example, isolation) or too much intimacy (for example, engulfment creating a stress level that is either too low or too high) and experiences anxiety as a result of the imbalance. These feelings initially develop in the family and then, by way of repetition-compulsion, or projection, either are re-created by the individual or are projected to exist by the individual in his or her late life experiences. In the individual, this process can lead to the immediate investment of the group with frightening, familial transference in the first or second group meeting. When this happens, a patient may experience so much stress that he or she runs out of a session in terror. Trying to induce such a person to return to the group to face and analyze his or her projections may be a formidable task. Such a member has probably been prematurely ushered into the company of other patients. The analyst must try to discern in advance the patient's distortions of reality. This may be accomplished by waiting for the development of a working alliance and/or more positive transference in prior individual treatment, followed by more intensive preliminary study of the patient's particular projective devices. Apparently such an individual straightaway recreates his own threatening family with its intimacy imbalance in any small cluster of strangers, where original conflict is forced speedily and dreadfully near the surface, so that he takes flight hurriedly. A patient who behaves this way is commonly shy, withdrawn, or schizoid. He is fearful of a collection of people who may renounce etiquette and the super-

ficial social forms that offer him some safety. He runs from the bru-
tality he is repeatedly reincarnating. He is more comfortable in an
outside world that assures him a precarious security as long as it
remains conventional or distant. He rarely shows up in a group,
and if he does, his resistances finally give way to analysis, so that
he constitutes no serious indictment of group analytic technique.

An example will show how this pattern may manifest itself and
how it can be worked with.

Susan is an example of partial failure of self-representation due
to her mother's apathy rather than affirmation of her. The result was the failure of object relatedness of the self and the
failure in recognizing what the object or other might have had
to offer. When Susan entered group she was living with her
mother, and felt engulfed by her but too guilty to leave. She
felt engulfed, too, by her husband, whom she unconsciously
thwarted by gaining weight and being difficult and for whom
she had given up higher education and career, but who remained symbiotically attached to her. She felt smothered by
her divorced daughter and grandson, whom she cared for but
resented, since she felt they drained her time and resources.
She had no friends because she felt people were rotten and
only used her. It was soon clear that she would become either
engulfed or used by any relationship she had developed, as
she had in brief forays outside the family relationships. She
began group therapy by saying and doing anything that might
put people off and predicting that everyone would soon hate
her.

After observing her first two sessions, the following stance
was taken. The analyst tried never to be directive, as her mother
was. The way Susan might act to alienate the group members
became apparent to her and the group when she described
her previous experiences with people. She expressed to the
group her wish to have something different happen. She also
told the group when she was experiencing her old familial
feelings. For many months she was her old self, but the members did not allow themselves to engulf her, tell her what to
do, or reject her behavior since some had experienced feelings
similar to hers early in their group experience. She was a non-
attender at alternate sessions, which she could not initially tol-

erate, but was assured by the others she would be welcome at any time later. These therapeutic tactics allowed her to get past her initial mother transference.

Furthermore, just as an individual recreates his pathogenic family, there is the ever-present danger that the group, functioning as a recreated family, may become pathogenic as a family. Without adroit management, some groups end up this way. The therapist must watch for the elaboration of inbred and incestuous trends that bind members together as neurotically as in the original family. A recovering patient, for example, may be attacked as unready for discharge by a compulsively overprotective member who is parentally castrating. If a man and woman gravitate toward each with erotic interest, they may be invested with father and mother roles, and other patients may react to them with detached respect, voyeuristic aggressive interest, or moralistic disapproval that corresponds to earlier ambivalent curiosity about intimacy between the parents. These investments can be dispelled only by persistent analysis and working through. Occasionally a member or two will exhibit some reluctance to permit a patient who has recovered to leave the group. Such members show the same kind of envy or jealousy earlier directed toward a sibling and feel the family group or parental therapist is favoring the cured member with special regard that her performance does not deserve. The majority, however, generally welcome the improvement of anyone and take pleasure in their progress. Transference that denies discharge to a patient who has recovered is also analyzable.

An unfavorable situation that may arise in a group is the development of intense, generalized neurotic resistance, accompanied by hostile bilateral transferences and the formation of allies in groups of two or three, leaving some individuals isolated except for a relatively warm relationship to the analyst. Sometimes even this association becomes strained, because the patient blames the therapist for having been exposed to such a trying and antagonistic environment. Such forms of resistance must be analyzed; otherwise, the group may fall apart. Attendance may become low and demoralize those present. The therapist, while taking an analytic view of absenteeism, confronts those who stay away with the possibility of being dropped. He explores transferences that force aggressors into belligerent roles and points out their illusory character. He is equally vigilant about projective devices that impel the compulsively withdrawn to retreat further or to submit to the domination of other members. The analyst seeks to uncover the causes for resistance to participation on deeper levels, pointing out explicitly the destructive character of particular defenses and encouraging free emotional ventilation. All else failing, the analyst may be obliged to remove a patient here and there, one at a time, at varying intervals, introducing each retired member into a more constructive group. Such a crisis can usually be avoided by not organizing a group with a majority of strongly sadomasochistic patients. Too many such members in the same milieu provide an unfavorable climate for evocation of the positive resources that need to be expressed if the group members are to proceed effectively in object relational therapy.

Group Equilibrium

Group equilibrium is achieved when the patients constructively recreate the family—but with a new look. Cultivating a permissive atmosphere in which mutual tolerance and regard can flourish will enable the earlier prohibitive character of the original family objects to be projected with less intensity and to be more easily worked through toward the internalization of more wholesome object representations. Furthermore, the general acceptance and sense of belonging that follow will enable a similarly easy transition to correspondingly untroubled social relations beyond the confines of the group. The other patients, because of their numbers, provide more familial surrogates for transference evocation. Each patient comes to a realization of the extent to which he recreates his own childhood family in every social setting and inappropriately invests others with familial substitute qualities. The number of participants also clarifies the variety and multiplicity of central and penumbral transferences. In individual analysis the therapist tries to see clearly what perceptual distortions the patient makes of outer reality and what internal factors contribute to this social disfigurement, but the analyst is often misled, because he or she does not see the patient in action. In group, the therapist also is interested in what is happening at the moment so that the patient's unconscious warping of fact can be observed in motion. The patient can then be confronted with his projective trends and the inciting role he plays in precipitating the environmental disturbances he resents so much.

An illustration of how a group helped an individual see his misperceptions of the present as if it were the past will be offered to show the usefulness of object relational analysis in groups for this purpose and to show how group equilibrium can be achieved.

George is a man in his late fifties with schizoid defenses, including sarcasm, intellectualization and withdrawal. He has felt empty and incomplete for years and had periodic bouts with deep depression while being chronically somewhat depressed. His fantasy was of an idealized relationship with a woman who could make him complete. He had been married once and divorced by a woman whose demands enraged him and who he defeated by passive aggressively never meeting them, with such symptoms as impotency. Detachment was his normal modis operandi inside and outside of the therapy group. George was transferentially viewed by one younger male member of the group as an immovable controlling figure (his father). A second younger male group member also viewed him as very controlling and irritating but experienced as well as a positive feeling toward George. The younger member tried to help George to feel free to be less controlling (a wish he had for his father). A younger female group member saw George as manipulative and subtly controlling (like both her parents). A fourth group member saw him as talking down to her and treating her as if she were unintelligent (again like her parents), and yet a fifth group member saw him as a warm, good father (the father she never had). When the first four members described all began to express their feelings to George, the recipient of so many transferences and told him how he should behave, as a group they became transferentially his mother, who always had controlled him and told him how to act, and he resisted their efforts vehemently. Only after one by one each father transference was explored and the group came to see the defensive nature of his controlling behavior (warding off his own introjected mother) and after his transference to the group was clarified did gradual progress for many group members occur. Many individuals came to see how they related to present-day figures as people from their past.

These theoretical and practical problems of working through are one of the most neglected, yet most important, aspects of object relational analysis both in the individual and in the group setting.

Group Malequilibrium

Group malequilibrium occurs when group members are all comfortable with one another but do not in any way challenge one another's defenses. The group itself is in an unhealthy stultifying balance. Conflict-laden topics are avoided and everyone, in an unconscious bargain, avoids stressful but potentially growth-inducing material.

An example of a patient in such a group is the following.

Frank's love for the emotional climate of the group bordered on the ecstatic. He reveled in the luxury of what he considered an absolutely honest relationship. He was, mirabile dictu, in a family whose projections, having become at last analyzable and understandable, no longer alarmed or hurt him.

The danger in his case was that he ran from real life to the fabricated safety of an unreal laboratory. He found the group warmer and saner than most associations on the outside. He needed to be instructed in how to carry the affective closeness he had achieved in the group to large segments of society, beyond the confines of his fellow members.

This is a common objection to working in concert with other patients. How, it is asked, can one transfer the good fellowship of the group to areas outside it? Object relational analysis in a group lays no Pollyannaish or grandiose claim to making the world a big happy family. But group analytic technique offers the patient a means of making conscious the trends that stand in the way of his vigorous affective contact with others, whether loving or hating. We say "hating" as well as "loving" because there are some psychopathic influences in the world that can appropriately be hated.

Another example further illustrates malequilibrium in groups.

Shirley was placed by one of us in group and arrived at her

first meeting with a long cigarette holder and a very theatrical air and dress. After attending the session, she told the therapist, "These are not my kind of people. Haven't you a group of patients who have more in common with me?" The therapist, who was seeing a number of artists and theater people, was about to start a new group. He invited this woman and several other patients who seemed compatible into the group. Everyone immediately hit it off, laughed, joked, and had a marvelous time. Members never talked about themselves, their feelings, their associations, or their dreams.

This group was eventually disbanded and its members placed in more heterogeneous groups where the cultivation of the group came through the promotion of differentiated, complementary and uncomplementary, and conflictful and unconflictful personalities. People, through their growing individuality, learned through differences in realistic perception and unrealistic misperception to appreciate one another's mutually proffered gifts of vision, to appreciate their oppositeness and opposition, their mutuality and compatibility, the treasures of one another's perceptions, and the nonnarcissistic growth of one another's egos. While the analyst was misled originally by the patients plea for a more harmonious group and than organized a homogeneously resistive membership that sabotaged analytic scrutiny, he subsequently dispersed the members into heterogeneous groups. In these, each participant was accepted while his intrapsychic representations were explored, challenged and eventually worked through aided by the perceptions and acceptance of more wholesome and realistic external objects and internal representations. Here the pathogenic incorporations of childhood died from an atrophy of disuse.

6

Psychoanalytic Developmental Psychology Groups

Malcolm J. Marks, Ed.D.

This paper will attempt to demonstrate through a case presentation the effective use of concurrent individual and group psychotherapy (Sager 1959) with a patient whose fear of an intensive central relationship kept him on the periphery of a treatment relationship. Through the use of psychotherapy in group, many persons feel less threatened by the therapeutic relationship (Slavson 1964:155–157, 173) and are enabled to move toward basic trust, a belief that the therapist cares for their personal integrity and will not invade their psyche or weaken their boundaries and ego defenses (Wolf and Schwartz 1962:248 ff.).

The patient to be described was able to move from once-weekly individual therapy to concurrent once-weekly individual and group therapy and, in time, into an intensive individual process of three-times-weekly sessions along with his group treatment. The basic therapeutic approach was to accept the patient's fear of remembering early central relationships while gradually exploring the genetic roots of this fear as well as its base in a pathological narcissism (Blanck and Blanck 1979; Marks 1985). The group process helped to keep the intensity of the transference "replication" and the centrality of the therapist within bounds (Durkin 1974:9) while the therapist used the combined treatment procedure to develop and strengthen ego boundaries and ego capacities for self-regulation essential to any working-through process.

The concept of "transference replication" is taken from the work of the Blancks (1979:13) in their text on *Ego Psychology* where they indicate that lower-level structures whose egos have been modified and are hence not intact respond to the therapist as if he or she were the actual person out of their past whom they hold responsible for their failures and to whom they look for gratification, reward, approval as "real," "actual" parent(s). The neurotic may feel such attitudes—and feel like blaming the therapist or loving the therapist or whatever, but they still know that the therapist is not the father or mother out of their past. The patient to be described spent several years of the treatment—the core of it, in fact—relating to the therapist as if he had magical powers and was capable of regulating and/or gratifying him (the patient). This will be elaborated in the case presentation.

In 1971, Wolf and Schwartz stated the following:

> In individual analysis, the analyst believes that the intensity of the transference relationship is a motivating and ultimately therapeutic influence. He adheres to the need for concentration on the analyst as the means by which unconscious processes can be exposed most expertly. He is dedicated to the necessity to work out and work through parental transferences directed toward him as the central difficulty.
>
> The analyst in groups values interaction among peers as well. He believes in the necessity to work through sibling as well as parental transferences invested in the peers rather than in isolated reliance on the authority of the analyst. (p. 251)

> Patients in a group generally feel closer to one another than to the analyst. . . . Relatedness in a group is partly transferential, but there is a larger component of realistic, friendly intercommunication than in the hierarchical contact with the analyst. (p. 252)

> Because group members offer one another some fulfillment of mu-
> tual needs, . . . they feel closer to one another than to the thera-
> pist. (p. 253)

Wolf and Schwartz's (1962) thesis is that people also develop within
sibling relationships and that psychoanalysis in group offers a broader
field on which to play out and work through one's psychoneuroses.
They do not dispute the value of traditional psychoanalysis, but see
it as limited (pp. 270–271). In essence, the core of this paper agrees
with Wolf and Schwartz's thesis and attempts to demonstrate how
psychotherapy in group served crucial goals.

One can be analyzed solely in group if a classical analysis is what
we have in mind. Essentially, this is because life begins for all of
us in the dyad and I follow the work of Hartman, Jacobson, Spitz,
Mahler, Anna Freud, and other brilliant theorists of metapsychology who have their theoretical roots in the work of Freud. These
theorists have studied processes of individuation and identity formation from a structural and object relations point of view (Blanck
and Blanck 1986). Jacobson (1964) integrated instinctual drive theory, structural theory having to do with the development of ego
and superego systems, and object relations theory in her classic work,
The Self and the Object World. One needs good ego endowment
(Hartman 1939 (see 1958)) and a good (average expectable) environment in beginning life if there is to be the development of the
psychic system, the id, and "the taming of the drives." Otherwise,
the human organism will be subject to the tyranny of the instinctual
drives and will tend to function at a primary process level (p. 35).

The patient to be described managed to somehow reach adult
life and to marry and, after a third attempt at marriage, to have a
family and a responsible position. He was, nonetheless, continuously assaulted by his instinctual drives and rarely in a state of psychic
equilibrium. Hartman (1939 (see 1958)) stressed that successful adaptation in its deepest sense requires the capacity to use one's syn-
thetic, organizing ego function (1) to achieve harmony and equilibrium between the self and the object world—the environment; and
(2) to achieve a harmony within the id so that the drives are working in concert rather than in opposition; and (3) to achieve a har-

mony and equilibrium within the psychic structure, that is, between the systems id, ego, and superego (pp. 39–40).

The patients come to therapy because their ego defense system is breaking down and their adaptive capacities are failing. This may manifest itself in outer relationships with spouse, family, work associates, but this is essentially symptomatic of a loss of psychic equilibrium. Hartman is noted because the use of group psychotherapy by theorists like Yalom (1975) addresses itself to interpersonal relationships rather than intrapsychic failures or deficiencies. The use of the group is a modality of reaching the individual (Wolf and Schwartz 1962), and the effort in psychotherapy in group is to use this medium in the service of the individual. Group cohesion is not sought, nor must all members be good group patients devoted to helping or treating each other. Therapy groups need to be more introspective and less interactive at times, although the leader should strive to reach a balance of feeling and insight in the group process. The members' reactions to each other can be used to consider their projections and introjections, their unconscious identifications, and the genetic roots. Thus, the patient in group is, in essence, turned back upon the self as a treatment goal. In the course of this, as the patient in combined treatment understands and resolves his or her inner conflicts, he or she is better able to develop more meaningful relationships within the therapy group and in the outside world.

The basic concepts of analytic group psychotherapy are drawn from Freudian theory having to do with transference and countertransference phenomena, to which group therapists like Slavson (1964) add other constructs such as "multiple transference." In group psychotherapy, the patients develop transference to each other, representing one or another parent, siblings, oedipal or pre-oedipal parents, and even transfer to the group itself as representing the magical good breast or the threatening oedipal father and so on (Kutash and Wolf 1986:334–336).

To the concept of unconscious resistance, group theroists introduce the concept of group resistance (Wolf 1974:134–135), the dictum being to analyze the group resistance before you analyze the individual resistances. A powerful group resistance in which the total group may insist on the therapist being or representing the omniscient, omnipotent early mother, may render the therapist impotent. Unless this is interpreted, the patients will look to the therapist's magic rather than to their own egos for help.

The defenses employed in treatment in group are more clearly manifested than in the individual sessions. The patient in the dyadic relationship may fix on a positive transference/neurosis or on a negative therapeutic reaction as a major defense as well as a resistance. In group, such defenses do not work as well as a result of the group interaction and the multiple transference phenomena where members challenge each other, especially as they see their own adaptive stance mirrored before them. This does not mean that it is productive to analyze defenses in group. To the contrary, the therapist must protect the individual member's capacity to defend until stronger structure and more sophisticated defenses are developed. So the therapist needs to be active in protecting weaker "structures" (whose expressions may be more at a primary process level) from overexposing themselves, or from attack by group members who are threatened by too raw exposure to their own primary processes by such developed structures (patients).

Following concepts of psychoanalytic developmental psychology, patients in group are not encouraged to act on their primary processes. Rather, the model is held up for self-regulation and better reality-testing. Hartman (1939/1958) noted the following in his thesis, *Ego Psychology and the Problem of Adaptation.*

> Many problems relevant in sociology are peripheral in psychoanalysis. Sociology centers on social action, on success or failure in the tasks set by society (i.e., tasks of adaptation), and is interested in the psychology of conflicts, the fate of aggressive and libidinal impulses, etc., *only* insofar as these are manifested in social behavior. (pp. 20–21)

He noted further that psychoanalysis is concerned with *how* the individual *masters* his difficulties through ego capacities that are conflict-free as well as conflict-borne. Many group psychotherapists tend to be more concerned with the interpersonal conflict resolution (Yalom 1975). The essential use of group as a medium of treatment within the sphere of metapsychology (Wolf and Schwartz 1962) would focus on man's inner structure, his capacity for internalization and his capacity to live with himself as having primacy over his capacity to live with others (pp. 72–73).

In this context, the use of group as a treatment modality might be seen as requiring higher level development so that the patient in group is addressing matters in his or her adaptation to the external world, which includes siblings, rivals for libidinal needs, and socialization. These adaptations rest on a core of solid identity formation and adaptation to the self. Within this context the group modality has much to offer. While the focus of this case presentation is on the use of the group as enabling the patient to develop tolerance for more central relationships and to aid an intensive treatment procedure that can effect better internalizations, I do not see this as the sole value of psychotherapy in group. I have seen patients in group treatment following an intensive analytic procedure in which they are able to use the group to work toward entry into the broader environ and to work out fears of sharing the self and object with others. The group is an aid to the more pathologically based narcissist who sees others as needs objects designed to bolster his or her flimsy self-esteem. The heterogeneity to symptom and structure in groups (Wolf and Schwartz 1962: Chap. 2) enables a fuller testing of the outer world of reality. As will be indicated in the case presentation, the therapist took the role of the father in introducing the patient to a broader world (Abelin 1971)—a more real world—within the group as an aid to development and as an intervention to his dwelling on the symbiotic dyad endlessly. (Kutash and Wolf 1986:338–342).

Case Presentation: Harold

Harold had had a succession of failures in his relationships with women and in his object relations in general. His first marriage was a failure after two attempts. His next relationship ended with a hospitalization for what appears to be a severe depression and ego regression and an inability to function. As he described the situation leading to his break with reality, Harold told me that he had been so enmeshed with this woman and so hypersexually active that he panicked and felt a loss of ego boundaries. After his hospitalization, Harold saw a psy-

chiatrist once weekly for fifteen years until the therapist moved
to another area. It was then that Harold was referred to me.

Harold came to this therapist as if he had no other choice
and as if he would be seeing him for another 15 to 20 years
once weekly. He expected to be in such a treatment procedure for the rest of his life. It was clear that this man had no
motivation for conflict resolution since he experienced no conflict. He was accustomed to losing control at home and at work,
boasted of how he had picked up a chair to throw at his boss.
He made clear his failure to develop adequate regulatory
mechanisms and was now ego-syntonic. He lived between being,
as he characterized himself, "a workaholic," on the one hand,
and on the edge of catastrophe on the other through the tendency to tantrums in his work relationships. He virtually avoided
familial relationships by staying late at work and going to work
on weekends, thus having little to do with his wife and four
children. He characterized his wife as a fierce, screaming, rigid
creature who controlled his life even to the extent of not allowing him to buy professional journals related to his work.
He characterized his bosses as "stupid," insensitive and failing
to appreciate his creativity and brilliance in his work life. In
effect, he had powerful creatures at home and at work to regulate him along with his obsessional, poorly organized work
habits and to keep him from acting on his instinctual drives,
in terms of promiscuous sex and violent outbursts. He was
truly not interested in a basic attitude that would place him
within his own structure, with a good reality testing ego and
well-developed discharge-regulating and stabilizing superego
structure (Blanck and Blanck 1986; chs. 2, 3, 4). He sought,
rather, to be maintained on a once-a-week dosage of therapy
while he went on his undisciplined course, convinced that no
one in the world could really care for him.

While too desperate not to come to treatment and too in-
sulated to feel the loss or abandonment of the previous therapist, Harold was not interested in a treatment procedure aimed
at strengthening him to the point of his being able to leave
treatment at some point in his life. In this way, there was a
perfect resistance. He would come passively to treatment, dis-
course on life or music or whatever, and remain untouched
and unthreatened. He was told that the therapist's aim would
be to prepare him not to need treatment forever, but it was

clear that this was not Harold's aim. He basically took a position of never accepting himself as a patient while agreeing to come at a regular time once a week. After several months in treatment, Harold came in one day and told the therapist that he did not like his (the therapist's) face. It was old and unpleasant—wrinkled, etc. The therapist understood this in terms of Rene Spitz's (1965) concept of the second organizer of the ego. When the baby has reached three months of age, there is the first organizer of the ego—the smiling response— any reasonable, kind stranger who bends over the baby will bring a smile. But, by eight months, the baby now cries when a strange face appears. This means that the baby's psyche has so organized its perceptions and attachment to the mother that only the mother's face will do. The stranger's face means to the infant of eight months that it has lost the mother. Thus, the centrality of the object and anxiety have their origins with the highly developed capacity of the organizing ego at this developmental phase. Harold was now able to feel the loss of the original therapist and to complain about the stranger—the new therapist—whom he had not really accepted. This was a positive sign in the developing therapeutic relationship since it meant Harold had at one time been able to have a central object in whom he had invested and had experienced a narcissistic wound when he "lost" her at the time of his sister's birth. Within several months, Harold was invited to enter a therapy group in conjunction with his individual therapy (Bieber 1971; Sager 1960). He resisted the initial offer but in time agreed to try the procedure. This could have been experienced by him as another loss but was aimed at enabling him to test out other relationships and to achieve a certain distance from and boundary in relation to the therapist that would prove ego-strengthening.

The group into which Harold was introduced was an analytically oriented psychotherapy group. It was an "open" group, in that members entered and left according to treatment aims and goals and also according to unconscious resistance in which they, at times, left the treatment prematurely. This group had been meeting for close to one year at the time Harold entered it. It was also a cotherapy group (Rosenbaum 1971:501 ff.) led by the therapist and his wife who was also analytically orientated. The composition of the group was usually balanced be-

tween four men and four women who fell in the range of borderline and neurotic categories. Harold was seen as functioning
as a seemingly low-level neurotic or high-level borderline, but
his was essentially a psychotic ego structure with depressive
and manic features. He did not differentiate central objects
present from central objects past, and early on in treatment
tended to see the therapist as representing an anal-phase
training mother. He tended, over time, to see the group cotherapist as the good, attuned, nurturing mother and the therapist as the disciplining, demanding mother. In individual sessions, he would complain about how hard it was to make his
early morning appointments (which had been arranged to accommodate his work schedule), how tired he was, and also
how angry. After twenty minutes or so into the individual session, he would begin to calm down and there was a more
available ego for the work of treatment and considering his
distortions. This, however, did not occur until the second year
of treatment with a pattern of two successive individual sessions and the weekly group session. In the third and fourth
year, he was seen for three successive individual sessions and
the weekly group therapy session.

In the group, Harold came gradually to feel safe in expressing his feelings of frustration in life and especially in his
marital relationship. He felt, over time, increasing trust in the
group members and experienced the group as a good family
and the one place where he felt both comfortable and understood. Yet, as a defensive adaptation, for a full year he managed to block out the group session from week to week and
the group members as well. He did not remember people in
the group or their "problems"—he did not think about them.
Over time, however, Harold came to be the most affectively
involved member of the group, keenly attuned to the other
members and even brilliantly insightful. Several of the men
in the group were psychologists who tended to be reticent in
the group, although a certain male camaraderie developed between Harold and one male professional in particular. Yet it
was Harold who had greater insight into self and other group
members.

This was a major contribution to Harold's overcoming a defensive adaptation to life by not letting himself feel other people's needs, concerns, or hurts. He was too narcissistically in-

vested in licking his own wounds. So, the milieu of group therapy had a humanizing effect on Harold and furthered his psychic development. The latter was effected through his developing trust in other humans and his developing trust in the therapeutic relationship. Since several other members were in intensive treatment with Harold's therapist, transference neurotic manifestations expressed by others toward his therapist in group enabled Harold to feel safer in coming to experience ambivalence—love and hate to his therapist. He also came to feel safer in the increasing intensity of the dyadic therapeutic relationship. His marital relationship was basically one in which he was the bad boy who did not do the chores around the house with a wife whom he could not feel any tenderness to or from. He avoided his three daughters and his son through his work patterns. In the course of this combined treatment, he came to feel much more empathic toward his children just as he came to develop his capacity for relationships in the therapy group. He shifted his familial position from the bad boy to the responsible father and by the last year of treatment, he was more of a protector to his wife. She came to appreciate his calming influence with the children and to look for him to be more of the ego-regulating force in the family.

Within the group, Harold came to work out some of his confusing attitudes toward women to whom he looked for sexual discharge and nothing more. He came to "fall in love" with one young woman in the group whose features and ethnic origins were similar to those of his mother. Through most of the four years of treatment, he tended to image his mother as self-invested and as having monologues with him when he did call her or visit her. Through his relationhip with "Joan" in the group, he could recall the idealized image of a libidinal mother. While he came to speak of his sexual fantasies of Joan and his erotic impulses, he was able, in time, to see Joan as a whole person rather than a needs object for sexual gratification. Joan, initially put off by Harold's primitive approach, eventually came to feel more womanly through the transference relationship in group with Harold and was enabled to express warmth and even tenderness toward him as his feelings of impotent rage gave way to feelings of sadness, aloneness, and despair.

Thus, there was provided through the medium of the group

and the group phenomenon of multiple transference an opportunity for Harold to work out his distorted images of women
as seducers, engulfers, and sex objects, and to see them more
in a total dimension. It was considered in his individual treatment that he had experienced his mother as sexually seductive
and responded at one level to feeling sexually overstimulated
and at another level to feeling sexually inadequate. This led
to feelings of impotent rage which were manifested in adult
life in his work relationships with bosses (representing the
training mother). As basic trust emerged within the combined
modality of treatment and the therapist became more deeply
representative of an early mother and, in time, of an oedipal
father, Harold was able to resolve problems essential to his
incapacity for drive regulation and reality testing. Living close
to the border of the pleasure principle with a flimsy reaction-
formation as defense, Harold was always on the brink of discharge and disaster. His instinctual drives were so dominant
that he could be overwhelmed by homosexual as well as heterosexual impulses and fantasies. On business trips and conferences, he fainted several times and had several hysterical
reactions initially diagnosed as heart attacks (suggestive of homosexual panic).

A central focus on the treatment was to strengthen ego ap-
paratuses that would enable him to better test reality and to
make ego-dystonic his thinly concealed pleasure in making
messes and to make ego-syntonic his being under his own regulation. To this end, as intensive individual treatment went
on, his rages at his bosses were related to a displacement from
an early rapprochement-subphase mother (Mahler 1971) who
failed to appreciate his creative efforts to individuate and to
be his own person. When his bosses, who in reality gave him
superior ratings, did not take the time to talk with him and
acknowledge his creative achievements on a complex project
at work, he tended to rage. Efforts were made to help him
to differentiate his bosses from an early mother who did not
understand little boys and who was ill-attuned to him.

Within the transference, interpretations were made in terms
of his feelings that the therapist did not appreciate or acknowledge the tremendous exertion of ego he was making in his
work and family life. While the therapist supported Harold's

developing ego capacities and better reality testing as he became an attuned parent and husband, the acting out within
the work situation took Harold to the brink of disaster. The
repetitious acting out caused the therapist grave concern. It
was curious that this was not manifested in the group directly,
although it took form in terms of Harold's subtle criticisms of
the therapist and his (Harold's) overt expressions of appreciation of the cotherapist whom he considered to be much more
insightful and attuned to him. While it was true that the cotherapist had insights into Harold which were significant, what
was meaningful was how Harold used them to denigrate the
central therapist. This, too, was helpful to the working-through
process in which Harold could use the group and individual
modalities to rework his denigration of the father and his
idealization of the mother and to finally feel more masculine
and adult toward women in the group as well as toward his
wife.

Harold used the group modality to work out unresolved
problems toward a younger sister with whom he had had some
sexual involvement—short of intercourse. He saw Joan not only
as the idealized mother but also as the erotic sister. He responded to several other women in the group as sexual figures
representing this younger sister. In the last year of the group
and of treatment for Harold, an older woman entered the group
who was overtly seductive to Harold. He experienced her as
engulfing and threatening and was fearful of her for some
months. In time, he was able to work out his fear of what
Mahler (1971) designates as "the reengulfing mother after separation" and to deal with "Cindie's" seductions. He was able,
also, to express erotic feelings toward the cotherapist and, in
time, to deal with his love feelings to the central therapist who
led him into the world of reality out of the symbiotic orbit
(Abelin 1971) where he could work toward giving up the quest
for the symbiotic mother and develop an attitude of pride in
his being under his own regulation.

From an entry point of hopelessness—he would have to see
the next therapist for as many years as he lived; he would
always need a powerful wife and bosses and a soothing therapist to function on his behalf—he developed a more hopeful
and healthy wish to be *out* of treatment and to manage his

own life. The intensive individual treatment offered a milieu for internalization of a better object who attuned himself to Harold and helped him over time to be kinder to himself and protective of his ego and sanity as against yielding to the power of his instinctual drives. The more real world of the group provided what Abelin (1971, 1975) wrote about in "The Role of the Father in the Separation-Individuation Process." It is the father who introduces the child to the world of reality outside the protective and magic world of the symbiotic orbit. The experience in group with many different persons with their own reality and their own distortions provided a protective milieu. Here, Harold could test out his relationships, past and present, without danger of destruction. There was time to work out his fear of remembering early experiences of being flooded by sexual stimuli beyond his ego capacities to deal with (hence, the pervasive impotent rages). There was also time to work out relationships of trust with decreasing fear of being set aside and of remembering thereby early painful narcissistic wounds. In short, he had the chance to venture out into a world with less of his defensive hostile projections and an enhanced capacity for love (Wolf and Kutash 1986:347–350).

I should like to offer here an excerpt from an individual therapy session with Harold. On Monday morning, he told of a dream in which he was "sitting on the 'pot,' facing 'Joe,' the guy who took my job. I was talking to him. Joe would beat up anybody who got out of line. . . ."

Monday's session had to do with Mother's Day and with a brother-in-law who had left his wife and children eleven years before and had never supported them after that. On his return, Harold's wife made a huge family gathering and feast for her brother (like welcoming the prodigal son). Harold identified with his brother-in-law but also felt outraged that this guy should be welcomed while he, Harold, who had kept his nose to the grindstone, got no appreciation from his wife, only complaints. This seemed reminiscent of Harold's father on his return from his travels as a salesman and tapped early feelings of bitterness at being set aside. This is the background for Tuesday morning's session.

HAROLD: I really worked yesterday. I felt so good. [This represented a change from his tendency in the past to complain bitterly about work in all its ramifications.] *(The therapist remained silent.)*

HAROLD: I think I'm going to have to deal with my anger if I'm going to get anywhere. *(A long pause; then the word* SPITEFUL *is thrust out.)* I seem to fuck up out of SPITE . . . [He refers to his relationship with his wife, then he talks of his envy of "John" a fellow group member.] He's such a success . . . seems to be making such progress [in treatment]. He's so bright . . . it's hard to deal with myself when I feel so ORDINARY. *(A silent pause.)* I feel apprehensive . . . about the long break between now [Tuesday morning] and Friday [his next individual session]. It makes me feel angry.

THERAPIST: [first comment in 25 minutes, associating to Monday's dream that someone who took Harold's job was keeping things in order—someone "tough"] So who's to do your job between now and Friday? [An appeal to Harold's ego and to his taking on the functions of the object/analyst by being his own reality tester and his own regulator.]

HAROLD: A good question . . . ME! *I don't want to.* [This awareness that he does not want the burden of self-regulation is followed by primitive thoughts and expletives about colleagues.] Prick! Fuck-off! *(There is no intervention—a pause . . . Harold waits and then resumes.)* With a computer, I don't need anyone [a profound unconscious wish]. Maybe that's what gives me such joy at work lately.

THERAPIST: Whose job is it to regulate you between now and Friday?

HAROLD: I don't like to think about that. [He would rather discharge than delay discharge and address his feelings.]

THERAPIST: Isn't that what your dream is about?

HAROLD: To have someone take care of the messes . . . a very ORDERLY dream . . . smells, etc., but [matters were] under control [in the dream] . . . I had Joe there threatening to punch out anyone who got out of line.

THERAPIST: What does that mean to you?

HAROLD: *(insightfully and now thinking):* Something in me is threatening to erupt—a way to keep me in check . . . to hold me down . . .

THERAPIST: Is that what you envy in John? That he's under control [his own]?

HAROLD: Yes, I guess so. He seems to have the lid on . . . to be in control at work. [While this is currently true, John was discharging all over the place several years before.]

THERAPIST: Is that the CHANGE you were talking about earlier?

HAROLD: *(Says something about discharging and making messes)* Out of anger! Out of spite! I feel so HURT [This is one of the rare times he has recognized how deeply hurt and narcissistically wounded he has been in life. His usual adaptation has been to rage, make messes, discharge, and to avoid his feelings of having been wounded as well as his sense of impotent rage.]

THERAPIST: [Attempts a reconstruction in terms of Harold's having been pushed precociously to master urethral and sphincter control without his mother having appreciated what a burden it placed on his ego.] You did master it at great cost to your child's ego.

HAROLD: [in response to the reconstruction] I feel some pressure to . . . change.

THERAPIST: Whose? [Taking care not to repeat the attitude of his training mother and impose change from without, forcing on Harold thereby a standard of self-regulation which is not his own.]

HAROLD: I feel it's from you but I know it comes from me.

THERAPIST: Isn't that hopeful?

HAROLD: Hopeful? *(with some bitterness)* I don't want to give up my anger . . . my spite . . . being a kid. I DO think of you as taking care of me . . . between now and Friday even though I don't see you.

THERAPIST: That's an important thought—that you feel I'll be with you. [Evidence of the process of internalization of a good object at work, even while Harold is able to express his reluctance to give up being the bad boy or "enfant terrible."]

HAROLD: It's not new . . . been there for months. I'm not so fearful of what I might do . . . or might not do at work.

THERAPIST: [reflecting his latent thoughts] You are fearful of what you might do and what you might NOT do.

HAROLD: FEARFUL! A good word!

THERAPIST: A good dream? [referring back to Monday's dream]

HAROLD: *(reassuring himself)* I wasn't gonna get beat up . . . someone *cared* about me.

THERAPIST: Who?
HAROLD: Who? I don't know . . . John? I've got a lot riding
   on him. All the work I did [on previous job] which John
   [not the group member] took over. My own PRIDE . . . He
   could also destroy me . . . turn over everything I did. It's
   so hard to pin it down (all said with feeling and pain).
THERAPIST: Oh . . .
HAROLD: I know. It's ME . . . OF COURSE!!!
THERAPIST: If you listen to yourself . . . your fear is that you'll
   UNDO everything. [Out of spite! Undoing proved a major
   mechanism on Harold's part over the years. By this time in
   his treatment there was some working-through process taking place and he now experienced anxiety as a signal warning him of his tendency to undo his painstaking work as
   well as his work in object negotiation. In the above material, Joe as well as John represented Harold's new internalizations working for him. They also represented his wish
   to have his therapist do it for him as well as be tough with
   him and not let him make a mess of his life.]

In closing, I shall note the effects of the intensive individual procedure that was supported and enabled by the group psychotherapy
experience.

The appeal to Harold's ego was made over an extended period
of time (five years) and included the following:

1. The developmental phase on which he was focused (a mix of the
   practicing and rapprochement subphase in which there had been
   a gross lack of attunement by the mother) was identified.
2. The frequency of individual sessions was increased to three times
   weekly with the aim being to provide soothing of the inner rage
   as Harold reexperienced insults at the hands of wife, boss and
   therapist.
3. It was explained to Harold that he was intent on reproducing
   the relationship of a past early phase in which he was wounded
   by a narcissistic-unattuned-artist-mother (a) in his marital relationships, (b) in his central work relationships, and (c) in his
   therapeutic relationship. The daily examples were prolific but the
   explanations did not suffice.
4. Through patient exploration and explanation, it slowly became
   available to Harold's self-observing ego that he was experiencing

narcissistic insults because he was investing in these current figures a capacity for empathetic understanding that was inappropriate in his work relationships and not available in his early subphase mother, in his present-day mother, or in his disturbed obsessional wife.

5. The therapeutic relationship itself with its transference–countertransference vicissitudes proved the central medium in reaching Harold's ego (Loewald 1960:16–33). His sense of betrayal and disillusionment was accepted as his genuine experience and came to be understood in terms of his fear of remembering or experiencing basic trust. He had had a previous fifteen years of therapy once weekly that essentially made no demands on his ego. The approach to Harold's treatment was, from the beginning, aimed at strengthening structure. There was a basic honesty including free admission, where valid, of the therapist's failure to understand Harold. As his open distrust was accepted along with his cynical attitude to psychotherapy, Harold began to be less deceptive. His affective mood states and his attitudes to self and others required less self-deception. When he found he could be more genuine in the treatment relationship, he was able to experience mourning for his first therapist whom he had lost, as well as anger at the therapist's departure to another area. He could relate this to the loss of and deficiency in fathering he had repressed, and he could take the risk, not without fear, anger, tantrums, contempt, and other defensive maneuvers, of trusting another person's caring for him as a full person rather than as someone to indulge or infantilize.

It became evident that there was a regressive indulgence in his years of tantrums at present-day, recreated parent-surrogate for not appreciating his ego capacities. There was more indulgence than mastery in this repetitive pattern.

Nonetheless, the work of therapy had somehow strengthened the self-and object-representations of Harold through a developing trust and more positive internalizations of the object world (Jacobson 1964). This was seen (1) in his improved relationship with his wife where he became the protector rather than the tantruming child; (2) in his acceptance of himself as a father to his children with whom he could empathize and yet keep appropriate boundaries; (3) in his ability to now use his self-observing ego to see that he was already experiencing a new boss as a parent-figure and looking to be guided, appreciated and judged by him; (4) in his coming to shift from valuing pleasure (oral and anal self-indulgence) to valuing self-regulation (Marks 1985, 1986). This served to build up self-esteem and components of superego structure; and (5) to give him the freedom of thinking of and wishing to be separate from his therapist.

In time, Harold began, almost without awareness, to indicate his "ambition" (Jacobson 1964) to function autonomously and without the need of the therapeutic relationship. This was considered and a time for termination was agreed upon jointly. Over this phase, Harold often expressed doubts, including doubts as to whether the therapist could really care for him if he could let him go, that is, terminate. In the working through of this phase as one in which Harold could experience loss and mourning related to early object loss (through his own loss of respect for the object world), there was evidence of his moving more toward Jacobson's phase of idealization basic to the attainment of object constancy (Hartman 1939/1958; Jacobson 1964; Mahler 1971).

Over the four years in this analytic group of men and women, Harold had evolved as the most real, insightful person in the group. He had begun with a shy facade, gradually moved toward expressing his more primitive unconscious in his verbal expressions toward the women in the group. One woman in particular, along with the cotherapist, served the process of drive neutralization that enabled him to recover feelings of tenderness and memories of longing for the early object. He was especially tender and idealizing toward the cotherapist and could experience himself as more manly and adult toward "Joan," the woman whom he fell in love with in the group. He could experience warmth and closeness toward two of the male members in the group without fear of his homosexual impulses. He offered his insights and his feelings to group members and his termination was received with attitudes of hope and admiration as well as with a deep sense of loss by his fellow-members. It was a moving expression of appreciation for this man and of a letting go out of love, which was something his narcissistic mother could not do. Yet, within the latter years of Harold's treatment, he was more accepting of his mother's limitations as well as of those of his wife. He did not see women as powerful, exploitative, and engulfing any longer. His transference to the therapist as the un-attuned, foolish mother was worked through. He worked through sexual problems with the seductive mother through the group experience with "Cindie," including his early sense of impotent rage. This served him in being more under his own drive regulation with greater abundance of psychic energies available for ego functioning.

Harold's pronouncement on entering treatment that he would continue another fifteen years or more as he had with his previous therapist—meaning he could never be free from a tie to an object who would test reality for him, regulate him, and take responsibility for his life—had given way to the *ambition* to live his own life rather than to spend it manipulating the object world. This was a profound achievement in which Harold's ego involvement caused a shift from an attitude of hopelessness and helplessness to an attitude that implied hope that he could become his own person with his own goals and his own capacity to realize those goals. This was no longer a goal or culture of pure narcissism but one in which his ambition included the goal of being able to love and to have a meaningful relationship with wife and children and colleagues based on a meaningful relationship with his self.

7

Self Psychology Groups

Frederic Arensberg, Ph.D.

Heinz Kohut (1979; Kohut and Wolf 1978) found that certain patients did not work through basic developmental problems in standard classical analytic treatment. Kohut (1971) saw that the working through of oedipal issues and their derivatives did nothing to accelerate growth of feelings of well-being, energy, verve, and confidence in these patients. Often, they still approached the world as frightened, tentative people, with feelings of small, undeveloped selves. The most analyzable of these people Kohut classified as having narcissistic behavior disorders and narcissistic personality disorders, both coming under the rubric of primary disorders of the self. Narcissistic behavior disorders are marked by perverse, delinquent, and addictive behavior, whereas narcissistic personality disorders are characterized by feelings of enfeeblement, enervation, depression, and an oversensitivity to failings or shifts in the environment and slights from others.

The current paper deals with the theory and technique of analytic group therapy from a self psychology perspective (that of Kohut and his disciples). This includes patients with primary narcissistic disturbances, and also those with secondary narcissistic disorders (those patients with structurally undamaged selves who are reacting to the vicissitudes of life with broad shifts in self-esteem). It must be interjected that Kohut himself neither conducted group therapy nor approved of it; his reasons for this are stated later. Therefore, what follows is based on adaptations of theories and applications of self psychology to the body of analytic group therapy work.

The methodology of the self psychologically informed analyst is empathy. Empathy is hearing the patients' experience through their own words, images, and feelings, and accurately relating this back to them. Empathy is nonevaluative and neutral, containing as little as possible of the differentiated observer, and reflecting as much as possible of the patient. In the analysis, as in the original dyad between mother (qua analyst) and child (qua patient), empathy must be imperfect, because the parenting object has a self of his or her own, and cannot always be perfectly reflective. Therefore the patient will necessarily experience failures in empathy, sometimes at crucial points in his or her development. Hopefully, in the analysis, this will occur within the context of a "good-enough environment" from Winnicott's (1960, see 1965) point of view and an "optimally frustrating environment" from Kohut's (1966). Oscillating degrees of empathy from the analyst within a firm, grounded, optimal environment lead to the revivification of early needs and emotionally laden memories within the patient. These needs (Kohut 1971) are thought of as universal in the development of a strong, vital, and energetic self that can sustain the vicissitudes of life. They are rearoused in the psychoanalytic treatment. The required response to these needs is from their "selfobjects." When these needs are thwarted either in life or in analysis, a reactivation of the original dyadic constellations occurs, and if the self state is in a sufficiently weakened condition, "fragmentation" (Kohut 1977) may occur. Fragmentations reflect damage to the self state, manifest in rage, depression, and paranoia, and in losses of self-esteem and confidence. In secondary narcissistic pathology, these states are minor and fleeting; in primary narcissistic conditions, the states may be more lasting and incapacitating.

The reactivation of these selfobject needs in psychoanalysis leads to the formation of transferences around specific poles (Kohut 1977), called mirroring and idealization. Later, twinship or alter ego was incorporated into Kohut's system (1984) as a third pole. Idealization (Kohut 1971) is the need for a lively, energetic, strong, and soothing selfobject. Mirroring is a selfobject function that accurately reflects the subject in his grandiosity, creativity, aggression, sexuality, fears, hunger, and so on. Twinship is a selfobject need rooted in the wish to have another person with exactly the same values, feelings, ideas, and attitudes. When these basic needs are overly frustrated in the infant/baby's development, and inadequately repaired by the parent, a developmental arrest is likely to occur. This can lead to oversensitivity to injury in particular areas, especially those constellations reactivated in the analysis. The purpose of the analysis is to activate the transferences through empathy, and help the individual to understand his deepest selfobject needs—both in the present and genetically.

Natural and inevitable empathic failures (the misunderstanding of selfobject needs) are recognized by the analyst and related to the patient's experience; this ultimately leads to analytic working through. When the current self is strengthened through an understanding of archaic selfobject needs, the process is called transmuting internalization (Kohut 1971, 1977, 1984).

In traditional analytic group therapy, an often chaotic family and environmental structure is reproduced in the group, so that with a multiplicity of transferences elicited, conflicts and residual drives can be analyzed (Wolf and Schwartz 1962; Yalom 1970). Prior to my familiarization with self psychology, I would seek to maximize conflict, transferential distortion, and highly charged emotion in groups so that a virtual laboratory could be established within the clinical setting. All would be analyzed within the patients' dynamics, connected to present situational problems, and related to genetic history. Such groups were especially effective in treating ego-syntonic character pathology.

However, it was found that certain patients could not benefit from arousal of these familiar conflicts; they either became worse in group, more defended, or could not remain in group due to the degree of upset. Interpretations seemed accurate, but the degree of emotional distress was overwhelming, interfering with life outside the group as well as within. In general, regardless of what meaning one could attribute to the conflict, the degree of narcissistic injury was too painful to benefit the patient. Frequently, this was unbeneficial to others in the group as well, and the group would become "stuck." In some cases, where the person was in combined treatment, individual sessions helped to lessen the impact of injury, but were not sufficient to offset the hurt. Another approach was needed to help these patients.

Kohut (1978) spoke of a "group self" that had a life of its own, could regulate its own patterns, and had a specific narcissistic configuration. He saw an exact parallel between group and individual selves, each with its own selfobject needs motivated by narcissism. In personal communications with Kohut, the author established that Kohut's negative attitude toward group therapy was grounded in his fear that the leader's potential power could be misused. Kohut felt that there was a great danger of the leader's charisma overshadowing the patient. If the leader's own narcissistic need dovetailed with the group's selfobject need for powerful idealization, the patients' needs might be sacrificed. In this manner empathy could be used to exploit the individual rather than help him, especially since he felt that group pressure leads to regression and greater vulnerability. Although it is vital to keep these factors in mind as cautionary measures, the following should demonstrate the overwhelming value of applying self psychology theory to group.

Harwood (1986) asserts that Kohut valued healthy narcissism in his later writings. Narcissism filled with a sense of joy and reciprocity with others is certainly an admirable group attribute. She emphasizes that since the group as a whole has multiple selfobject functions, it helps members move from narcissistic positions to those of mutuality. Harwood (1986) speaks of the selfobject functions of individual group members, the group as a whole, and the leader, emphasizing the importance of the idealized parent imago that was so vital for the child in his quest for self-structure. She stresses that as the group supplies empathy and understanding, the patient becomes strengthened and can recognize his own strength and uniqueness as well as that of others in the group (and in the larger world). Stone and Whitman (1977) emphasize that self psychology establishes a group milieu that supports narcissistic needs as valid and encourages their expression. Such "difficult" patients like "monopolizers" or "help-rejecting complainers" who would be frustrated and frustrating in ordinary groups, can have their narcissistic needs understood in self psychology groups; the disruptive and negative aspects of these character traits are ameliorated. Bacal (1985) relates to the value of the group providing an opportunity for transferences to shift from one member to another (including the therapist). For example, the rage at a failing ideal might be mollified in that others could pick up this function. Consequently, patients could risk significant anger and/or disappointment at the leader.

Technique

The composition of a self psychology–oriented group cannot be quite as heterogeneous as a conventional analytic group (Arensberg 1985). Patients need to have significant experience in individual analytic treatment. Through individual or combined analyses, patients should already have become attuned to, and fairly accepting of, their selfobject needs. A person who is rigidly contemptuous of archaic developmental needs can perpetually disrupt the calm and support of the group. He or she may damage the constancy of selfobject ties established in both group and individual treatment. Severely developmentally arrested people may be particularly vulnerable to these disruptions, especially where they are prolonged beyond optimal frustration. It is not as much a matter of diagnosis, as of readiness to receive empathic responses without excessive defensiveness, that determines readiness for group.

Preparation for group should involve a clear statement of its nature and structure, and what the patient is likely to gain. The more trusting and safe the dyadic contact between patient and analyst, the better the odds are of a successful group experience. A respectful alliance with at least potential solidity, should be established. It is desirable for the prospective group patient to have a working knowledge of some of his dynamics and a basic acceptance of the transference. He should have had ample opportunity to express fantasies and feelings about the new experience he will embark in, and to analyze dreams. The analyst should supply an attitude of optimism and hope regarding the group, that of a new adventure.

The purpose and goal of a self psychology–oriented group is to supply the patient with another arena where his selfobject needs can be experienced, understood, and sometimes gratified. An empathic milieu, constancy of structure and composition, and seriousness of purpose allows for the emergence of selfobject transferences toward the leader, group as a whole, individuals in the group, and combinations of individuals. The group can elicit every conceivable transference, and these can be linked to the patient's presenting problems as well as genetic issues. Group provides a generally safe environment where the deepest feelings can be expressed without danger of catastrophic humiliation, retaliation, or disappearances. (Group members usually return following turmoil and conflict). Thus, the ultimate threat of dissolution and disintegration is greatly reduced. Now that selfobject needs and feelings are empathically mirrored, developmental blockages are alleviated. The energized, revitalized self can traverse new territory with a sense of vigor and joy. The structure of group should emphasize reliability and consistency, so that it feels safe and allows for free self-expression.

The role of the leader is as analyst and model. He creates a milieu through his demeanor, projection of his sense of himself, respect and interest in the others, warmth and understanding. It is essential that the group analyst have a good knowledge of each patient's dynamics, issues, and goals, and that these be remembered and applied in group. Interpretations should be empathically relevant to the individual. Other group members usually acquire an empathic and analytic attitude merely by being in the group, but also by receiving empathic interpretations. Great skill is required from the leader when two or more group members are involved in serious emotional conflict, especially a seemingly unresolvable one. It is important not to interpret too quickly so that the transference can be maximized within optimally frustrating conditions. After things have quieted down, the analyst should make interpretations, respectively relevant to both patients, providing maximum empathy to each. The statements should be individualistic, reflecting specific knowledge of each person.

Self psychology groups have a marvelous capacity to elicit the three poles of selfobject transference. These will each be illustrated in the clinical section. Some patients perceive group as a soothing, positive, healthy, ideal place, while others see group as a collection of rejects and losers. In both cases, memories of early family experiences are elicited, respectively inducing the wished-for idealized parent imago and parental disappointments and failures.

Patients who have had their feelings and thoughts mirrored by the analyst in individual therapy are in a particularly favorable position to provide this for others in the group, as well as receiving empathic responses. The self is greatly strengthened by the accurate mirroring in the group. With a stronger self, there is less vulnerability, less oversensitivity to minor injuries in the outside world, and greater feelings of vitality and resilience. In other words, with transmuting internalizations, it takes a greater external stimulus to create fragmentation.

Twinship has no equivalent. Anyone experiencing the feeling, "Oh, that could be me talking," knows twinship. It is more than being known or understood; it is hearing an exact response of the self coming from another person, and is usually experienced with delight and amazement. Dramatically, a person will enter group feeling heavy and dragged out, receive a twinship remark, and light up like the electricity has been turned on.

No issue has been more misunderstood than "aggression" in self psychology groups. Self psychology groups are not "goody-goody" places where everyone is nice and sweet. Because the milieu is one of safety, where one enters with a reasonable expectation of understanding, extreme conflict and rage are tolerable. The group constancy allows one to know they will not be abandoned and fear of dissolution is minimized. In general, rage and hostility are viewed as fragmentation products, responses to severe empathic failures, or reactions to an agonizing memory of past selfobject transgressions. A primary purpose of the group, initially, is to reactivate these disturbing constellations, so they can be empathically analyzed. Aggression, on the other hand, is seen as a healthy developmental expression of the self, full of energy and vitality, in need of accurate mirroring.

In self psychology groups, resistance is usually analyzed as an attempt of the self to restore and protect itself, when it anticipates damage to its selfobject needs. Defenses are utilized to protect against fragmentation and ultimate disintegration of the self. When the group functions well, one trusts that his or her selfobject needs will be empathically understood, and resistance diminishes. A typical interpretation would be "it is understandable that you came fifteen minutes late to group today, because after what you experienced at the end of last group, you must have expected to be further beaten down tonight."

Working through in self psychology could well be called "cure through empathic failures." Just as the original mother could not get inside her infant to provide perfect empathy (since the mother and baby are two separate entities), the same is true in the analytic situation. The original injury was due to the mothering figure's inability to calmly, nondefensively, and evenly tolerate the child's response to selfobject failure. These failures, inevitably occur in group. The analyst and group understand the failures, trace their origin within the group, recall the rearoused constellations, and empathically mirror the patient's experience. The frequent repetition for this leads to the transmuting internalizations evident in a stronger revitalized self.

Countertransference reactions contain some specific facets for the group self psychologist. Primarily, the group analyst may have a need to be the perfect empathic parent (one without failures) and, through repairing his children, be vicariously repairing himself. If it ultimately represents a "life and death" situation for himself, he may be internally intolerant of these inevitable failures. As much as possible, he should be attuned to these issues.

Clinical Examples

Mirroring

Kenneth entered training analysis at age 28; two years later he entered group therapy in addition to individual treatment.

He was a loving, emotional man, who had an excellent relationship with his wife and children, but felt very nervous and inadequate around other men. As an analyst and student, he felt stupid and inept. His older European immigrant parents doted on him. (He had one sister, nineteen years older, who was out of the house when he was born). He felt very loved, but weak and unaccomplished. As an adolescent he felt like a freak. He loved individual therapy, felt appreciated by the therapist, and developed a solid idealizing transference.

Group was initially rough for him; he thought of himself as the "stupid guy in group" and behaved accordingly. He would make the most inane comments, and seemed to talk only for the sake of talking. The women regarded him as their "poor baby" and the men saw him as impotent and quite dispensable. He, however, loved group and felt it was a warm and nurturant place. He accepted his role as the "group schlepper."

Sometime later Bill entered the group. He felt contempt and disgust for Kenneth. He would say to Kenneth, "How can you be an analyst; you'd be the last person I would go to." One of Kenneth's patients called him a "worm." Now, he began to feel humiliated by his behavior, and to get more in touch with his feelings of self-loathing. He began to isolate himself and shut his mouth. When he expressed these feelings in individual sessions, he was encouraged to bring them into the group. He now disparaged the empathy given by the analyst. He felt this weakened him and that he needed some "toughening up." As the group expressed deep understanding of his experience of shame, humiliation, and vulnerability, he began to express violent anger by shouting and banging his fists on the table. Every act of self-expression was welcomed by the group, and even by Bill. His aggression was being mirrored, allowing him to traverse a developmental barrier. His parents couldn't do that for him. Gradually, he began to talk about feeling a sexual attraction to Nan in the group. She enjoyed this greatly, and it led to the expression of many sexual feelings by both parties. Bill became very competitive with Kenneth. The group applauded all of Ken's powerful and adequate behavior. Kenneth talked of new, very potent feelings in making love to his wife. He said his penis felt stronger, bigger and harder. As an analyst, he felt smarter and more in control. He began to make wonderful interpretations in group. Kenneth felt he was an attractive and significant figure as he walked on the street. The group marvelled at the changes they were beholding, and he relished all this. His grandiosity, never mirrored as a child by his loving but timid parents, was now receiving attention and this made him feel wonderful. One could see, by the week, his growing energy, confidence, and self-esteem. His infantile rage turned to effective aggressive behavior in work and play but he lost none of his sensitivity or capacity for tenderness. A sense of grandeur gradually supplanted the infantile grandiosity, although it never totally disappeared.

Twinship

Paula was a 60-year-old social worker who had been in orthodox analysis for seven years with another analyst. She came to group because of difficulties in her work as a group therapist at a local hospital. She felt intimidated by her colleagues, supervisors, and patients. She expressed boredom and lack of confidence, and thought of leaving the field. Initially, she became enamored of the leader in the group, observing all of his therapeutic moves like a hawk. She asked direct questions of the leader concerning his methodology. "You're playing therapist in the group and isolating yourself from us," said the group. The therapist then intervened, "Paula is asking these questions in order to establish her place and value with me and within the group, however, it is understandable that you experience abandonment when you feel she is keeping herself separate from you and placing herself above you." The therapist could have emphasized the obvious oedipal and competitive meaning, or the defensive aspects of her comments, but he felt the timing was bad and it would be empathically incorrect. The group then started to understand Paula. Gradually she became more connected to the group. When the leader admitted errors as he made them, and openly expressed vulnerability, she became both amazed and relieved. Her own experiences as group leader paralleled these but she was frightened and ashamed of them. She said "you are exactly like me; we are peas in a pod." She began to make brilliant observations in group, often discerning things the leader hadn't thought of. The importance of the twinship experience was interpreted, and was connected to her feelings of profound isolation as a child. Paula became one of the most highly esteemed, valued, and cared-for group members. When she expressed her own deep vulnerabilities, others were only too glad to respond and connect with her. At this time she stated that in the therapy group she felt like an excellent thinker, but that this feeling did not carry over into the groups she was running.

The continuing experience of twinship with the analyst's feelings, attitudes, and techniques accumulated during the following three years in group. She had never before felt that anyone else had the same feelings as herself. She had been an only child with a peculiar, schizoid mother and an arrogant, critical father. She gradually began to feel like the others in the group. For the first time in her life she said she felt like an insider, not an "onlooker from beyond." For a while Paula often experienced herself as one with the leader, sometimes as the leader himself when leading her groups. When speaking to her colleagues and supervisors, she perceived herself to be an intelligent, significant and thoughtful person. In time, she no longer felt fused with the analyst, but her skill and vitality remained very much her own.

Idealization

Myron was in a four-times-weekly self analysis for five years prior to entering group. Myron had entered analysis because he felt very lonely and anxious, was ashamed of his homosexuality, and could not control his drinking. He was an only child whose father abandoned his mother before he was born; he never knew him. He had an intensely close symbiotic relationship with his mother, taking pride in being "mama's good boy." Upon entering treatment, it was suggested that he also join an alcohol self-help group, which he did. Myron was an extremely handsome, 40-year-old businessman who felt unattractive, unsuccessful, and doomed to a life of failure. He had a history of no stable relationships.

Individual analysis proceeded well, and a powerful mother

transference developed. Predictably, he did everything to please the analyst and was the model of a well progressing patient. Outwardly, he entered into a successful, lucrative business, formed a long-term stable relationship with a lover, stopped drinking, and never displayed displeasure with his treatment. Inwardly, predictably, he remained anxious, depressed, and continued to hate himself. Empathy led to renewed symbiotic ties with a mother figure who allowed him to manifest success in the outside world, but whose price for love was that he remain weak and impotent inside. Although these interpretations were continuously made, there was little change in his level of aggression and self-esteem.

He readily agreed to enter group, with the understanding that group could facilitate internal changes. In the group he met Carol who was his ideal of a woman; she was stately, beautiful, sophisticated, successful, and empathic. Myron marvelled at how wonderful it was of this leader to have such a prominent "goddess" in his group. Carol and the group as a whole became his idealized parent imago. He started to feel much better about himself, and became more optimistic and assertive in his relationships. He was able to tell others off in the group, to criticize their weaknesses (particularly the other men), and expressed great rage when a woman was dominating the group space. At the same time, he fought more with his lover, feeling safer and stronger in the relationship.

The most dramatic shift, however, occurred when Carol decided to terminate. He felt crushed, saddened, and outraged. He understood her need to leave, but he began to despise the group. He dreaded coming, missed quite a few sessions, and was agitated and miserable when he did attend. He expressed disdain and disgust toward the leader, for the first time doubting his ability. He called it the "group of losers" and asked why the leader wasn't adequate enough to bring in another Carol. He had a dream (the night after a group session) in which he was sitting in his dreary childhood kitchen in North Carolina with his mother and several crippled men. He couldn't escape and felt imprisoned. He screamed and no one heard. When he came into group the next week he immediately knew that the group, without Carol, was his hopeless and desolate childhood family. Carol's disappearance represented a loss of the idealized, uncastrating mother who gave him value. At the same time, the male group leader had an adequate presence for him, as long as he could produce a "Carol." Without Carol, the leader became a fallen ideal.

Myron's insights allowed him to reestablish the analyst as an ideal figure, but he retained his anger at him for failing to produce the group he needed. Even with insights, group remained too painfully reminiscent of his depressing childhood, and although he acknowledged its great value, felt he had to terminate. He remained in individual analysis, continuing to utilize these insights. He vigilantly regarded his need for an ideal as valid, whether it was the analyst or an outside figure, and felt that his disappointments in these idealized figures were justified. The analyst's lack of perfection was tolerated, but not welcomed, and he left therapy feeling solid, hopeful, sexual, and proud.

Idealization of the group seems to have a power far greater than the sum of its individuals, or toward any one person. To the same degree, when idealization of the group falters, the entire atmosphere changes and there can be a somber, dead quality affecting everyone. Sometimes, one individual or a specific constellation of people can shift the mood of a group in either direction. Analysis in a group is necessary but not sufficient; a group must have vitality and energy. Both the leader and members supply this spirit, which is the source of idealization. Obviously, this is a factor in deciding on the composition of the group. This energy is also what sustains a group through its low points.

Working Through of Empathic Failure

Finally, let us briefly consider two vignettes of empathic failure, the first unresolved, the second resolved. Tina was a happily married woman in her early forties. She married as a young teenager and was leading a steady, but unspectacular life. Paul, the "group celebrity," showed special interest in Tina, telling her that if he could ever find someone like her, he'd marry her. Tina was very flattered. His ardor continued for several months. Tina felt a new sense of herself as a woman; she felt more sexual than she had ever felt before.

In time, a new woman, Ann, entered group and Paul's affections shifted. During all of this, each person's feelings were carefully analyzed. Each member of the group responded characteristically; vengeance, envy, jealousy, competition, submission, and aggression were all expressed. However, analysis didn't temper Tina's humiliation in front of the group. She could not get in touch with feelings of rage, envy, or competition in herself. She could only feel a humiliation that was described as more painful than anything she had ever experienced. The closest situation we could come to in analysis was the birth of her sister who was two years younger, but the pain remained untouched. Tina appreciated the empathy toward her internal experience, but surprisingly this did not even provide temporary relief. She terminated group as it felt too painful to endure. She appreciated the group, but left feeling as a failure. I believe in retrospect that she was not able to mobilize her rage at the leader for putting her through this humiliation, and for not sufficiently helping her to find the strength to survive. She felt too small to manage this without parental help, and insufficient analysis of this issue constituted the empathic failure. If this failure had been analyzed and repaired, it would have strengthened Tina.

An empathic failure with a more favorable outcome occurred with Sylvia. She was a 22-year-old woman who had been in group for two years, and announced that she planned to leave in one year to join an all-woman commune. This plan was positively received by the leader and most members. However, with only three sessions remaining prior to the planned termination, the leader analyzed certain dynamics in her leaving group and entering a commune (among them isolating herself from an opportunity to be with men whom she had been afraid of). Sylvia panicked. The mirroring of her positive movement was now suddenly withdrawn, just when she was becoming most excited about it. Understandably, she regressed back to old patterns. The leader, investigating his countertransference, realized that he was unconsciously acting on his own separation anxiety, and was not fully allowing himself to feel the loss of Sylvia. That would explain his original failure to analyze the patient adequately, and his sudden, nonempathic, untimely comments at the end of treatment. In the following session, the leader admitted his error. He spoke of caring for Sylvia and his feelings of loss. He also dealt with how this "sudden analysis" affected Sylvia, and that it dove-tailed with similar defects in mirroring from her mother when Sylvia was young. The leader commented that his analysis of her defense was probably correct, but the timing of it was most hurtful. He added that it might be important for her to try the commune at this time in her life, and when she was ready to leave it, there still would be plenty of time to work out her issues with men. She was very relieved. Sylvia felt good about the experience in group, optimistic about her move, and solid in herself. She (and the group) felt especially good about the leader's openness, viewing it as a parental strength that had been absent in their own families.

In summary, self psychology theory and techniques are appro-priate to group, especially with Kohut's warnings kept in mind. In no way does this supplant or replace the more traditional ap-proaches regarding group, but is necessary in the treatment of nar-cissistic disorders or in the ordinary narcissism that is in all of us.

8

Group Dynamic Treatment

Saul Tuttman, M.D., Ph.D.

The purpose of this paper is to explore the use of combining group dynamic theory and individual dynamics in conducting a group. Several psychoanalysts who have appreciated and clarified the application of *group dynamics* in their groups are the British theorists and practitioners: Bion (1959), Ezriel (1950), Foulkes (1964), and Pines (1981). American analytically oriented psychotherapists who also believe that group dynamics can be "exploited" therapeutically in treating patients in groups include: Durkin (1964), Fried (1954), Glatzer (1960), Scheidlinger (1982), and Stein (1963). More recently, Horwitz (1986), Kauff (1989), Kibel (1989), Kosseff (1989), and others, including myself (Tuttman 1989) have considered group dynamics as well as intrapsychic factors in conducting group treatment.

Early Group Dynamic Theories Applied to Therapy

In 1921, Freud's monograph on group psychology appeared. Although he did not describe the psychotherapeutic aspects of groups, he did examine psychodynamic factors involved in groups and offered several interesting hypotheses about the motivation and functioning in groups. He referred to the importance of leadership but mentioned that a "leading idea" can take the place of an actual leader. Further, he distinguished transient and permanent groups, homogeneous and heterogeneous groups, organized and unorganized groups. Freud contended that the basic dynamic underlying group formation and functioning deals with the mechanism of identification. Freud also considered empathy important since it permitted group members to experience through one another. This not only furthers positive feelings within the group but also limits the danger of aggression interfering with cohesion.

One of the first psychoanalysts who actually developed a theory about working with groups in an effort to achieve therapeutic aims was Wilfred Bion, the British Kleinian analyst whose important book, *Experiences in Groups* (1959), presented what has come to be influential in the field of group dynamics and treatment. He (Bion 1959) stated: "I am impressed, as a practicing psychoanalyst, by the fact that the psychoanalytic approach through the individual and through the group are dealing with different facets of the same phenomena. The two methods provide the practitioner with a rudimentary binocular vision" (p. 8). Bion utilized Kleinian hypotheses and his own intuitions to examine attitudes of the group-as-a-whole toward leader and other group members as well as toward the group itself. He noticed that recurrent themes and episodes could be monitored and this led him to his unique propositions concerning group dynamics. "First, every group meets to *do* something. The group is thus geared to a task in some way related to reality and attempts to utilize rational methods and cooperation. This constitutes the 'work group' orientation; its characteristics are similar to those attributed by Freud to the ego . . ." (Tuttman 1989; 221).

Bion (1959) stated: "When patients meet for group therapy sessions, some mental activity is directed to the solution of the problems for which the individual seeks help" (p. 144). But this work group functioning, Bion added, is often blocked or diverted by unconscious mental activities present in the group participants that lead to anxiety that, in turn, leads to powerful emotional resistances and drives in a special form Bion called "The unconscious basic assumptions." He found these assumptions to be prevalent in all groups. For Bion, to do realistic work in the group requires discipline, cooperation, and good reality testing. The unconscious assumptions do provide the energy for group activity but also generate resistance to reality work. They must be appreciated and harnessed if the group is to transcend them and function as a working group. Any group completely governed by unconscious assumptions will be counterproductive. Thus the working group and the leader must create a therapeutic alliance and together monitor, observe, and harness the archaic assumptions underlying the primitive energies at work.

Bion, as Kleinian analyst, focused on archaic pre-oedipal fantasies involving paranoid, schizoid, and depressive features in contrast to Freud who related group functioning to family ties (with the father as leader) and oedipal issues. Bion described the basic assumptions that interfere with working group activities. These include dependence, pairing, and fight-flight orientations. It is useful for the group therapist to read Bion's (1959) descriptions of such processes (as well as Scheidlinger's [1980] summary and critique). Bion also focused on the primitive Kleinian mechanisms of projective identification and splitting, which he found to be operant in group behavior. Understanding these dynamics permits a working-through process within the group. Bion's theory of group dynamics is essentially bipolar in that he recognized an interaction of the manifest group and the latent group clearly reflecting the psychoanalytic understanding of the conscious and unconscious dimensions of individual personalities.

Ezriel (1950, 1957) was also interested in the interaction between manifest and latent group manifestations. Originally he worked with Bion and eventually postulated an underlying *common group problem* that results in manifest tension and is a ". . . common denominator of the dominant unconscious fantasies of the group." Foulkes (1951, 1964), also in London, integrated his psychoanalytic concerns, group therapy interest, and his insight that individuals live in a social framework. This he called a "network," the natural group in which patients live. It must be understood in order to enrich the comprehension of the group analytic situation (which Foulkes referred to as the group "matrix"). He concluded that only by appreciating the individual's functioning in both *matrix* and *network* can one appreciate the patient's pathology as a social process.

Foulke's dynamic focus relates to his underlying hypothesis that mental disturbances are due, at least in part, to psychopathology involving several interacting individuals. Disturbance is conceived in terms of relationships involving nuclear and extended families and other social groups. Foulkes concluded that one can help the patient to effect change only as his network changes; furthermore, effort or success at change will create disruption. Thus, even the cure of emotional disturbance with a particular individual will result in a disequilibrium among the various members of that individual's network. These dynamics must be explored in meaningful group treatment if change is to be accomplished.

Whitaker and Lieberman (1964) applied Thomas French's (1952) concept of *focal conflict theory* to groups. French considered any individual's current behavior to be that person's technique for solving personality conflicts experienced in the present but originating in very early experience. These early focal conflicts need to be appreciated and understood. Whitaker and Lieberman (1964) suggested that each group member is affected by different *group focal conflicts* and these differences result in group conflicts. As the group interacts, hidden conflict begins to emerge and requires interpretation and working through.

Recent Group Dynamic Concepts and their Application

Henriette Glatzer (1975) believes that certain patients may progress further in group psychotherapy than in dyadic treatment. They have serious developmental defects that make them too emotionally vulnerable and disorganized to utilize individual therapy effectively. In such cases, the group often serves as an incorruptible superego that will not allow a patient to dissolve in "acting out" or self-pity. In such instances peers, who are fellow-patients, can reinforce reality values when such individuals are blocked by superego resistances. Thus, Glatzer (1962) believes, group interaction and a focus on group dynamics accelerates the therapeutic alliance. Group structure provides support and helps overcome resistances. Group members actively and usually effectively interpret defenses and underwrite reality. The greater activity of group members' functioning as cotherapists mitigates the otherwise needed ongoing active intervention of the group leader–analyst. For certain patients this is very helpful since their backgrounds may motivate them to react with resistance when the leader is active. As a consequence, such patients can come to experience the therapist as a more "palatable" object who is available for constructive identification. The group as a whole becomes a therapeutic matrix and the group therapist becomes less of an awesome, powerful, inaccessible figure.

Several psychoanalytic practitioners agree that *group dynamics* are invaluable in furthering group treatment in some cases. I shall refer to those group leaders who utilize the group dynamic aspects in conducting group psychotherapy. Edrita Fried (1961) noted that patients in the group seemed more inclined to express feelings directly by action or reaction rather than by intellectualizing or reporting them as was their inclination in individual sessions. The group situation encouraged active confrontations and more dynamic exploration, which facilitates changes in response patterns and leads to new attachments. Thus, fresh adaptations and meaningful structural change may result, in some instances, more through *group dynamic* factors and group-as-a-whole interaction than through dyadic psychoanalytic treatment.

Durkin (1975, 1983), another analytic group therapist, has also been impressed by the application of dynamic field theories of Kurt Lewin (1951) on her work. Furthermore, she was influenced by the British group therapists who, in addition to analytic concerns were very interested in the group-as-a-whole approaches to treating patients. Durkin (1964) agreed with Scheidlinger (1964) that a group dynamic focus was complementary rather than contradictory to analytic group therapy. She (Durkin 1975) referred to the importance of understanding the stated ". . . relationships between each person's unconscious motivations and the mutual influence of group members transactions with one another, . . . the relationship between the individual inputs and those of the group-as-a-whole" (p. 10).

Ganzarain (1959), also analytically inclined, nevertheless began to contemplate the applications of *general systems theory* (Bertanaffly, 1968) to group psychotherapy. Durkin (1975) also came to consider these group-as-a-whole approaches along with *general systems theory*. She expressed the possibility that this could provide a scientific metatheory that might demonstrate the interconnections of all complex multivariable phenomena by pointing out their structural parallels and spelling out the laws by which such organization operates. In that context, she has struggled toward developing both psychoanalytic and group dynamic conceptual subsystems.

It is interesting to observe that so many psychoanalytically inclined psychotherapists, in the course of leading groups, have learned to value the relevance and applicability of group dynamics. For example, Leonard Horwitz (1977) concluded that "both group forces and individual personalities . . . actively influence the process of group therapy" (p. 23). Over the years, he has come to appreciate the limitations of holistic approaches *and* of dyadic psychoanalytic approaches as well, and he has attempted to correct for these limitations by seeking a balanced treatment approach. Horwitz (1989) recognizes the "common group theme" hypothesis adopted by holistic therapists. This is similar to Bion's (1959) "basic assumption" concept whereas Ezriel (1950) discussed "common group tension" and Whitaker and Lieberman (1964) referred to "the group focal conflict." All of these terms and ideas assume that unified underlying shared conflicts take place in groups. It is important that group leaders be aware of this factor. In 1971 Horwitz described the advantages of a group dynamic or group-as-a-whole approach. When using such focus, the therapist need not be concerned about equal time for each patient since the ongoing elaboration of shared conflicts is applicable to all members. The reiteration and reappearance of a group theme in the communications of many members in a group eventually leads to a clearly emerging group context. This will make it clear to each individual as to what is occurring. Such manifestations also decrease the likelihood of therapist error. Greater "contagion" effects of group-centered interactions are more likely.

At the same time, there are shortcomings to a group-centered approach; the therapist may be too restricted by the need to respond to the common group tension; as a result, individuals may actually feel ignored (since each person's needs and reactions are dealt with as secondary to the group's overall needs in such an approach.

Another danger in the group dynamics orientation is that the leader may appear too knowing and too powerful and peer transferences may be neglected. In the last decade, Horwitz (1989) has extended his holistic approach by exploiting the merits of the group as a whole while minimizing its limitations. He now advocates the following protocol: the leader's earliest focus is on the individual personal idiosyncratic features of *each* group member. As other members respond with emotion, there may emerge (with the aid of the therapist's involvement) the elaboration of a group theme. So the main technical sequence becomes first: the focus on individuals by the group and by the therapist and then, second: the offer later of holistic interpretations. In this way the individual needs of each patient tend to be less neglected since all patients have done the groundwork and the group-centered themes that emerge are clearly applicable universally and each individual's predicament is acknowledged.

Aaron Stein (1964) was another psychoanalytically oriented therapist who came to value the group dynamics approach in conducting group therapy. He also recognized that when the group-as-a-whole approach was applied alone, it lacked a specific method for integrating treatment for the multiple aspects of transference and focused either on the individual in the group context or on holistic phenomena minimizing member-to-member peer transference. And so, Stein and Kibel (1984) stressed peer interaction among individuals in the group. These group interactions ". . . consolidate to yield a collaborative group-as-a-whole response" (Stein and Kibel 1984: 318). Their work encouraged selective variations in a leader's style that could utilize to therapeutic advantage either each person in the group or the powerful group-as-a-whole forces at work.

I find it impressive that psychoanalysts who have ventured into the domain of group dynamics have learned to appreciate the value of utilizing the group dynamic aspects of the group treatment situation. The group-as-a-whole (group dynamics) vantage point leads to an enrichment of the group interaction and increases the likelihood of therapeutic results.

Applying Combined Group Dynamics and Individual Dynamics in Group Treatment

Most dynamic group therapists appreciate the role of projective identification and splitting in groups as well as in dyadic treatment. These Kleinian notions have been richly applied to the understanding of the borderline syndrome (recently by Otto Kernberg in 1975, and before that by Wilfred Bion in 1959). In the *group* psychotherapy literature, papers on treating borderlines (Horwitz 1989; Hosseff 1989; Tuttman 1984) have appeared despite the fact that these concepts deal with *intrapsychic* dynamics. The operation of these mechanisms involves an interaction with other people. In the group atmosphere, it occurs frequently that the projections from one person are transferred to other group members. Clearly both intrapsychic and group dynamic factors are at work. Similarly, the construct of a group "matrix" (Foulkes and Anthony 1964; Scheidlinger 1974) involves both intrapsychic and group dynamic processes. Application of this "group matrix" concept to therapy of the difficult-to-treat patients (borderlines, narcissistic, and psychotic) has recently appeared (Tuttman 1989) in the papers of Kauff, Kibel, Kosseff and others. This work follows from an appreciation of the great difficulty these patients had developmentally in completing the individuation process. Often such patients and their therapists both find dyadic treatment very stormy since it involves a recapitulation of past traumas in their difficult developmental histories. Therefore, therapists sometimes find unique advantages afforded by the group milieu for dealing with such matters. Again, we are dealing with an interplay of intrapsychic and group dynamic factors.

For example, applying "combined" theories may facilitate the working through of Mahler's separation and individuation phases in groups. Here the parallel of caretaker and child; individual therapist and analysand; and group-as-a-whole matrix and the group patient has meaningful applications. The group provides support, holding, and a nurturing base (Scheidlinger's 1974 paper on the "mother group"), which offers security and identificatory possibilities in a manner somewhat similar to that which a caretaker provides for a child or certain psychotherapists provide in individual treatment. There are advantages utilizing the group matrix in working through.

This will be demonstrated in the following illustration. In this instance a patient had experienced a dyadic developmental history that was traumatic. Often such individuals are frightened of the intimacy of the dyadic situation since it generates anxiety, aggression, and resistances. In the context of the group situation, it is possible to work through therapeutically such internal problems because of the group dynamics operating. Hopefully, this is illustrated in the following description.

Clinical Example

This central figure, a patient we will call Jim,* has been treated somewhat effectively in individual treatment; although for reasons that become clear in the illustration, group dynamic factors made a vital difference in what was attainable. This example reflects, in my opinion, the value of a group dynamic approach in dealing with certain problems for particular patients under special conditions. In a sense this demonstrates the effective use of a combined approach in which both group dynamics and intrapsychic dynamics play their role in the effective resolution of the patient's problems.

Jim's father was an army officer during World War II. Though stationed in New York, he had a family in another city. In the course of a brief affair, his girlfriend became pregnant and Jim was born. Since his father was devoutly religious and a well known professional figure, he was determined to maintain his marriage and avoided any publicity and contact with this child of a secret alliance. Jim, never having met his father, lived with his mother until her boyfriend asked her to marry him (with the provision that she send away the little boy of two). Placement was arranged at a nearby orphanage. At that time, the caretakers of this particular religious institution were assigned to care for unwanted children. Apparently, it was their

---

*This illustration is a composite of several groups and patients I have treated over the years. The details are basically accurate but the names and features that might have been identifiable have been modified so as to assure confidentiality. For purposes of convenience to author and readers, I have employed the same clinical material for illustrative purposes in different papers, although the context has varied and the mode and purpose of presentation has been different. The group incidents reported here have appeared in Tuttman 1980, 1984, 1985, 1989.

philosophy that emotions and feelings were not to be involved in child-care since that type of emotional intensity was potentially sinful. The staff was frequently changed as a means of discouraging personal involvements. As a result, Jim never developed an ongoing consistent relationship with any person. The atmosphere was one of anonymity and change. There was no opportunity to experience a long-range trusting relationship.

Now an adult, Jim has continued a rather impersonal lifestyle. Whenever sexual needs have become strong, he would seek impersonal homosexual contacts, usually at waterfront bars. He avoided personal involvement as completely as he could. He was aware of fantasies involving longings for caring, reliable parents, but he quickly repressed such yearnings and lived his life wandering from one bar to another. As soon as there was any indication that emotions might be aroused, he would run away and seek alternative indiscriminate contacts.

He entered treatment as he became aware of painful emotional isolation, and when he panicked at an inkling of feeling for someone. In the course of a year's individual psychotherapy, he began to feel frightened about his developing emotions toward the therapist. Understandably, his transference reactions were filled with longings, rage, apprehension, and anticipated disappointment. It was clear that this patient could not tolerate dependency needs nor was he comfortable with intense displaced anger. Despite these difficulties, gradually his ego functioning improved. I was impressed with his sensitivity and intelligence, but it was clear from his life history that there had not been opportunity for him to learn how to verbalize and communicate needs and reactions. Clearly, he panicked at the prospect of needing anyone and experiencing personal feelings. He was anxious about the intensity he was often on the brink of experiencing.

Because transference needs and reactions were *so* strong (and since I considered Jim sufficiently able to control his behavior), I suggested that he join a psychotherapy group. My understanding of his discomfort in personal relationships led me to conclude that a splitting of the transference might prove helpful to him therapeutically. His dread of intimacy and his intense rage could be more easily "contained" (Bion 1959) in a group situation. In addition, it was my hope that a reality group of caring individuals could provide a good group matrix and might help him face the patterns of his past while, at the same time, provide a group structure that would encourage exploration of his history and patterns. This could conceivably help him (through feedback and experience) to generate insight and learn new modes of adaptation. This particular group was very cohesive and experienced. The participants and leader had worked together for a long while before Jim entered. The group was well functioning from the standpoint of group-as-a-whole processes and on psychoanalytic levels of working through as well.

And so, Jim began group psychotherapy. Quickly members of the group in their accustomed manner offered acceptance and feedback: Jim seemed belligerent and provocative in turn and most group members disliked this and explained themselves. Jim was unaccustomed to feedback of any kind and he was shocked to hear that he could have such impact on others. He had no idea that he conveyed such intense feelings nor that words emanating from him or directed to him could have such power to provoke and to cause pain. The therapist observed how, even during initial sessions, the group was providing feedback and potentially useful understanding. It was clear that this isolated individual was finding himself in a meaningful and contemporary human situation that involved relationships. With the help of the group (since most group members by now had experience in monitoring and observing their own patterns and reactions), Jim was quick to learn that he desperately avoided facing needs, feelings, and anger. He and group members related this to his history of having been rejected, negated, and ignored. He also came to appreciate his dread of risking closeness, given the profound disappointments throughout his life. With the help of other group members and the leader's limited but "empathically" gauged interpretations, Jim came to consider the possibility that a function of his rage, apart from ventilation, was to lessen the possibility of arousing in himself and in others the closeness and intimacy he dreaded at least as much as he desired.

Jim was very sensitive whenever there was criticism or irritability toward him in the group. In one session, when he felt disapproval and lack of concern, he suddenly remembered a feeling he had experienced often when, at around the age of

four, the children at the orphanage were brought routinely to
a large bathroom and were instructed to sit at assigned places
in a long row of exposed toilets. Each boy was to promptly
defecate. The matron, as Jim recalls it, walked down the row
wiping every child with the same sheet of paper. At this recollection, the therapy group seemed restless. Some expressed
disgust and shock yet sensed the significance of this painful
memory. Several laughed as if to relieve tension and this reaction aroused Jim's rage. He spoke emotionally about his father who never existed, the disloyalty of his mother who abandoned him, the orphanage ritual that inflicted such indignity,
isolation, intrusion, and anonymity. And now, the last straw:
the mocking, rejecting group. The passion of his anguish and
his emotional expressiveness reached group members and leader
as we came to share those memories of his painful past.

Such interactions in the group were catalytic in furthering
ongoing individual treatment as well as making the group a
place in which Jim learned to work hard, to communicate, and
gain respect from his peers.

Group members supplied feedback. The night after Jim reported the orphanage routine, a group participant had a dream
she discussed the following session. Although from an econom-
ically privileged background, this woman felt strong identification with Jim's poverty and anguish. She dreamed that she
provided porridge for Oliver, the orphan hero of the Broadway
musical she had just seen a few nights before.

One winter night, as Jim tried to sleep in his cold, slum
apartment, an alley cat, who had apparently been climbing on
the fire escape, scratched on his window sill, interfering with
his rest. He reluctantly let the half-frozen creature in and a
battle-royal ensued over the next few weeks. The cat eagerly
awaited his return home every night, crept into his bed, leaned
against him and purred. He was both delighted and terrified.
The group members sympathized and were also annoyed when
Jim became anxious and enraged at the cat's intrusiveness,
neediness, demandingness. She seemed to assume that he
"owed" her the comforts of life! But he so enjoyed indulging
her that he felt guilty when he tossed "Matilda" off the bed.
He soon stopped doing that. The group members supported
his goodwill, helped him control his irritability, gave him
counsel and advice and appreciation until Matilda came to be

a welcome member of his simple household, his first companion other than the group itself.

Gradually, Jim increasingly risked allowing painful memories to vividly appear. There were indications of feeling more contact and increasing sensitivity to group members as well. Clearly, group therapy offered a meaningful arena in which Jim could bring up old problems, try to "work them out" and dare to experiment with what would be new modes, new patterns of responding, reacting, verbalizing, and communicating. The therapist remained neutral. Jim increasingly looked to the group for support and feedback. In an atmosphere of exploration and acceptance in which it became safe for all feelings and memories to emerge, Jim succeeded in working through what had appeared as disruptive resistance in individual treatment as the ambivalent transference grew. The result of the experiences in group has facilitated depth psychodynamic work in both individual and group treatment.

This was the first time Jim began to feel closer to others and safe enough to open up his feelings and share his life's details with a group of empathic, respectful peers. Group members have also benefited from his empathic, respectful peers. Group members have also benefited from his experience. "Those who participate in an ongoing, evolving history of any particular group gradually develop a form of emotional shorthand, a shared vocabulary, an argot, which serves us all in our joint search for further insight and still more enhanced communication" (Tuttman 1985).

In considering the usefulness of group dynamics in aiding the resolution of intrapsychic difficulties, as in the previous example, an interesting question arises: *Are there any group dynamic factors unique to the group therapy situation that are not available in dyadic treatment?* One way of approaching this question is by posing a series of related questions: Is there something about the structure of the group that provides a significant difference from the structure of the individual psychotherapy situation? In individual treatment and relationships there is the constraint of the one-to-one. As Theodor Reik stated (1948) in another context: "Dere's No Hiding Place Down Dere." (Reik was referring to the black spiritual that implies that omnipotent God knows about Man's digressions despite efforts to hide.) A parallel may exist in the youngster's early life view of the parent (or the patient's view of the therapist in dyadic treatment). Sometimes the pressure is too great in that there does not appear to be an available hiding place or a space for expressing or disguising the unacceptable frustration or rage. The group provides alternate outlets and so offers enough "space" (Winnicott 1965). The group contains the therapist and the patient *but it is more* than both of them (Kosseff 1975). There are many ways to express or hide emotions. They can be projected onto other group members or expressed through the "group voice." Others can be engaged as spokespeople for the secret thoughts so dangerous that the patient cannot take responsibility for them. The one-to-one relationship often does not leave the space needed by certain patients with certain dynamics. The group provides: the presence of several interacting people with buffer potential; the space and alternative individuals to project onto (to evade one by getting close to another, the choice of sitting in one space close to patient B or C or the therapist, or chosing not to); the possibility of pairing, of alliances, of utilizing, directly or indirectly, the voice of someone else to represent an aspect of oneself. All of this is made possible through the group structure. It is less likely to occur, at least on the level of reality, in individual interaction.

In conclusion, various theories, techniques and strategies dealing with group dynamics in group psychotherapy (as well as a brief historical overview) have been offered in the hope that the reader finds some clarification regarding the use and value of group dynamics in group treatment.

PART II

Neopsychoanalytic and Postanalytic
Group Psychotherapies

Postanalytic group psychotherapies, like psychoanalytic group therapy, can be divided into two distinct branches: postanalytic humanistic group therapies and postanalytic behavioral and directive group approaches. Humanistic psychology gives priority to human experience, values, intentions, and meaning, while promoting personal growth and change through interpersonal interactions. Philosophically these theories embrace Rousseau's concept of human nature as good but corruptible, rather than the Freudian/ Hobbesian view of human nature as more evil and requiring directive interventions. The humanistic view contrasts sharply as well with the Lochean/Behavioristic view of the human as "blank slate" molded by environmental conditioning.

At the other end of the spectrum from the postanalytic humanistic approaches are the postanalytic behavioral and directive approaches. Behavior therapy in groups is therapy that aims to alter people's maladaptive behavior through experimentally derived procedures such as conditioning. These approaches contrast with the psychoanalytic model's concern with treating intrapsychic organization or utilizing factors that lead to maladaptive behavior as a symptom in a group member, or as a group-as-a-whole theme to be addressed on the basis of its latent causation. An approach of growing utilization in behavior therapy groups is cognitive behavior modification, which emphasizes cognitive processes as mediators of behavior change, including thoughts, images, self statements, sets, and response strategies.

In essay 9 Herbert Holt describes existential group psychoanalysis as a group therapy for individuals who have difficulty in finding meaning and purpose to life and maintaining their identities. The theoretical background of existential group analysis is based on the phenomenological philosophy of Edmund Husserl who focused on unconscious intentionality and phenomenological description of the self, and on the existential theory of his pupil, Martin Heidegger, who focused on the concept of Dasein (being-in-the-world in a threefold manner of Eigenwelt, Mitwelt, and Umwelt). These Husserlian-Heideggerian explanations of being-in-the-world underpin Ludwig Binswanger's interpretation of Freudian psychoanalysis and are biologically grounded on the modern genetic triune brain theories of MacLean. In essay 9 the application of these theories to actual case histories of participating group members are clinically evaluated. Each person's problems are discussed while ellucidating the theme (Leitmotive of the group) and while illuminating the psychological place and development of the different participants in the group (Sitz im Leben).

In essay 10 Gary Yontef reports that since the 1940s group therapy has been central in Gestalt therapy, and Gestalt therapy has been instrumental in its use. The interactive environment of group therapy, he believes, is perfectly suited to Gestalt therapy, which never considers the individual apart from the interaction of person and environment, especially the person-to-person environment. True to its existential and phenomenological roots, Gestalt therapy emphasizes that awareness, growth, and healing emerge from the dialogic meeting of self and others.

The group environment, he believes, provides rich possibilities for experimentation with contact between therapist and patient and between group members. This potential, he advances, can be fully utilized in Gestalt therapy groups since the theory and clinical methodology of Gestalt therapy supports, guides, and encourages the full use of human resources and has no theory-derived limitations on presence or experimentation. The full personal presence of both therapist and patients, confirmation through dialogue, emergence of awareness by phenomenological awareness and experimentation are all encouraged in Gestalt therapy groups.

Yontef stresses that the Gestalt therapy system has no "shoulds" and does not attempt direct manipulation of patients' behavior to move them to better functioning. Rather, the therapy is based on the paradox that the more people know, affirm, and identify with who they are, the more they grow. Change based on self-rejection does not work, he contends, and that Gestalt therapy uses active techniques that restore or establish patient self direction and esteem, especially by focusing on how awareness is developed, blocked, or distorted by each person.

Goals in Gestalt therapy are process goals—people knowing how to be aware of what they are doing and how they are doing it. He believes these tools make the existential values on responsibility and choice meaningful. These include being able to distinguish between true immediate experience (e.g., observing the obvious) and ideas added by inference, prior learning, external pressure, and so on. By being aware of what is happening and what is needed in the organism/environment field, the individual can make real choices among options rather than merely responding habitually.

In essay 11 the development of psychodrama is traced from its origin in Moreno's notion of spontaneity/creativity. The devices of improvisational drama are described as being employed to draw memories from the past and hypothetical imaginings of the future into the immediacy of the here-and-now where spontaneity can exert its influence for creative change. The roles of director, protagonist, auxiliary ego, audience, and the physical setting are explained. The techniques of self-presentation, future projection, hypnodrama, monodrama, and soliloquy are briefly described while the techniques of the double and of role reversal are detailed more fully. A case of writer's block with severe social inhibition is presented.

In essay 12 Phillip Reichline and Jeanette Targow apply Gestalt, transactional, family systems, and humanistic techniques to the treatment of couples groups. This essay reveals their philosophy as it relates to couple group therapy as a modality of choice in the treatment of relationship problems. They use several taped exerpts from ongoing couples groups to highlight effective communication patterns, defenses as coping mechanisms, the importance of a safe climate for all productions, the weaving of interpersonal and intrapsychic phenomena, and the modeling of cotherapists' differences.

In essay 13 Uri Ruevini introduces the reader to the process of family network intervention and to a variety of group encounter techniques designed to mobilize and empower ailing family members in times of crisis.

The postpsychoanalytic behavioral therapeutic approaches are presented in essays 14 and 15. In essay 14 George Bartzokis, Robert Liberman and Robert Hierholzer present behavior therapy in groups. They describe the application of the principles of learning derived from psychological experimentation to the modification of dysfunctional behavior in a group of individuals. They stress behavior therapy's emphasis on (1) specifying problems and goals, (2) using principles of learning to facilitate change, and (3) measuring change in behavior. They have found that behavioral methods in groups have become more structured as they have been infused by social learning theories.

Group Cognitive Behavioral Group Therapy is a recent development based on the cognitive theories of Ellis (1962), Beck (1972, 1983), and Meichenbaum (1977). The cognitive theory differs from the behavioral in that it deals with what people are thinking and seeks to modify maladaptive thinking patterns. This emerging group of techniques is represented in this volume by the work of Albert Ellis and the application of his rational-emotive therapy to groups.

In his paper, Albert Ellis contends that rational-emotive therapy (RET), while especially designed for individual psychotherapy, is also suited to group therapy for several reasons: (1) It largely follows a teaching model, so that a number of individuals can be simultaneously and efficiently taught how to overcome their emotional and behavioral disturbances by a single therapist. (2) It encourages group members to use RET with the other participants and thereby to learn to use it better with themselves. (3) While being heavily cognitive, RET also steadily employs many emotive-experiential and behavioral methods, which are described in the essay. These methods, he believes, can often best be done within, as well as reported back to a therapy group. Ellis hypothesizes that RET is more effective in a shorter period of time than most other forms of group psychotherapy.

In essay 16 Robert Goulding describes his Redecisional approach to Transactional Analysis, which while based on, also has some important differences from the original Transactional Analysis theory of Eric Berne. Goulding combines TA theory with techniques from Gestalt therapy, family therapy, psychodrama, and behavior modification. Transactional Analysis is described as an interactional therapy based on the assumption that people make current choices based on past, often outmoded, premises. The approach emphasizes cognitive, rational, and behavioral aspects of one's personality. The goal of this treatment is to aid people to make new decisions that fit their present life circumstances. Transactional Analysis and redecision therapy focus on factors such as injunctions, early decisions, strokes, games, rackets, the life script, and redecisions, all explained by Goulding in his paper.

Section 1

Humanistic Group Psychologies

9

Existential Group Analysis

Herbert Holt, M.D., F.A.A.P.

Existential analysis is a modern psychotherapy based on clinical experiential findings derived from work with patients and under-pinned by the philosophies of E. Husserl's phenomenology and M. Heidegger's existential analysis. Basic existential phenomena were integrated with Freudian psychoanalysis by post-Freudian psychoanalysts such as Menard Boss and Ludwig Binswanger, among others. In this paper I will focus on Ludwig Binswanger's inter-pretation of Freudian psychoanalysis and his attempt to theoreti-cally integrate it with existential philosophical concepts. Binswanger found the Heideggerian philosophical paradigm useful in clinical psychoanalytic practice. He used the concept that all human ex-periences are phenomena of reality. Under phenomena he under-stood to mean any personal experience whether that experience is conscious, rational, emotional and interpersonal, or intrapsychic such as delusions and hallucinations. In this paper I will make an attempt to underpin the above derived data that have been explained psychologically and philosophically by the Heideggerian and Husserlian theories with the most recent findings of our modern brain research, especially with Paul MacLean's theory of the living triune brain.

Most clinical existential therapists can share this paradigm, which Heidegger called *Dasein* (being-in-the-world). He means under Dasein specifically that these phenomena of reality are the only reality we can experience subjectively. A person experiences himself as having been born into the world without his choice. As he grows up, he becomes gradually aware of the fact that he lives in this condition of thrownness and this is his subjective existence. Having become aware of himself as a living person and so become responsible for himself, he has now a personal choice to decide to give consent to his life or to kill himself. This is his responsibility and his choice not only in relation to himself but also to others. This state of being, Dasein, creates a special anxiety in man that is mostly experienced as rage, terror, a general feeling of unhappiness, and utter isolation. People become aware that they live and die in their own skin and no one can live or die for them. This basic complex phenomena Heidegger calls basic existential anxiety, and he feels that this is the basic elemental frustration with and condition of life as a human being.

Through self-reflection we gradually become consciously aware of ourselves, of being alive and of other people being alive sharing the world with us and that we are alive in the surrounding world. (The corresponding German concepts of Heidegger are Eigenwelt, Mitwelt, Umwelt.) The paradigm of Dasein has considerable explanatory power in not only being aware of ourselves through introspection but also aware of other people in the world through our visual, auditory, and tactile sense perceptions. Since we communicate through language and nonverbal behavior to other human beings, no absolute objective communication can be achieved since the limits of language hinders us in sharing our thoughts and feelings fully with other people.

Ludwig Binswanger, a Swiss psychoanalyst and pupil of Sigmund Freud, was a classically trained analyst who applied the Heideggerian paradigm to psychoanalysis and called it Daseinanalyse. He believed, with Freud, that it is the task of psychotherapy to over-come anxiety and internal resistance, and that by understanding the origin of these deep impulses and feelings and bringing them to the level of consciousness a patient has a chance to enjoy life. While Binswanger's existential analysis denies the Freudian position that all behavior is caused by a few instincts, he accepts the ideas that behavior is underpinned by instincts. With the help of the phe-nomenological point-of-view focusing on meaning and purpose of life, he enlarges the view of man holistically.

If we look at man's life from a biological genetic evolutionary point of view, we could see the human being and his world from a different perspective and angle. Paul MacLean theorized that each part of our living triune brain experiences itself, other people, and the world differently. Each brain influences the total view of man and according to his theory, each brain has a different awareness of itself, of other people and the world. He distinguishes the basic archaic brain, which is the primitive, emotional brain, controlled by the limbic midbrain. Both brains are controlled by the neocor-tex, which is divided into two hemispheres connected by a neural bridge. He feels that the archaic brain is dimly aware of itself but not conscious of itself. The limbic brain is aware of itself but not fully conscious. Only the neocortex can consciously be aware of its functioning and make rational, appropriate decisions based on this awareness. This theory suggests that these three separate views of the world are integrated automatically and this integration is with-out awareness and is a holistic experience of the total brain.

Existential analysis attempts to understand these brain functions by taking a Gestalt position. Even the smallest unit (a dream, il-lusion, delusion, or interpersonal experience) is a holistic experi-ence and must be understood in the context of a network of thoughts and feelings that occur in time in our mind, with more or less inner awareness. Conscious, authentic awareness of self in one's experi-ence with other people and in one's world is an essential goal of existential therapy. At the same time, we keep in mind that per-sonal experience and the holistic character of any living experience are very difficult to conceptualize and therefore to communicate. Explanations are often incomplete since, in the communication of an experience, we are not automatically provided with the principle of explanation. When theories move toward more abstract explanation, we can lose the subjective character of the statements, and we have to come to the conclusion that it is difficult to communicate subjective experience.

Man, being "thrown" into life (Heidegger), is a social, group animal and is always born into the social unit of the family whose members are usually bound to each other emotionally, be it negative or positive attachments. When we speak of group relationships, we think of the relationship of parent, or their substitutes, to their children. It is the emotional dynamic of dependency and fear of rejection in children that leads to group social anxiety. Certain group attitudes are established within families, be they control, submission, cooperation, or independent, which in modern families are hopefully not authoritarian but voluntary. If not, the family unit can break down and group social anxiety is reinforced.

The purpose of existential group therapy is to help individuals in their ability to develop and maintain themselves as unique human beings in their world. The ability of the "self" to maintain itself in balance not only against the pressures of group and social forces but also against inner drives coming from the organic structure of the living brain, is the characteristic of our human dilemma.

Group Leader

In coping with their own Dasein, group leaders have the choice of facing and overcoming their own mental pain and suffering, which can be subjectively overwhelming, or to suppress these feelings. They often need the help of long training and personal therapy in overcoming their chronic unhappiness and to learn to deal with their own life experiences. After having gone through their personal training analysis, they are in a position to help patients overcome their suffering and to choose whether or not the patient wants to overcome their psychic misery and live a life potentially of hope and responsibility and creative care for others.

The existential group therapist tries to establish a milieu within the group in which emotional and verbal regressive states and structural conflicts, which date back to earliest parental relationship, can be experienced openly in a new climate of acceptance.

In group therapy he can help his patients to a new openness of their emotions and traumatic experiences and can help them to overcome their feeling of stress and anxiety. Existential group therapy leads to a reinforcement of the concept of uniqueness and the experience of awareness of the self while belonging to the cooperative network of helping group members.

The group leader selects people according to the three modes of being-in-the-world: (1) people who function predominantly in the archaic brain and who experience the world symbolically, as in a dream; (2) people who live in the daydream mode of wishes, hopes, and fears and experience themselves from this self-centered point-of-view; and (3) people who function in the neocortex and have predominantly interpersonal, emotional, and/or rational logical conflicts and problems.

An existential group includes these three modes of relating, which helps people in time, while attending the group, to become aware of the differences of life styles and point-of-view each group member brings to the group.

Some Techniques in Existential Group Psychoanalysis

The following techniques are used in existential therapy and can be applied to group therapy. They are used to help group members experience verbally, emotionally, and by acting out problems in group, their projected and externalized lived-out patterns of thinking, feeling, talking, and behaving.

1. *The epoché* is a method of bracketing thoughts and feelings.
2. *Paradoxical interventions* is a scenario method in which the patient verbally acts out hypothetical situations in group that they experience as real based on internal image patterns that have to be understood by them.
3. *Discussion and illumination* of guided fantasies, daydreams, dreams, hallucinations, and delusions help members become aware of how they actually feel and think.

These techniques are based on the fact that an effective method is necessary to help a person separate out from the emotional chaos caused by past mental and emotional memory structures and to help find new ways of thinking and feeling. The patient tries to cope with the new realities and tries not to live in an imaginary past or future but in interpersonal daily life. The experience of other people and one's self in memory are structures in the mind and can be experienced as verbal and visual imagery whether it be daydreams, dreams, or as subjectively experienced, realistic relationships.

A Protocol of a Segment of Existential Group Psychoanalysis

The composition of this group is limited to eight women and five men who meet once a week for one hour with the group leader. Before the formal meeting, there is an informal, leaderless meeting. After the formal meeting, some group members meet again over dinner to discuss and clarify issues that were discussed during the group. They often experience new insights and further their understanding through self-help.

This is the 47th meeting of the group and it begins with Anne, a 28-year-old social psychologist who opened the group by saying that Jack, another group member present, has misunderstood and misrepresented her motives concerning her husband. She accuses him, a 65-year-old businessman, of having willfully and maliciously distorted her story to suit his own prejudiced point of view.

[The patient begins with a hostile projection onto Jack: externalization and projection reveal how she has misunderstood herself and her husband. It is she who has "willfully and maliciously" distorted her relationship to her husband, and she uses Jack as a living symbol of this distortion.]

Anne is an attractive woman who recently obtained a legal separation from her husband because she feels that she "doesn't need him anymore." Anne told the group, "I married him to escape my very rigid, Methodist parents, but I don't love him anymore. He still demands that I pay sexual attention to him, though, and I resent it bitterly."

Jack angrily interrupts her, "You never loved him. You said yourself that you used him as a means to an end because you couldn't support yourself."

[Jack has understood Anne's story accurately based on what

she has told the group and from his own perspective and point of view. Anne really has said in past sessions that she doesn't love her husband and Jack is responding to that from his own feelings of being a husband.]

Anne replies furiously, "How dare you say that to me! That is very cruel! Of course I loved my husband."

[She has given her reasons for marrying her husband truthfully, but the group leader knows it is only a partial truth because he has her in private sessions and knows a fuller spectrum of her reasons. The group leader asks himself why she focuses on this particular part (escaping her parents and marrying for money.) What is missing is the other "opposite." On the midbrain level in which Anne functions, thoughts and feelings are organized in pairs of opposites: good/bad, love/hate, marrying for money/marrying for love, staying/escaping. Expressing one "opposite" necessarily implies the unconscious presence of the other, so when Anne says she married for money, the necessary opposite reveals that she did, in fact, think she was marrying for love—a typical adolescent, midbrain way of thinking. Anne is furious because she doesn't believe she married her husband for money. She is unaware that she links love and money together in her mind.]

Three other women in the group responded to Anne's outburst like a Greek chorus: "Yeah, yeah, yeah! You loved your husband, all right—you loved the money, position, and status he could give you because he's a rich investment banker!"

[The women reinforce Jack's position and won't let Anne deny what she has said in the past about her motives for marrying her husband. However, the group thinks that money is money—they don't know that money is a concept for Anne that represents love. The labels people give to feelings and concepts can be deceptive, especially when one mistakes the names or labels for reality. The midbrain confuses labels with facts, when in actuality concepts and percepts have no being in the concrete world. Anne is unaware that the group does not share her confusion that money and love are the same.]

Matthew, a 35-year-old computer programmer who has great trouble with his own wife because he has an idealized vision of her feminine tenderness and compassion and feels that she has despoiled everything he holds sacred, said, "Look, Anne. How can you sit there and tell us you loved your husband when we knew you before you married him! Every week, you came in here and told us how wonderful it would be to marry such a rich man. You never told us that you loved him for his own sake." He then added sarcastically, "Congratulations! You got what you said you wanted!"

Anne began to weep from anger and frustration, crying out, "Why do you keep saying I married him for money? I loved him in my own way!"

Another group member, Joan, 38 years old and unmarried, said enviously, "What's wrong with marrying for money? Lucky you! Please, Anne, if you ever want to divorce your husband, give him to me! One woman's reject is another woman's joy, after all."

Anne responded, "I will never introduce you to my husband! I'll never divorce him even though we're separated— even though we don't have sex anymore, we live in the same apartment, and he's my security blanket."

[Because Anne cannot describe her real feelings about her husband, Joan has misinterpreted the group exchange to mean that Anne has separated herself from her husband and doesn't want him anymore. In fact, she has revealed that she sees her husband as a daddy whom she loves, a "security blanket." She has communicated that she speaks from her midbrain, and this is an earlier stage now than even the adolescent stage in which she began the session. The conversation is not helping her to advance to a realistic mode of thinking where words mean what they are intended to mean. If she said, "I see him as a loving father," it would be clear why she does not have sex with him: it would be incestuous.]

Marcel, a French university professor, who although homosexual, has a successful nonsexual marriage, sums up Anne's response by saying, "So you live together like sister and brother."

Anne screams at Marcel, "You evil man! Who are you to make me feel so terrible?"

So far, the group leader has not spoken and is sitting outside the group, implying that he is functioning as an observer-participant and not a group member. The group leader wants to help Anne see the underlying issue of mislabeling of thoughts and feelings because, although she thinks and feels like a child, she is not a child. The group leader says to the group, "Look, let's see what the underlying issues are. You've had a chance to communicate your feelings about what Anne said, but let's make rounds and see what each one of you has to say from an observant, descriptive point-of-view.

Most members perceive that the group theme (leitmotive) for the session is the relationship of human beings who live together and their motivations for choosing each other. Each group member then has an opportunity to discuss the leitmotive in terms of their own life situations: man living with woman, man living with man, woman living with woman, or men and women living alone. They discussed their first memories about their relationships with their mothers, fathers, and siblings, and gradually with the help of bracketing their own thoughts and feelings, they discuss the "hidden agenda" each one has about what a relationship ought/should/must be like as an ideal standard. Some are able to compare this idealized standard to what they think and feel a satisfactory relationship would be for them. This was not an intellectual exercise, but an experience utilizing a method of determining for themselves their "seat in life."

Continuing with the leitmotive method over the next few sessions, Joan, a 38-year-old unmarried schoolteacher, examines her relationships, and why she has been unable to marry. When she was 5 years old, her parents staged a mock wedding between her 8-year-old brother and herself. While the adults found it humorous, she took it seriously at that time. With the help of both private and group sessions, Joan discovered that she could not marry because she felt she was in her mind already "married." She loved her brother very much as a child, but he found the episode ridiculous. As an adult, her brother was living as a homosexual. Even after she realized that the "marriage" was a joke, she felt rejected and bitter toward her parents, and decided never to marry.

"But I don't know," Joan said. "In the last session we discussed why I wasn't serious about getting married. I had a dream in which I saw myself as a beautiful, dangerous witch, and all the men were afraid of me when they found out who I really was. I know the dream is a projection of my unconscious, and that I must be seeing myself as a dangerous, elemental earth-mother type, but I still think I want to get married, even if my unconscious implies that I don't.

[Joan is missing the "necessary opposite" of this witch image, which is a puny, frightened child. She is frightened by the demand she makes on herself to control men, who she realizes she cannot control. Her dream reveals a profound truth in mythic images (there are no witches in real life!) and symbolic and imaginative language. Joan never was and never will be a dangerous person, nor is she a puny frightened child. She is, however, truly frightened by her demands on men. This underlying fear is not a fantasy.]

A further variation of the leitmotive was brought out by Jack, who had the romantic idea that he married his wife "for love." "After all," he said, "she didn't have a pot to piss in. I even had to buy her wedding dress, so surely I couldn't have married her for money or position, could I?"

[In actuality, Jack's wife is a very powerful, controlling person who ended up owning the business she developed with his help. He was, therefore, very sensitive and angry with women like Anne, whom he perceived to have married for money.]

Matthew had to face a different variation of the leitmotive cued in by Anne's encounter. He said, "I looked at my wife recently and realized that I don't particularly like her and don't want to be married to her anymore. I used to see her with the eyes of romantic love—I guess I was projecting an idealized image onto her. But now I see her as she really is—a bitter, mean, man-hating woman. But I have a really hard time accepting the fact that she's not the woman I want her to be or thought she was. I feel awful."

[Matthew is describing the "necessary opposite," or counterimage to the ideal mother and now he projects the counterimage—the despised, mean mother onto his wife because she did not respond to his idealized image.]

Marcel was always afraid that his wife would find out he is a homosexual. Being a Roman Catholic, he suggested to her before they married that they have a nonsexual union, a religious, spiritual marriage. To his surprise, his future wife accepted this arrangement. But he felt there must be something wrong. One day, he came home unexpectedly and found his wife in bed with another woman. He felt devastated! His wife said, "What do you want? We have a good marriage. I'm a 'dyke' and you're 'gay.' We have a spiritual marriage. We have companionship—we eat together, travel together, share money together. As far as sex is concerned, don't worry about me." And he said, "But what about me?" To which she said, "You can do whatever you want with your sex organs. We have a good marriage and I won't let you break it up." That night, he had the following dream:

In the dream I am comforting and talking to a small girl, around 3 to 5 years old, and she wanted to tell me something. Then suddenly, a ghost-apparition appears and he is an old, gray-bearded man. It was her grandfather and I realized it must be a ghost because he is dead. I angrily accuse him of being immoral in his behavior toward the little girl. He laughs and says he has done nothing against her will. I am furious with him for saying that because I believe grown-ups have the responsibility to teach the child that you can't just do what you want to do. There are certain things you just don't do! He says to me, "Well, I will prove it to you." He than asks the girl to come to him and she runs over to him and immediately starts to fondle his genitals. I am shocked by her sudden change in behavior. I tell her to stop and she asks me, "Why? I like to do this."

Marcel explains to the group: "In this dream, I liked to be a little girl and as a child I always wanted to be a female."

Anne held desperately to the belief that she "loved" her husband, which had been discussed several times by the group. The cynical remarks of different group members have to be neutralized or they too develop a fixed idea of why they have relationships with other people.

One of these people was Alice, a 39-year-old high school teacher who comes from a family of five children. She is the youngest. Her mother told her she came from Budapest, Hungary, and always said what a wonderful town it was and what a great life she lived going to operas and balls. Alice, who was raised in the Midwest and was never in Hungary, and who was always a "good" girl, tried to fulfill her mother's dreams and wishes. She was never happy. One day, she visited an aunt, the only living sister of her mother who was living in Florida. She told her aunt about the "glamorous life" her mother had while living in Budapest and her aunt was amazed.

Her aunt said, "We were pig peasants living in a little village and the only thing your mother knew about Budapest

is that when she was 18 years old, she became a maid in a
middle-class home. She never went to a ball, never went to
an opera. She just dreamed about things like that."

Alice was deeply shocked by this revelation and couldn't
accept it. She confronted her mother who, after repeatedly
denying it, broke down and confessed that it was a daydream,
a wish, a hope that kept her going. When she left to come to
America, she kept this image of a glittering life in Budapest
and sold this idea to her children who evaluated their life according to the story of their mother and always felt they "never
made it." Whatever they achieved academically or personally
was minimized and they were very unhappy.

When Anne told the story to the group of her "fixed" idea
that she married for love, Alice broke down and started to cry
and said she always felt she could never seem to get the life
she thought she wanted to have. She said she wanted to be
married, to have children, and to live an upper-class life, but
in actuality she did everything to prevent it. She divorced her
first husband, married again, but divorced her second husband
and never had any children. As Alice began to see that what
she thought she wanted was what her mother wanted for her—
to be married to a glamorous man, go to the opera, concerts,
parties, etc.—she realized she did not like operas, nor concerts, and at the one ball to which she went she felt very
uncomfortable and left early. She never considered asking herself if she wanted to be married.

When Anne was confronted with all the other life experiences of the group members, she had to gradually face the
fact that marrying her husband "for love" was a fantasy and
that she doesn't need it anymore. She could consider whether
or not she wants to divorce him or if she really holds onto
him because he is her "security blanket" or because she would
like to have a relationship with this man if it is possible.

When a child decides to leave his family and early environment and tries to create a life of his own based on his own
gifts, talents, and abilities to work, he is often in a kind of
total absorption with what he is doing. It is like being in an
intense play mode secure that his parents knowledgeably support his activities. This intense feeling of total absorption we
see also in grown-up-men and women who have successfully
left their families and created a life style of their own. But

some closely knit families do not like this and will treat such grown-up family members as a kind of traitor to the aspirations and world view of their families that they left behind.

If Anne and Alice had tried to create their own unique life style, they would have been "excommunicated" and been made to feel guilty by their families. Many daughters and sons take over the unconscious dreams of their mothers as their own and try to fulfill them out of love and to make their mothers happy. But there is a seed of unhappiness. They don't ask themselves if they really want to get married and have children, or if they want to live a single life as in previous times women could do by renouncing their obligations to their families and becoming nuns.

Clark, a 50-year-old accountant, who very seldom talked in the group, has never been married and focuses life on his work. He is a private person and doesn't like to share his thoughts and feelings with anyone and kept mostly to himself while being in the group. He once told us that he imagined that if he did not talk, nothing bad could happen to him and if he doesn't experience any feelings consciously, he would have no problems. He communicated that he was trying to deal with his mother's dissatisfaction in her life and ambition for him in this manner. He felt he has a difficult juggling act to do, a kind of emotional conflict between obedience to his mother's wishes versus rebellion, which he could only overcome in his search for order in his life by choosing for his work accountancy and by repressing and suppressing his thoughts and feelings. In his oedipal disillusionment, he rejected his dead father and was angry even with his memory. He only communicated to people in his work and in private life what he considered essential and functional.

While the leitmotive was beginning to be worked through in the group, he became gradually agitated, started to cry and burst out angrily, "I had a dream! Don't you think you should listen!"

The group members became startled and kept silent, but the group leader encouraged him to tell his dream.

The setting of the dream was a nondescript place where suddenly his mother appeared and in a sad and crying way addressed him: "Clark, I will leave you now. I should have left twenty years ago."

"Oh, no!" pleaded Clark, "please don't leave me."

She said, "I've been dead for twenty years. I'm just a shadow. I should have gone where all the dead people go."

Clark felt very panicky and pleaded with his mother not to leave him. She is the center of his existence. Without her, he felt he could not go on and he would have to kill himself.

In the dream his mother said, "I should have left a long time ago. I stayed out of love. I knew you would kill yourself without me. But I have to leave now. Goodbye, Clark."

Clark awoke from the dream. He felt beside himself. He could not contain himself physically, vomiting, and urinating on the floor. He realized that he had loved his mother so deeply and for so long that he could not marry. He felt he needed her and that she needed him, but realized it was time for him to be related to other people. He cried in the group. Anne and Alice embraced him. He couldn't stop crying, saying, "So I don't have to die. I won't be alone. I will be able to have friends," which he repeated over, and over, and over.

[Clark's feelings of wanting to die was not a desire to kill himself but was an expression of his experiencing the "death" of his internalized, dualistic mother/child image. When patients give up images, they often describe feelings such as "dying," "loneliness," or "nothingness" because their identity was perceived while in the midbrain as the "child" or the "mother."]

I explained to the group that people hold onto fixed ideas to which they attach a great deal of emotion as an expression of living in the midbrain. For a short period of time, Anne was able to transcend her fixed idea that she married her husband for "love" or the counterimage of marrying for "money." While in the mid-brain there is an unconscious tension between two extreme feelings, for example, love and hate, and there are two possibilities of overcoming living in this mode. One is by automatic regression to the archaic brain with its consequent feeling of anger with oneself, other people, and the world.

A second possibility is bracketing the fixed idea and its associated feelings and seeing the multitude of possible realistic reasons for having a relationship with another person. With the help of the group and the group leader, Anne might be able to have a new life experience by gradually overcoming living in the midbrain, which after all, until recently, has encompassed her whole life philosophy. Only then can she live in the adult personality and realize that she can develop her own life style and choose a meaningful and purposeful life with her husband or with someone else or live a private life. With the help of the total brain she can then live a predominantly conscious interpersonal life in the world with people of her own choosing.

Conclusion

The question is often posed, "We know the treatment, but what is the disease?" Existential analysis would answer, "There is no dis-ease, and consequently, no cure." We do not deny that the biological brain can malfunction under certain circumstances of trauma and infection and for such states of malfunction we need medical and chemical treatment. Existential analysis, however, understands dis-ease to be a state of fundamental subjective discomfort that individuals experience because they are human and because our psychological reactions are the by-products of our contemporary existence, which state we label existential basic anxiety (Dasein's Angst). Human beings are actually very sturdy and our genetic endowment and constitution enables us frequently to live with many inherent contradictions and in an often constant state of anxiety without breaking down emotionally or physically.

The dis-ease of human experience according to our theory arises from both the tensions of Dasein as well as our problems of relating and establishing communication with other human beings who might live in a different mode of experience than we do. The tensions of Dasein are caused on the one hand by the neurological impulses of the two lower brains that try to control the neocortex, leading away from conscious choice toward compulsive, obsessive, unconscious behaviors while on the other hand the total brain is trying to communicate with other individuals in the interpersonal world.

Existential group analysis tries to deal with the tensions and conflicts patients have not only in daily life but also in the group. We can help patients to become aware that the fundamental dis-ease of Dasein with which every human being has to cope underlies but is not the cause of physical, organic, and genetic diseases. We try to help patients come to terms with "life as is" and hope thereby that when they accept their life as is in the here-and-now, they can reduce their mental suffering. Existential group analysis can show the patient that he has the freedom to choose his own mode of being-in-the-world and is personally responsible to himself and others for his choices of what he does and what he is. By choosing his own values, he can also consciously try to change these values and can have the experience of becoming a different person in relation to himself, his fellow man, and his world.

10

Gestalt Therapy in Groups

Gary Yontef, Ph.D.

Group therapy and group training modalities have been central in Gestalt therapy since its inception in the 1940s. In the 1960s Gestalt therapy was in the forefront of the movement toward popularizing group therapy. A recent survey found that 98 percent of Gestalt therapists surveyed had a part of their Gestalt therapy training in groups and 85 percent had over 50 percent of their training in groups (Frew 1988).

The interactive environment of group therapy is perfectly suited to Gestalt therapy practice, "an approach which has as its starting point the inevitable and continuous interacting of the individual and the environment" (Frew 1988:77–78). In Gestalt therapy theory the individual is never considered apart from the interaction of the individual/environment field. Although "We speak of the organism contacting the environment, . . . it is the contact that is the simplest and first reality" (Perls, Hefferline, and Goodman 1951:227).

A unifying clinical methodology distinguishes all Gestalt therapy modalities, including group, individual, couple, and family therapy. Influenced by existential thinkers such as Martin Buber, Gestalt therapists believe that awareness, growth, and healing results from the meeting of self and other (dialogue). The framework is an operationalized existential phenomenological approach that uses and enhances interhuman contact and phenomenological awareness and awareness experiments.

Basic Theory

Living requires regulating contact, that is, establishing and maintaining a boundary differentiating and connecting the person and the rest of the individual/environment field. An individuated identity requires separation from the rest of the field, yet living and growing requires connecting. People need to take in from the environment, taking ideas or good wishes from others, and also need to put into the environment by caring for others, creating art, or excreting excess. Psychological processes are functions of the boundary. That boundary is lost if awareness of either differences or connectedness is lost.

There are two contrasting processes for accepting input from the environment: assimilation and introjection. Gestalt therapy theory accentuates assimilation, the process of determining for oneself with awareness what is true, acceptable, fitting, or healthy. Introjection is the process of taking in without full awareness and assimilation. Introjecting, a central process in all psychological disturbances, results in introjects or "shoulds," which are fixed and rigid beliefs taken in without determining one's own position. In order to assimilate one must destructure observations, ideas, or suggestions and pick and choose for oneself what aspects to accept or reject.

Although most interactions are regulated by habit, organismic self-regulation requires that, as needed, people direct the contact process with awareness of the dominant need of person and environment and discriminate who, what, and how to contact, when to withdraw, what to accept, what to reject, what to seek, what to attack, and so forth. This contrasts with "shouldistic" regulation, (regulation determined by shoulds rather than fresh discrimination) and self-absorbed regulation (regulation determined by one's own need apart from consideration of others).

"Live and learn" the saying goes. People observe, sense and have the ability to successively learn how to reach better levels of self-regulation and to achieve the best level of satisfaction that conditions allow. This is a cyclical process, in that awareness enables contact and it is through contact that awareness is enhanced. Therapy is needed when awareness does not develop as needed, when the person repeats mistakes without learning from experience and is unable to create new solutions and opportunities.

Awareness is not looking inward (intrapsychic), but is an acknowledgment of the relationship between the individual and the environment. Knowing oneself requires a boundary, as in awareness of the difference between self and other. Awareness connects the needs and resources of the person and the needs and resources of the environment and is a function of the boundary between the individual and the environment.

The heart of the Gestalt therapy concept of change is called the paradoxical theory of change. It holds that natural growth is an inevitable aspect of being alive when people identify with themselves as they really are. This theory states that the more people try to be who they are not, the more they stay the same (Beisser 1970). Trying and seeming to be something other than one's true self is self-rejecting and not self-supporting. Self-improvement programs are frequently disappointing since they are usually based on self-rejection—which is not a good base for growth.

When people regulate themselves by exploring, sensing, and acknowledging what is, they are in the best position to whole-heartedly experiment with alternatives and sense suitability for themselves. Hence Gestalt therapy uses the vitality of here-and-now sensing and feeling to explicate those life themes and dynamic developmental patterns that are essential to the person's current life using direct experiential methods that emphasize personal experience, interhuman contact, and experimentation rather than either reconditioning or attempting change based on speculative, obsessive methods such as free association, interpretion or analyzing "why."

Enid's husband complained that although she made excellent contact physically, she didn't make very good verbal contact. Although she worked on this in individual Gestalt therapy, it still mystified her when she joined group. Her spontaneous interactions with people suffered, but she didn't have support to do better. One of the steps in her learning in group was watching a more experienced group member look at her (and others) with sparkling and clear eyes, make silent contact with others, and then express herself with clear "I" statements. She was very affected by this and began experimenting, at first in group and then between sessions, with looking at people.

Then Enid could touch and look, but was still not able to verbally express herself with clarity, accuracy, vitality, or fluidity. When another group member used the phrase "going with the flow" Enid suddenly had the idea for the first time that she could be spontaneous in interpersonal verbal communications, as she could with dancing. This "aha" was a different reality for her and she began to experiment with different ways of "dancing with words." Being with others in the group and experimenting resulted in more effective learning than mere talking.

Gestalt therapy theory is based on dialogue and awareness of what is. The Gestalt therapy system has no shoulds. Even our awareness and contact goals are only compass points for the therapist to organize his or her thoughts and interventions. Individuals decide for themselves when to be how aware of what, and when to be in what kind of contact with whom. The goal in Gestalt therapy is a process goal, which is for people to have sufficient awareness, contact skills, and sense of responsibility for organismic self-regulation.

The Therapeutic Methodology: Phenomenology and Dialogue

Phenomenology

Maximum therapeutic growth does not result from just any kind of contact or awareness, but from a special kind of phenomenological awareness and a special form of interhuman contact called dialogue (discussed in the following). That is why Gestalt therapy in the 1940s moved away from the "why–because" interpretations of classical analysis to be closer to patients' actual sense experience.

This phenomenological focus emphasizes what patients do know rather than what they are not aware of. That which is out of awareness is brought into awareness through sharing observations, experimentation, dialogue, and awareness of the process of avoiding awareness. By basing therapeutic work on here-and-now sensing rather than theory-driven interpretations Gestalt therapy helps patients to learn for themselves to be truly responsible for knowing what they need, guiding action, and resolving impasses.

Larry was a 60-year-old man who never really talked to anyone when he spoke in group, never looked lively nor seemed emotionally congruent. He readily accommodated by saying "yes" to anyone's feedback. He didn't know what he felt or needed and his behavior didn't change. The therapist suggested that he do the following experiment: look at each person in the group and tell the person what he observed at that very second and then share what he felt in his own body. As he did this experiment Larry started becoming, sounding, and looking more alive. As he used his senses, got in touch with his body, and interacted with others, he became more animated, spontaneous, and was better received by the group.

Larry learned to contact based on sharing immediate awareness. Immediate awareness is neither "subjective" nor "objective," neither internal nor external, but is a bond between a particular perceiver and that which is perceived in an actual individual-environment field. There is no single objectively valid reality. Unfortunately, immediate awareness is often interrupted, distorted, or colored. People often "perceive" what they expect to perceive rather than perceiving freshly. Instead of sensing (internal and external), feeling (emotions), and understanding (meaning) of oneself in the world and the world in which one lives, many are "aware" in an obsessive and disconnected way.

Learning phenomenological discipline enables people to interrupt the interruption and purify the awareness process in order to know their immediate, naive perception and direct their own therapeutic exploration so that they do not have to depend on the interpretations of others. By putting prior beliefs in brackets one can know what is actually experienced, needed and preferred.

In Gestalt therapy patients learn the difference between what is observed and what is inferred, between what is actually felt and what one expected to feel, between actual taste and what one be-lieved was tasty, between expressing that which is actually felt and talking about feelings.

Jackie had a prior belief that men were angry, aggressive, and mean. When Gary joined the group he was extremely tense, tightly squeezing his face and fists. He was surprised when Jackie said she "felt he was angry at her because she was a woman." This wasn't a feeling, it was an inference that she mislabeled as a feeling. Gary actually felt scared, not angry. Gary on the other hand had believed that he liked independent women. In fact he actually experienced fright when with independent women, and contrary to expectations, he enjoyed women who were more accommodating. Prior to this work he had chosen partners based on his expectations and not his actual experience and these relationships did not work out.

Awareness training helps patients define their own interests, preferences, evaluations, solutions, etc. Independence of judgment is encouraged in relation to the therapy process, to the therapist, and other patients.

People bring their natural awareness process into the therapy group, and together patients and therapist observe how the needed awareness does or does not develop. Patients learn to be aware of their awareness process by focusing and phenomenological exper-imentation and by a therapeutic dialogic relationship with the ther-apist and other group members. In a sense, Gestalt therapy pa-tients acquire tools. They learn how to learn. This work can focus on any area of concern for the individual, the family, the group, or larger social units.

Gestalt therapists are most likely to ask questions such as "what are you seeing or hearing right now?" "What are you sensing or emotionally feeling in your body right now?" "What do you want or need right at this moment?" Group participants are encouraged to give feedback to others expressing that which is directly ob-served or felt rather than projecting, interpreting, or problem solv-ing.

Gestalt therapists are trained to put their biases into brackets and clear their mind to observe the obvious. Gestalt therapy ac-tively focuses not only on what patients think, feel, and say, but also on enteroceptive, exteroceptive and proprioceptive awareness by the patient, and therapist observation of body gestures, posture, movement, sound, syntax, and so forth. Thus when patients keep themselves unaware of something, a Gestalt therapist often uses these observations, for example, commenting on a patient's gestures, rather than interpretation.

An important aspect of awareness work is being aware of unawareness, including resistance to awareness. Gestalt therapists do not say that patients should discard their resistance. Often awareness does not develop because of self-protective forces once necessary for psychological survival. Resistance to awareness is a process to be owned and brought into awareness so patients can be responsible for continuing or altering it.

The goal in this therapeutic dialogue and phenomenological exploration is insight, although the concept is very different in Gestalt therapy than in other therapies. Insight is the simultaneous comprehension of how the parts of a process fit together with the whole ("aha"). It is the emergent process of knowing who is doing what and how. It is a feeling understanding in which a person knows what he or she does, how it is done, and takes responsibility for it. For example, what am I doing and how am I doing it? If I am avoiding being aware of and taking responsibility for my negative impact on others, how do I do it? Do I turn away and not see? Or rationalize? Do I hold my breath and numb myself so that I don't feel my grief at seeing pain in others?

As patients sharpen their contact, improve self-regulation, and are more insightful, they gain mastery over their lives and tools to experiment with options. Sometimes insight involves relating current events to past events, as when remnants of the past, such as currently felt emotions about the past, introjects, or conditioned responses, interfere with interaction in the group. Developmental themes are made foreground as currently needed, using present centered and experiential methods rather than prizing connections that are primarily cognitive.

Tina was considered a bulwark of support to others in her group. She seemed solid, had learned to share her reactions in an open, insightful, and caring manner. However, she just couldn't listen to

Tim, who had recently joined the group. She would find herself emotionally gone, thinking about something else, as she had at the very beginning of her therapy.

Tim was very wordy. His contact was marred by using a lot of words, not getting to the point, deflecting, withholding affect. Tina discussed with Tim her observation of what he was doing and her reaction. While this dialogue cleared the air, it did not alter Tina's emotional reaction to him.

She worked on this one-on-one with the therapist in the group and what emerged was that Tim's verbosity without contact reminded her of her mother. Tina's mother was so out of touch while talking that she seemed psychotic. Tina used isolating defenses against being overwhelmed and disappearing under the constancy of her mother's wordiness without contact. These defenses were reactivated by her interactions with Tim. As a result Tina did important work on bringing into the foreground the remnants of past interactions with mom that still impeded her current interactions.

The dialogue with Tina, her subsequent exploration and their continued contact in group gave Tim important insight into how he affected people and also what often lay behind immediate reactions of people to him. It led to his learning how to support better contact and also aided the group by bringing into the open processes that unexpressed would have interfered with the formation of group cohesion.

Exerimental Phenomenology. One of the most basic of all clinical interventions is empathic reflection of the patient's experience. This is a vital aspect of both phenomenology and dialogue. While it is quite supporting to have the clarification of the therapist's empathic reflections, this is not state-of-the-art use of the phenomenological perspective. In Gestalt therapy we use more active techniques and still maintain the advantages of the phenomenological perspective.

This was not possible in traditional psychoanalytic psychotherapy since the accepted methodology was based on free association rather than focused awareness and the active techniques used in short-term therapy or behavior modification were considered antithetical to long-term intensive therapy. In traditional psychoanalytic groups participants were encouraged to explain feelings or behavior, to search for genetic causes, but active expression and experimentation in the therapeutic hour was limited. This put an unnecessary limitation on the liveliness and power of the therapy.

With discrimination Gestalt therapists use active techniques in both short-term and long-term intensive psychotherapy. In doing this the Gestalt therapist shifts from just empathic following, but does not shift to one of active change agent.

Gestalt therapy experiments are done without attachment to outcome (Jacobs, in press). The purpose of experimenting with new behavior in Gestalt therapy is to be more aware, to know options and to feel consequences. All interventions and suggestions in Gestalt therapy are considered experiments in awareness and not efforts to direct, control, recondition, or change behavior.

Many therapists of other persuasions use active techniques to change patients' behavior, but not simply for increasing awareness through experimentation. Such approaches lack a methodology for phenomenological focusing and exploring. For example, expressing emotions can be suggested as an experiment or as a substantive goal of being more emotionally expressive. If the therapist is attached to this goal, the suggested "experiment" is not genuinely experimental.

Enhanced awareness and experimentation enables people to expand horizons, develop new skills, improve human relations, and work through old wounds. Patients develop autonomy and skill at the same time that the therapeutic search for insight is developing. It is important that the tools a patient acquires be strong enough to support the new awareness, experimentation, and contact. Without the development of these tools a patient is left with an unfortunate choice between not moving forward (e.g., as in "supportive therapy") and moving forward with insufficient self-support.

Expanded techniques include training the patient in phenomenological focusing, creating phenomenological experiments, using shared phenomenological reports (dialogue). When the therapist shares his or her observations, emotions, past experience, creative ideas while maintaining the therapeutic focus, the patient has more possibilities for his or her phenomenological work. The increased interaction and technological interventions are means of aiding self-direction, support and expansion and not for therapist-directed change.

There is a much greater range of experimentation that naturally fits in groups. One person's phenomenological work becomes a stimulus for another's work or vicarious learning. Interaction between people provides sharing of phenomenological perspectives and new data for phenomenological focusing and exploration.

People in group live, act, and learn from results, just as in nature. However, therapeutic experiments have several differences: First, the experiments arise out of a therapeutic relationship. This means patients have a place to explore with some protection from ordinary accountability and consequences. For example, in group one can experiment with aggression or flirting with less risk. Second, experiments are guided by the therapist who takes account of the therapy context, makes the experiments suitable to the person and of graded difficulty. Third, the avoidance of awareness is itself the central object of observation and experimentation, as when explicit comment is made on process in therapy and the patient becomes aware of the awareness process.

Awareness through Dialogic Relationships

Awareness and growth emerge from contact. Since genuine dialogue is never controlled by either person, it has a quality of emergence that is inherently experimental. Gestalt therapy groups encourage and facilitate participants to risk exploratory dialogue. By trying things out together and discovering how they feel, participants create more self-support, self-definition, and interpersonal responsibility.

From the beginning of its divergence from psychoanalysis, Gestalt therapy has emphasized the active meeting between people, basing the therapeutic relationship on the full manifest personal presence of both patient and therapist rather than the traditional strategy of keeping the person of the analyst in the background. The analyst was not encouraged to experiment or facilitate patient experimentation and was forbidden from making personally expressive statements in order not to taint the transference. Gestalt therapists enrich therapy by trusting what emerges from actively revealing themselves. Far from hurting the therapeutic exploration, including exploration of the transference, this personal presence of the therapist increases therapeutic effectiveness. The therapist judiciously, appropriately, and with discrimination shares his or her observations, personal reactions, emotions, past experience, suggestions for therapeutic activity by the patient, and so on.

Louisa reported feeling more distance between herself and the therapist following the therapist's return from a long vacation and that something was different and "not right" about the therapist's manner. The therapist felt refreshed, crisp, working more effectively than before vacation. At that point numerous interpretations and confrontations were possible that would analyze the patient's problem (material related to separations, reactions to crisper interventions, narcissistic injury, etc).

The therapist listened and inquired about exactly what Louisa was observing and experiencing during two recent interactions in group. In the first incident the therapist confronted Louisa when he saw her doing a monologue and she perceived herself being contactful. Louisa "saw" the therapist as looking resentful, negative, and she felt left alone. The therapist then asked her about a more recent incident in which the therapist both confronted and frustrated her by not answering a question and thereby putting pressure on her to provide her own answer (which she did, discovering a feeling of self-hate behind a self-directed "why question"). In the latter situation Louisa did not feel the distance and did not feel left alone.

The therapist got in touch with the fact that in the first instance he had been frustrated and his contact had not been full and congruent; not expressing his frustration interfered with being fully involved. Louisa confirmed that the confrontation in the second incident did not leave her feeling abandoned, but in the first instance it had. By the therapist listening, going further into his own awareness and then sharing the result, there evolved a clearer awareness for both the therapist and the patient. The patient went on to work on her feelings of loss and disappointment as she gained a more complete and accurate picture of the therapist.

In group the contact is sometimes between therapist and patients and sometimes among group members. Group participants are encouraged to express their feelings, wants, creativity, ideas and so forth using words, sounds, gestures, movement, art.

While James was working on his dissatisfaction with the woman he lived with, who complained that James judged her to be inadequate, he felt distracted by Betty's fidgeting and disinterested look. The group's attention shifted to the dialogue between them. Betty identified with James' woman friend, and shared with James that she often felt stupid around him. James told her that he felt unheard by her that night, as he frequently did with his woman friend. Betty was afraid that if she just listened to James while he worked, she would surrender her autonomy and be caught up in his perspective. This fear was part of her not marrying, which she said she wanted. Betty concluded that if she expressed herself sooner she could listen more and be more secure from being swallowed up by the other. James became clear that in spite of his appearing to be in the one-up role in relation to women, that he felt quite vulnerable to not being understood and loved by them.

Following this dialogue Eliott departed from his frequent custom of telling current events stories that frequently appeared to be of little interest to him or the group and instead shared directly with Betty that he had a similar problem in that he too had a longstanding unmet desire to get married and had trouble maintaining a relationship of intimacy without merger and suggested that they work on this together in the group.

In the past there had often been friction between them, with Eliott wanting attention from Betty and Betty discouraging any connection between them. In fact, Eliott shared that in spite of Betty's aloof manner, he was afraid that if they had contact, Betty would "glom" on. Betty felt unseen by Eliott's compulsive and insensitive approaches.

The therapist suggested an experiment in which for ten minutes in group they would pretend to have an ongoing relationship and would express themselves to each other making only "Here-and-now I . . . " statements. After initial difficulty, both found this very useful in building specific awareness skills necessary to establish and maintain intimate contact and wanted to do more of such focusing and experimenting with contact.

People can become aware of resistance to awareness by watching others (as Eliott did) as well as hearing feedback and identifications by several other participants. When one patient is missing the obvious in a consistent pattern, the fact of distortions, avoidances, biases in the awareness process often becomes clear to the observer with greater ease than to the protagonist. This can promote the question: "How do I avoid awareness?"

Above all the Gestalt therapy relationship starts with the therapist respecting the patient's awareness and facilitating the patient to begin the vital process of learning to respect his or her own experience and growth potential. In dialogic Gestalt therapy the therapist practices inclusion (Buber 1965). The therapist practicing inclusion swings himself or herself fully into the other person's phenomenology while maintaining awareness of his or her separate identity. This has been described as "imagining the real," as making of the other person an independent person and confirming the other person's independent existence and the validity of multiple realities.

Confirmation means accepting whole people (although not necessarily everything about them), meaning how they are and also how they could be. Inclusion means experiencing as fully as possible the viewpoint of the other, and at the same time confirming the other as a separate person. The test of the accuracy of inclusion, as in empathic reflection, is the patient's experience of being understood. No one knows the patient better than the patient does and no can feel another's feelings.

Gestalt Therapy Styles of Group Therapy

In the mid-1960s Fritz Perls popularized Gestalt therapy with workshop demonstrations and training films in which he used a style of working one-on-one in groups that enabled him to quickly demonstrate some aspects of Gestalt therapy (Harman 1984). Unfortunately his style became erroneously equated with Gestalt therapy and it was assumed that all Gestalt therapy was done one-on-one in group and that there was no interaction or emphasis on group process. In fact, since its inception in the 1940s Gestalt therapy has been practiced in a wide variety of individual and group therapy styles (Harman 1984).

In a recent survey 83 percent of Gestalt therapists surveyed declared that their leadership style used at least two of the three group foci (one-on-one, interaction, group as a whole), and 60 percent reported a style utilizing all three. Only 4.4 percent report an exclusively or primarily one-on-one ("hot-seat model"). The mixed model is by far the most frequently encountered (Frew 1988; Harman 1984). Since the "hot-seat" model has been so influential in how Gestalt therapy is represented, I will describe it first.

The typical hot-seat group starts with "rounds" or "checkin." Each person expresses, usually to the therapist, what is experienced, what is felt, wanted, observed, and so on. This might be about momentary mood, the state of one's life, a focus on a theme that is occupying the person, feelings toward someone in the group, or feelings about the group as a whole. There would often be some brief interaction or facilitation between the therapist and the person who is talking that might lead to interaction among group members.

When rounds are over the therapist would typically ask: "Does anyone want to work?" In the earliest days "working" meant someone would come up to a special chair ("the hot-seat") and work with the therapist in front of the group. This was especially effective for quickly demonstrating Gestalt therapy. The staging was under the control of the therapist who could arrange chairs so everyone in the group could see therapist and patient.

That style quickly softened into the "floating hot-seat." In this style the person still worked one-on-one, but the hot-seat was wherever the person was sitting. In the earliest forms the group was kept out of the interaction until the work was over, and then asked to share feedback. Group members were asked to share observations (note: not interpretations) that might have been missed, feeling reactions in the present, and any sharing of one's own experience with the theme in question. In no case was a member encouraged to continue the work, to do further work for the protagonist, problem solve, analyze, or interpret.

In spite of the form of the leader being the hub and all interactions going through the leader, these groups often are quite dynamic and cohesive and strong bonds are formed by the group members. The work is often very intensive and has profound impact on patient's lives, in part because the focus is channeled by the therapist and patient and less fragmented by "too many cooks" (see discussion in Harman, 1984).

This work often deeply touches the observers and a strong and enduring sense of community and loyalty is developed. Unfortunately, in that style the group dynamics are seldom commented on by the therapist. Of course, there is nothing in the theory of Gestalt therapy that made this so, but rather it became a custom in some circles because of the influence of Perls' style.

The observers form a background, like a Greek chorus, adding to the intensity of the experience. Often the therapist would use the group during a piece of work. Roger, a young therapist in group therapy reported competitive feelings with the therapist. The therapist suggested that as an experiment the young man go around the group and say to each person: "There is enough room in the world for Jim [the therapist's name] and I." It was clearly not what the patient thought at the onset. He tried the experiment. As he went around the group repeating the phrase it became less mechanical, and he truly felt, at least for a moment, that he need not compete with the therapist, that he need not submit or rebel or compare in a judgmental way. He discovered that there was "enough room." This was a revolutionary and liberating discovery to him. (Since it was an experiment, results could have been different and still successful. The goal is to discover without attachment to any particular outcome).

Later in the group Roger was being immovable and uncompromising and Jim proposed the same experiment. This time Roger was to say "I won't . . ." to each person. In this experiment the "I won't" changed tone from the beginning to the end. In the beginning it appeared to others and was experienced by Roger as half-hearted, stubborn, and withholding. By the end of the round Roger's "I won't" sounded and was experienced as powerful and contactful. As a result of this experiment, he discovered that his stubborness had a lot of power, power that he had a choice of how to express. "Won't," with awareness and directness, was very powerful.

Some Gestalt therapists use a pure group process approach in which the interaction of the members in the present is the focus. This approach makes maximum use of the healing effect of inter-human interaction with its concomitant increase in awareness and contact skills. When conducted by a skilled Gestalt therapist characterological discoveries also occur with this approach. However, it is more difficult with this approach to get clear on the mechanism of distorting awareness and on the unfinished business with non-group members.

Therefore, many use a mixed model, one in which the group sometimes does one-on-one work, sometimes works on interactions in the group, sometimes work on a theme together, and sometimes focuses on the group as a whole. However, in working on awareness of group interaction, Gestalt therapists always also work with individual awareness, and when working one-on-one focus on the constantly present and shifting relationship between people.

A borderline man entered a therapy group run by his individual therapist. In the first session he appeared lively and contactful, although he didn't share very much of his own life issues. In the second session he did work, starting to talk about very intense early material relating to his mother and himself. The material was brought forth with great feeling, but with a great deal of psychoanalytic jargon about his oedipal complex. Although the material appeared consistent with an oedipal interpretation, the therapist knew issues of abandonment and aggressive intrusion by the mother at a much earlier age were more central.

The patient was going very far beyond his support. He had not made contact with other group members and on that evening was also not contactful with the therapist. He talked about meaningful material in an emotional way, but was not in sufficient contact with the other group members, not sufficiently aware of himself in the current situation and did not have sufficient tools to discriminate and utilize the kind of information he was talking about. It was important for the therapist to interrupt him and establish contact between the patient, himself, and the other group members before the patient prematurely plunged into a cathartic whirlpool of prim-itive emotions about past events without relating to the current context—the group—that would lead to fragmentation and regres-sion and not integration.

The patient was able to look at and connect with other group members, share his feelings, get centered, and become authentically excited about the contact. He started to learn what support he needed for healthy contact. He could deal with his unfinished situation with his mother at a later, more appropriate time.

Integrated Eclecticism

There is no single Gestalt therapy group style. Gestalt therapy is inclusive and eclectic and does not prescribe or limit practice to particular techniques or styles. Gestalt group therapists are encouraged to create and borrow forms, styles, and techniques from diverse sources. Gestalt group therapy is particularly varied, creative, vibrant, flexible, powerful, and fertile for integrating a variety of interventions.

However, the Gestalt therapy framework is not eclectic in the sense of adding techniques, observations, and ideas together like a shopping list. Rather it is a system that transforms, assimilates, and integrates them into a coherent methodology. The Gestalt therapy philosophy, change theory, and methodology enable the well trained clinician to create a clinical approach that is appropriate to the needs of each patient, group, the personality of the therapist, and the needs of society.

Some Gestalt therapists use a lot of techniques, either in one-on-one or group work (e.g., group experiments or exercises), and some almost none. Some therapists are more disclosing than others. Some are relatively more confrontive, some more sympathetic. Of course different Gestalt therapists have different levels of skill at working with different processes. For example some are more skilled at working with body awareness, some with movement, some with the process of thinking. With all of these variations, the same basic Gestalt principles are followed.

Regardless of style, Gestalt therapy groups present a special opportunity to work on autonomy, self-regulation, self-knowledge, acceptance and experimentation. Integration is enhanced by public acknowledgment and expression of emotion and sharing reactions. A well run therapy group promotes self-acceptance.

To prevent conformity through identification, introjection, confluence, and group pressure the theory and practice of Gestlat therapy emphasizes awareness of differences, individual definition of needs, preferences and values, and assimilation rather than introjection. Gestalt therapy groups try to avoid directly or inadvertently encouraging the conformity generated by groups that exhort expressiveness, anger, love, analysis of transference, or other substantive goals.

Shelly, a relatively new group member, had an introjected belief that her presence in group was legitimate only if she "worked" one-on-one with the therapist in the group. However, when she did, the work was unsatisfying to her. One night when asked what she was aware of, she said: "I want to work." "I wonder," responded the therapist, "if that is what you really want or need tonight. You answered so quickly I wonder if you really checked in with yourself." He then asked her to get in touch with her senses, her feelings, her body, and feel what she wanted.

She did not really want to do one-on-one work, but wanted some legitimacy for being in the group. She actually wanted to use the group that evening as a haven, as a refuge in which she could be among accepting and emotionally expressive people. While legitimizing being in group without doing one-on-one work was important, and knowing she needed a haven was even more important, ultimately what was most important from this interaction was her getting in touch with the fact that she frequently acted on shoulds, mistaking them for needs or wants. Discovering that she could find her real need by using her own sensory awareness was an important step for her.

Judith was a borderline woman with years of individual therapy experience. One of the issues she was working on during the period that she was in the group was whether the kind of contact she wanted from her husband was realistic, healthy, and moral. She wanted contact that was tender, sensual, intimate, sexual, and so forth, but had been raised with the belief that any sensual contact was immoral. She reported that her husband recoiled in reaction to any of her advances or invitations. It was unclear from her description exactly how much of his reaction was a result of characterological issues (possibly fear of engulfment) and how much due to the hurt, disappointment, resentment, shame, and fear that seemed to be salient in their marital relationship. She said her husband told her she was clinging, crazy, incompetent, and mentally ill. She tended to introject this view and add it to negative childhood introjects.

It was tempting to represent a more progressive view to her, and to some degree the therapist and other group members did so. But more important than this was the issue of her being entitled and able to have her own position, to experiment and find out what was appropriate in her own judgment. As she experimented with contact in group several types of interaction occurred. Most of the group reacted to her vitality with interest, excitement, and admiration. In that sense she was a very positive addition to the group and served as a model of exciting contact. That alone would have been positively reinforcing and worthwhile. However two other kinds of interactions happened.

Mary reacted to the interaction between Judith and men with rage. For her Judith's seductiveness raised old and hurtful issues of how she was treated by men and the exploitive aspects of relations between the sexes. She had been hurt by the constant message of "you are not pretty enough" and believed that seductive behavior was demeaning and put men in a dominant position. This presented Mary with a lively situation in which she could work on the issue. It gave Judith some awareness of one aspect of her lively behavior since she actually did experience herself in a one-down position and had accepted the traditional female role of accommodating, entertaining men, and so on.

For Brian her liveliness and emotional lability seemed phony and manipulative. He reacted negatively, although not yet feeling safe enough to discuss this in the group. Later, after Judith had left group, he faced a similar issue with another woman in group (Lucia) with directness and tact. This initiated useful work by Lucia on her interaction with the group and learning that people were put off by her aloof style.

Judith worked in depth on the unresolved interaction with her minister father. Her family taught that it was a woman's duty to obey her husband in all matters. At the therapist's suggestion Judith imagined her father was sitting in an empty chair in the consultation room, and had a "dialogue" with him. She eventually pushed him back and with hand gestures and words asserted her right to her own position and time free of submitting in order to develop her own position. This was an important step in her development of separation and autonomy and led to working through intense issues of hunger, hurt, shame, rage, and so forth.

Conclusion

The Gestalt therapy approach deals with the full range of clinical conditions, personalities, and cultural variations. Symptoms are worked on directly, as they are not in some approaches emphasizing long-term personality treatment, while at the same time the long-term personality work is never neglected. This methodology can be used in short-term work that can either remain short-term or lead into intensive long-term work.

Gestalt therapy as an existential approach uses experimental phenomenological and dialogical methods to explore how people exist through how they behave, feel, relate, think, create, live, as well as psychophysical functioning and cultural and psychodynamic history that is influential in the current field and that is part of the meaningful background of the present moment. By clear insight into what is, Gestalt therapy establishes a ground for continued growth.

It has been successfully adapted for work with virtually all clinical conditions by Gestalt therapists who understand the theory of Gestalt therapy and also have a good professional background on the clinical conditions being treated.

Because of its emphasis on description, patient self-regulation, separate verification of all observation by patients, its wariness about introjection and teaching of skills of assimilation, and its suspension of any theoretical dogma when working with patients, there is a built-in correction process in Gestalt therapy.

By making the fullest use of the human resources of therapist and group members and vigorous assimilation and integration of the best from other forms of therapy without the restraints of dogma, Gestalt group therapy has been a changing, growing, and increasingly effective form of therapy.

11

Psychodrama

James M. Sacks, Ph.D.

Webster's defines *psychodrama* as "a form of cathartic therapy in which a patient acts out by improvisation, situations related to his problem, often before an audience and with others who represent persons near his problem" (Guralnik 1982). Catharsis was emphasized (J. L. Moreno 1940; Z. T. Moreno 1979; Nichols and Zax 1977) but there are now several thousand publications on the subject for use in every form of insight-oriented therapy (Greer and Sacks 1973; Gendron 1980). The founder, Viennese-American psychiatrist J. L. Moreno (1889–1974), elaborated a broad theoretical system that ranged from religious philosophy to microsociology in more than one hundred publications. His group-centered, interpersonal approach generally distanced him from the mainstream psychoanalytic psychiatry of his day although he insisted that his *sociometric* system did not negate psychoanalytic insight but only subsumed it. He was fond of saying that many couches will fit on a stage but no stages on a couch or that verbal behavior is only one kind of action available to psychodramatists. He saw signs of "rapprochements" especially among the works of French and English analysts and analytically oriented sociologists.

Moreno's central concept, what he called his *ideé fixe,* was spontaneity. It was a *sine qua non* for creativity not reducible to any more fundamental entity, conscious or unconscious, but inherent in human nature. Socio- and psychopathology were traceable to a deficit in this "s factor." Psychotherapy consisted in facilitating the potential for spontaneity in an individual or group. Spontaneity was clearly distinguished from uncontrolled abandon or impulsivity, its antithesis being compulsive or inauthentic behavior rather than raw instinct. It was measured by the twin criteria of adequacy and originality. Wild behavior fails the adequacy test. Spontaneity was thus seen as including the capacity for restraint as well as expression (Z. T. Moreno, 1965).

Moreno was fascinated by psychological time. Spontaneity is tied to the present, "the moment" or the "here-and-now." He focused on events *in status nascendi* since it was in origination that change was triggered by spontaneity or where spontaneity failed and neurotic repetition and rigidity aborted the creative leap. Moreno's emphasis on the present was certainly not based on undervaluation of the past and future. He sought instead to rescue vital but temporally distant events from being buried in mental archives or lost in dim speculation. The psychodramatist attempts to infuse past and future with the spontaneity of the present by reliving them in dramatic format. In make-believe, what was and might be, is. The approach differs from the "here-and-now" group therapies, which focus exclusively on intragroup dynamics. Since the unconscious has no past, interpretations delivered in the language of the past cannot be quite accurate. ("You must have resented Alex's insult" may not hit the mark. Only when the actor playing Alex says, "You're too fat!" can the patient reexperience the wave of resentment that is then available for reevaluation.)

Moreno distinguished his concept of spontaneity from Bergson's *élan vital* and his *hic et nunc* from Bergson's *durée.* He criticized Bergson for his focus on such an infinitesimal instant that it lacked all dimensions, like an instant in physical time, and thus it was not amenable to influence. For Moreno "the moment" could still be captured to test and to train. Despite the acknowledged paradoxical nature of his injunction "Be spontaneous!" he invented many ways to cultivate this elusive quality. Moreno (1964:130) notes: "Spontaneity training seems a contradiction in terms. How can spontaneity be trained? It consists of two phases: the liberation of the organism from clichés, that is, deconserving it and making it free for the reception of s. In the second phase, the increased receptivity and readiness of the individual organism facilitates new dimensions of personality development."

Psychodrama grew out of the theater of spontaneity that Moreno (1947) established in Vienna in 1923 to train actors. As budding psychiatrist as well as theatrical producer and acting coach, he could not separate the failed spontaneity of the inadequate actor from that of the inadequate human being. As a social scientist, he focused also on the entire population of the theater, actors and audience alike. Nurtured by the development of his scientific method of measuring psychosocial phenomena, psychodrama as a group psychotherapy soon evolved.

Moreno's sociometry has since taken its place as a standard research tool in social science. But for Moreno, sociometry was more than a method of generating diagrams of group preferences. It was a way of objectifying the whole of group dynamics, as important for understanding what happens in groups as is the psychodramatic reenactment of events that shaped the individuals who compose them. Moreno explains that the group therapist has no need of formal sociograms to know about the emotional forces, bonds, and repulsions that constitute the underlying sociometric structure of every group. Sociometric tests are merely ways of adding precision to these impressions.

Elements of the Psychodramatic Situation

1. The *audience* is that part of the group not taking an active part in a given drama. It is important that at least one member of the group remain outside of the action as it is for the sake of the

audience that the play is performed. It is the attentive parent. (In a well known cartoon a little girl falls off her tricycle in the first panel and lands on her head. The next three panels show her searching the house and yard. In the final panel she finds her mother and bursts into tears. We are hardly impelled to talk if no one is listening.)

2. Psychodrama has a designated *protagonist.* In this respect it stands in contrast to exclusively group-centered therapies that do not delineate such an uncontested position for the individual. At the outset of the session attention is focused on the group as a whole or moves from person to person. It settles ultimately on a single member whom every effort is made to accommodate. His rivals are held in abeyance and the therapist enlists the group to help appreciate the uniqueness of only one. The group finds it easier to bear their envy during this period knowing that they too will be as fully respected in their turn and will not be easily sacrificed to majoritarian needs. In later phases of the session, after the protagonist has achieved some sense of fulfillment in his personal drama, attention returns to the group.

3. The chief therapist is called the *director* according to Moreno's preference for using the terminology of the theater rather than the clinic. Similarly, on the level of observable action, the psychodrama director resembles his counterpart in the legitimate theater more than he resembles the conventional group therapist. He uses all means to facilitate the inherent spontaneity of the protagonist and of the group. He warms the players up into action, sets the scenes, calls out for role reversals, summons group members onto the stage and dismisses others, closes the action phase and leads the after-discussion. He may indicate to the auxiliary egos what line to pursue and he may even assume a role himself, especially that of the double, if no one else in the group seems able to introduce a necessary element. As active as these functions might seem, each intervention must be accomplished as simply and elegantly as possible so that the scene flows generally on its own momentum rather than being orchestrated. The drama, of course, cannot have a truly even flow because the protagonist himself is torn in different directions. One function of the director then, is to open

avenues for each of the opposing wishes to enter the arena of expressed action rather than to cancel each other out in the deadness
of repression.

Some of the issues to which the director must attend are these:
(a) He must not lose sight of the simple conscious intent of the
protagonist. This may seem extraneous to mention but overattach-
ment to a pet formulation can cause a director to miss or under-
value direct statements by the protagonist. (b) Like the analyst, he
must maintain "floating attention" to sense what might be happening unconsciously. Clues for these hypotheses come from spontaneity failures such as a disparity between content and tone of voice,
unnatural pauses, ignoring, grasping at, or dwelling inordinately on
a point in the scene or an event in the group, or a general note
of falseness in the patient's behavior. The explicit message may be
unconvincing because it is opposed by an unspoken counterforce.
(c) The director must monitor the protagonist's capacity to accept
and integrate new material. Based on this evaluation he may decide
whether to set up a scene designed to facilitate the expression of
the suspected feeling, whether to insert the idea through doubling
(see below), whether to set scenes to build self-esteem, or merely
to wait. (d) Despite his special attention to the protagonist, the director must maintain some thread of empathic contact with each
group member. (A was insulted to be chosen to play an obnoxious
person; B is sulking because he wasn't chosen at all; C is afraid B
will turn his passive aggression against him; D is disgusted with C
for being manipulable by B; etc.) There is much body language to
be read, often in low light, and decisions to be made as to how
long the group dynamics can safely be left unacknowledged during
the drama. The director may use natural breaks in the drama to
process group reactions or save them for the after-discussion. They
may be analyzed descriptively or psychodramatically.

4. The *physical setting* of psychodrama is unique to the form. In
psychodrama, the freedom to experiment with new ways of behaving and to experience the accompanying affects rests on the distinction between the real world as represented by the audience and
the make-believe world on stage. For patients who cannot always
keep this distinction clear it is especially important to delineate the

stage area. At the same time there must be a regulated flow between the psychological events on and off stage. If the stage is too small it confines the action and if it is too large, as a proscenium stage of an auditorium, the audience feels distant from the actors and the actors feel too much on display. Some psychodrama theaters have elaborate stages while others use only a large rug at one end of the room. Moreno's stages were in the form of three concentric circles rising one step each toward the center. He could then move the potential protagonist from the audience step by step to the highest level where the action took place.

As in legitimate theater the director controls the lighting. This helps focus attention on the action with stage lights or on the group with house lights. Windows need opaque shades if sessions are held during daylight. The full range of light including full darkness is useful especially with patients who feel safest when they are not seen. Lowered light should be used with caution, however, since some patients become anxious when they cannot see clearly. Colored light adds another dimension most directors find useful. Sound amplification is unnecessary as groups of more than 12 to 15 require too long a wait before each becomes the protagonist.

5. Moreno applied the term *auxiliary ego* or simply auxiliary to those who help the protagonist by playing roles, whether group members or cotherapists. As the group evolves, members develop skill at the special kind of improvisational acting required. Stylized impressions with accents, idiosyncratic gestures, etc., so charming on the comedy stage, are out of place. The talented psychodrama auxiliary ego portrays only what is necessary to achieve the psychological impact required. Group members with no pretensions to Thespian talent become surprisingly adept. Auxiliaries learn to listen for traits that the protagonist imputes to the character. (PROTAGONIST: "Did you hear what I said?" The auxiliary grunts affirmatively, looks attentive for a moment but soon stares vacantly.) The auxiliary ego is encouraged to remember material from previous sessions about the character he is playing. Soon everyone knows the stock ways each member perceives his significant others. Patients whose objects tend to remain split, may be helped to blend disparate images of others when the auxiliary ego revives some con-

trary trait he recalls from a previous session to combine with the image the protagonist is expecting.

Techniques

The director has numerous dramatic techniques available during the action phase. A usual starting point is the *self-presentation,* a straightforward enactment by the protagonist of his presenting problem. He plays his own role while auxiliaries play the roles of others. This may begin with a real event but the self-presentation is soon blended with deviations from reality (i.e., the protagonist's perceived reality). The drama can be used to experiment with alternatives for the protagonist and opportunities to behave in ways that he might have wished to or simply in new ways that seem to emerge in the psychodrama arena. Such deviations from the level of pure recapitulation, Moreno called *surplus reality.*

The *future projection* technique is one such surplus reality scene. A protagonist might be led to enact a future scene that is distressingly vague. A student, confused about career planning, might try life scenes from several professions. He may discover unexpected disturbances or gratifications that could not be experienced by discussion alone. The director and the group can also bring attention to unrealistic expectations that he imagines about these professionals. Often a patient is asked to play a scene some years ahead and to assume all has gone well. Despite this chance to construct an ideal future, many protagonists people the stage with the same kinds of objectionable characters or continue the same problems they suffer with in life. The lonely person forgets to include a spouse in his home or the exasperated father creates on stage a son who still requires his harsh advice. Such scenes enable patients to see how patterns projected on others have internal origins. Negative future projections if used with caution are helpful in exploring feelings of despair or fear. Psychodramatic worst-case-analyses often end unexpectedly. (A hypochondriac's fear of heart-attack led to a hospital scene in which he fought furiously with the nurses to go home. It became apparent, even to him, that it was not death so much as dependency on women that he feared and ultimately longed for.)

Future projections are also used educationally. Patients nearing discharge, for example, are given role rehearsal in the tasks of civilian life. Analytically oriented psychodramatists question the efficacy of simple training in overcoming psychopathology. "A man will not get a job more easily because he has gone through dialogues with a psychotherapist representing an employer; however, because a patient has been able to discover through psychodrama what his fantasied image of an employer represents in terms of displacement of his anxiety, he will be able to make progress toward recovery" (Lebovici 1974:299–300). Notwithstanding this insight into the nature of unconscious conflict, it is just as fallacious to forget that people, in fact, normally can learn by practice.

Moreno used hypothetical improvisations diagnostically to see how far a protagonist could diverge from his actual personality. A self-derogating patient might be cast as a proud, condescending character to see how compulsive or flexible was his need for self-abasement.

Moreno combined psychodrama with hypnosis as *hypnodrama*, and with drugs, music, dance, art, or whatever might open a new channel for spontaneity.

Moreno, in his usual disregard for the psychotherapy conventions of his time, had no hesitation in bringing significant others into the drama. Auxiliary egos and the therapy group were seen as substitutes if the real people were unable to attend and the psychodrama stage only substituted for psychodrama *in situ*. Still more radically, and here even Moreno laid out many cautions, he would encourage selected patients with sufficient experience to run minidramas in the course of their lives. Spouses might agree to reverse roles at home from time to time to improve mutual understanding.

Moreno dealt with dreams by first enacting the manifest dream, then allowing it to be changed by the protagonist to have an ending more to his liking. When a dream is dramatized, the protagonist can revive the attitudes, feelings, and systems of assumptions he held as the dreamer. The dream is extended beyond the remembered events. In this state, actions of a marvelously regressed form ensue, markedly different from the behavior of the individual in waking dramas allowing the protagonist to discover aspects of himself not otherwise easily available.

Sometimes the auxiliary egos are confusing. In such cases a *monodrama* is conducted in which the protagonist plays all the roles moving about on the stage speaking now for one and then for the other. After a monodrama, the scene may be rerun with auxiliaries to relieve the protagonist from the need to constantly change identity.

The psychodrama *soliloquy* functions (1) to allow the expression of thoughts that cannot be shared with the other characters, and (2) to interrupt the action. A particularly ephemeral feeling often flashes past in the heat of an interchange and would normally be washed away in the flow of events. At such a significant moment the director calls for a soliloquy and the action freezes. The protagonist then, may pace around the stage under lowered lights with his double behind. He can now muse on the deeper meaning of what has been triggered. What occurred in action and affect can be captured in words before it is lost.

In the *double* technique, an auxiliary ego is assigned to remain with the protagonist as a kind of alter ego, staying near him throughout the scene (Toeman 1948). This important technique will be discussed here in special detail. As with the other auxiliaries, the double is self-selected by the protagonist. He positions himself behind or beside the protagonist so as to remain out of his field of vision. The double generally follows the protagonist and adopts his gestures and postures as a way of enhancing his own empathy. From time to time the double speaks aloud saying what he imagines that the protagonist could almost say but has not quite. He is meant to be heard as part of the subjective self rather than an object to be focused on. The convention is established that the other actors cannot hear the double so that the protagonist must either reword or change what the double has said. No one speaks until the protagonist has been allowed to repair the double's interpolation. The double's words may be inserted as lines in the dialogue or may initiate a soliloquy.

The pause for the protagonist's correction gives the double great latitude for error and speculation or to speak for only one side of a conflicted issue leaving it to the protagonist to balance the final impression. Asking the protagonist to "say it in your own words if it is 'right' or change it if it is 'wrong,' " helps lessen any tendency for an obedient protagonist to parrot his double's words without conviction. When the words are changed, of course, the meaning inevitably changes. In practice, there is no qualitative difference between agreeing and disagreeing. Oppositional protagonists can consider a changed nuance as proof that an idea is entirely theirs while a compliant protagonist can change the sense totally and still view it as only a rephrasing.

Even when the double remains silent, the protagonist's awareness of a benevolent and accompanying presence expands his sense of himself and helps him feel stronger. (Even a woman who wanted to "work on her loneliness" was not isolated on stage. The auxiliaries mumbled softly while she soliloquized in a far corner with her double about her alienation.) The goal is always to help the protagonist find language to integrate experience. Since language and communication are interpersonal, the double as some melange of self and inner objects, may serve as the only conversational partner that can be trusted for certain delicate matters. If the director suspects that the double induces a paranoid fear of being followed or of being mentally invaded, the protagonist is reminded to feel free to dismiss or change doubles.

A double influences not so much the stand that a protagonist may take but rather what issue will be addressed. (A husband was psychologizing to his wife that she overspent in reaction to her father's miserliness. DOUBLE: "I have to earn the money and I get angry that you take it out on me." PROTAGONIST: "It doesn't make me mad; it scares me and I don't know why." The doubling shifted the protagonist from the subject of why she wasted money to how he felt about it.)

The double can intervene differently in regard to impulse and restraint:

1. He can speak as a reflection of what the prrootagonist has already said. If not overused this helps the protagonist feel validated through being understood. The process differs from Kohutian empathy or Rogerian acceptance since the double speaks from within. The affirmation comes not only from the other, the therapist, in the hope that it will be internalized; the double's affirmation is already partially internalized as stemming from a period when self and other were not distinct. The reflecting double blends with the

voice of the confirming, good mother/self with its unique power to lend solidity to the protagonist's identity; that he exists; has feelings and perceptions and words to communicate them. Kohut's (1971) therapeutic "mirroring" would seem to be at least as effectively accomplished in this form of doubling as in his own format. (Reflecting is easily oversimplified and abused. One exasperated protagonist snapped at his double, "I just said that!")

2. The double can voice latent impulses. Like the director, the double must sense how much beyond what he has already expressed is likely to be acceptable to the protagonist. Increasing the protagonist's defensiveness is counterproductive not to mention the danger of overwhelming him with feelings for which he is unprepared. Crude expression of intense emotion by the double in the hope of loosening some purgative abreaction is almost always a mistake. The protagonist either: backs off into an observing attitude to watch the show, allowing the double to speak for him; carries on with feigned emotion in imitation of the double, thinking that that's what's expected of him; calls up some related feeling from his emotional repertoire and dutifully directs it to the object designated; becomes frightened and loses rather than gains capacity to master the debilitating effect of a traumatic situation.

3. The double may join the resistance. With that pole strengthened, the protagonist tends to readjust the balance by some loosening on the expressive side. ("I'm not really upset by it," reassures the protagonist that there are limits to his vulnerability so that he is freer to respond with: "I'm not upset but it's starting to bug me.") It is vital that the double not try to trick the protagonist with a paradoxical reverse psychology that will soon be felt as manipulative. The double must have an inner ally, a real force of defense or resistance to which he lends support.

The double can help readjust the protagonist's level of abstraction. Some circumstantial protagonists flood the field with details without drawing conclusions. ("You took my comb away. I put it right here. It was my long brown comb. . . ." The double might break in with, "You always do things like that!") More frequent are protagonists who get lost in clichés and generalizations. ("You're not really there for me. You're so immature and not in touch with your feelings.") Specificity in itself may be threatening to these patients, quite apart from the content. The double must advance carefully. ("I'll give you an example of what you do," yields: "I can't think of an example but that's the way you are.") A better tactic for the double is to edge into specificity himself to test the waters for the protagonist. ("I don't like to go to restaurants with you any more because of this." PROTAGONIST: "I could hardly look at Phil after we left the bar Tuesday. You bent their ears for twenty minutes about your rare coins. It was so boring. . . ." The double could guess that the protagonist sometimes eats with others and that the trait referred to may appear anywhere.)

The double can facilitate the protagonist's capacity to describe his feelings rather than only the circumstances eliciting them. Sometimes it helps simply to name feelings that are conscious to the protagonist but that he does not feel justified in mentioning. ("I didn't want to upset you but now that it's over I can tell you I was scared.") Sometimes a double can simply refer to an emotionally significant fact without commenting on its meaning. ("I don't know if you can tell on the phone, Jack, but I'm crying and squeezing my fingers together.")

Doubling is also part of a technique in which the protagonist "writes" a letter aloud to the significant other (Sacks 1974). After the signature, the double adds a P.S. that the protagonist corrects with a P.P.S. As in the soliloquy, the protagonist can speak without interruption but here, he sends his words directly to the other person, with a different emotional effect.

Multiple doubles are sometimes used to externalize inner conflict. One double may tempt the protagonist to seek a mistress while the other one implores him to remain faithful. Role reversals between the protagonist and doubles illuminate various facets of the conflict as a step toward its resolution.

A director may also appoint a second double to move into direct confrontation with the protagonist. The primary double remains in the rear supporting position. The protagonist can then express feelings toward himself from a peculiarly separate stance. This technique is contraindicated for patients with insecure cohesion of the self. Satyanarayan (1987) cautions against all role displacements with such patients. The technique does have a special utility with passive, depressed patients whose aggression is bound in unconscious self-hate. They cannot defend themselves even in scenes of totally unjustified attack. They often can, however, change their style from passive to active if they do not change the object from self to other. They may attack themselves mercilessly in this psychodramatic arrangement. The double playing the target self, fights back with every kind of self-justification to function as a credible foil. When the protagonist becomes animated he is then confronted with a person from his life more deserving of his rage and he can often continue his momentum with the new opponent.

Moreno (1953) traces his technique of *role reversal* to this description of human encounter he had written earlier in poetic form: "A meeting of two: eye to eye, face to face. And when you are near I will tear your eyes out and place them instead of mine, and you will tear my eyes out and place them instead of yours, and then I will look at you with your eyes and you will look at me with mine" (J. L. Moreno 1914). When the director calls for a role reversal, protagonist and antagonist physically change places. The technique has many uses beyond modeling to instruct the auxiliaries mentioned earlier. It is used primrily to expand empathy. When a protagonist first reverses roles with an opponent, he may exhibit only a caricatured image. After being in the role for a certain time, however, a need to justify himself arises, even as a hated character, and he is unable to maintain his stereotyped version. Gradually, the comic-strip villain becomes three-dimensional complete with needs, fears, and hopes. Misplaced role reversal with a guilt-prone protagonist risks invoking a moralistic tone causing the protagonist to suppress aggression in favor of altruistic or broad-minded values. (A protagonist about to recapture rivalrous feelings toward a sister is asked to reverse roles. He is at once reminded that from her point of view she deserved none of it and that he, in fact, was the aggressor. While humanizing his view of his sister, it further submerges a hate that lives on unresolved.)

In role reversal with an intimate person the protagonist sees not only the world at large from the other's point of view but he is also compelled to see himself from their viewpoint. To his quotation above Moreno might have added, "I will look at me with your eyes and you will look at you with my eyes." A self-disparaging person may be able to see positive aspects in himself when in the role of an admirer. In the role of a detractor one is pressed to see one's shortcomings. When a protagonist resists this role it is sometimes helpful to remind him that assuming the other's role in no way indicates agreement. As mistaken as the other person may be, he has a mind that perceives the protagonist and the exercise is only to explore how this misperception must seem. Painful role reversal is eased somewhat because the auxiliary ego opposite is defending the protagonist perhaps better than he could himself. When role reversal is used in a natural relationship as in marital counseling, each spouse is more willing to see himself from the other's point of view in the hope of a *quid pro quo*, the relief of being understood in one's own terms by the partner.

Role reversal has a special usefulness with paranoid characters. They can often portray their enemies with surprising vividness. Once they have strongly identified with the motives and feelings of their persecutor it becomes easier to help them reown their projections.

Miltos

The following case is not selected to be typical but to illustrate stages of a treatment process. It contains a classical catharsis with recovery of a traumatic memory. Such massive derepression occurs only rarely and is not the stuff of which day-to-day treatment consists. When it does occur it helps clarify how certain therpeutic mechanisms work in more subtle situations. The need for continuous working through, of ego building and symbol formation is as important in less spectacular cases even when the rationale is less obvious. With Miltos an important abreaction was facilitated by psychodrama that exposed new material that could be further integrated, again with psychodramatic methods. The story has a happy ending that seems almost too pat but Miltos was a star patient with personality endowments we cannot generally count on.

Miltos was 26 years old when he sought therapy for a block preventing his completing a Masters thesis in political science. It was obvious that he had overcome great resistance to calling me. He was so reluctant to talk about any other aspect of his life besides his writing that I did not press him for a full history. He avoided all eye contact and flushed beet red at moments that seemed to have no apparent emotional significance. I saw him individually twice a week for several months as his story slowly emerged.

Miltos had been the only child in a poor but intact extended family in a Greek village. When he was 2 years old his father was killed in a political uprising and he lived another year with his mother and maternal grandparents. The strengths of his later years were built in these first three relatively happy years. His mother then remarried a farmer from an isolated community. The stepfather had two older sons by two previous marriages. The elder son was angry about yet another interloper entering the family. Both brothers whose mothers had died resented Miltos who still had a mother and they constantly teased him. The community was very religious and the stepfather was influential in the church. He was cruel, vulgar, and frequently violent. Miltos remembered the stepfather threatening his mother with a gun and firing into the air. It required all the mother's efforts to ingratiate herself with her husband with no margin to protect her son. No one in the family was educated and the mother had no idea that escape was possible. Miltos was the lowest on the totem pole in a sadistic social system. He recalled no playmates. He was kept burdened with field chores and attended school only irregularly.

Miltos no longer ate with the family after he was 10 years old. They had either banished him from the table or he refused to sit with them. He retained some capacity to rebel. On one occasion after being punished he methodically destroyed a field of melons. He spent hours in vengeful fantasy.

At 12 years of age, a large school opened nearby to which Miltos could walk. There he drew the attention of a male teacher who noticed his intelligence and caught him up on years of missed education. He also inspired ambition in this determined and emotionally hungry child. Miltos learned English, read widely and lived in an intellectual world that made him feel far above his ignorant family. By the time he was eighteen he had contacted a distant relative of his mother's in America, took a job on a boat and emigrated. He broke off all contact with his family.

Miltos entered college and, being no stranger to menial work, maintained himself for two years on scholarships and odd jobs.

He established only fragile friendships with other isolated male students. He played chess and enjoyed individual sports. He finished college with better than average marks and entered graduate school hoping to return to Greece as a politician, ultimately to use his power for social benefit. A job he had taken doing simple electronic repairs required no contact with people. The position led to more complex work and he began earning a good living while still a student.

As effective as he was at his other work, so was he paralyzed in writing. He berated himself over this but felt he could overcome it by will power. His growing sophistication finally induced him to seek psychotherapy. He had read some psychology and had theories on his own dynamics. He was strongly motivated to get better and lacked any sign of self-pity. The world in which he was reared had offered no pity and he expected none.

In the beginning Miltos could not speak without being questioned. Like writing, speaking and thinking were also affected. He spoke only in a curt functional way and then stopping as though there were no inner flow of ideas. When I asked what went on in his mind at the times that he blushed and sweated he only knew that he must try to talk and not leave the session early. I introduced the doubling procedure to help him fill in the language that he could not find. I stuck to surface and ego-syntonic material. He still fell silent sometimes and could neither agree nor disagree with what I had said.

Miltos had never had any interpersonal sex life. Fantasies were limited to situations, all highly contrived, to account for why the woman would have anything to do with him. They were forced by circumstance, mistook him for someone else in the dark, they were blind, and so forth.

After several months Miltos was able to introduce subjects other than his writing block. He realized that he "ought" to have people in his life besides the casual contacts at work.

I had not considered placing him in a group so soon since he was barely able to talk to me but he had heard that I did group therapy and asked to join. I placed him in combined therapy but did not reduce his individual sessions. In fact he withdrew completely in the group. When the other members finally pressed him to talk, he began to blush and sweat and

I had to rescue him on several occasions. Due to his pride in
not succumbing to anxiety and to avoid the shame of being
rescued again he, quite abruptly, began speaking in the group.
He explained that the right to pass of which he availed himself
so often, had helped him but that he would now like to tell
the group some of what he had already told me. Once begun
he continued uninterruptedly in a mechanical tone unaware
that he was consuming all the group time. They tolerated his
monopolizing since he had been silent for so long but eventually they complained that he could not "talk a little." I interrupted him occasionally to forestall too much aggression from
the group. After six months Miltos felt himself to be a real
part of a social entity for the first time in his life. He came
to the sessions early hoping to speak with someone in the
waiting room. He was now the last to leave at the end of the
session although he was careful never to try for extra time by
thinking of one last thing to say as another member had been
doing. He was now able to "talk a little."

I would have delayed making Miltos a protagonist longer
but he was eager and had progressed well. He was a protagonist five times in the next year. The first two times he spoke
with men from work and a woman whom he was trying to
approach. The third time I brought in his mother. Not surprisingly he fell silent and had his blushing and sweating reaction so I diverted the scene to more contemporary matters.
The following week he told the group how he had felt during
the prior session. He realized that, while he was now able to
talk about his mother with some equanimity and was no longer
upset when he last saw her, he was still overcome facing his
mother in the drama. Evidently the restraints that reality required prevented the upwelling of the emotions attached to
her as did the distance of the narrative talking format. Only
the psychodrama format elicited this overwhelming feeling in
her presence.

Miltos now began a regimen of speaking with his mother
out loud in his room to prepare for his next opportunity as
protagonist. When the time came, his anxiety was gone as was
most of his spontaneity. Nevertheless the danger of being
overwhelmed was greater than the danger of protracted arti-
ficiality and he was probably wise to make these preparations.
The gist of his session was that he himself was at fault for

expecting more of her than she was able to give; that he still resented her but did not hate her. Having survived this session he wanted to see what would come of the next one if he did not prepare it.

The next time Miltos wanted to take on his stepfather, bypassing the lesser enemies of his two half-brothers. The auxiliary playing the stepfather and Miltos both stood dumb, glaring at each other for a full minute and again Miltos began to flush and perspire profusely. Suddenly, he sank to the floor. He sobbed for several minutes while his double lay next to him. Several times he tried to speak but starting to speak caused him to break down again. After several attempts the double began to repeat, "I can't talk." Miltos then corrected this to, "I can talk."

After a long time, Miltos, explained what had happened. During the moments of glaring Miltos felt himself to be living in the one-year period of his life that he had not remembered since it had occurred between the ages of ten and eleven. At that time he had felt so alienated from the family that, not only did he not eat with them but he moved out of the house entirely and slept every night in the barn with the farm animals. He went into the house only when he thought everyone was out and took food to eat in the barn. At first they had demanded that he come back but he was too frightened and proud. He came to feel that he was the greatest of the animals rather than the lowest of the humans. The effect of this memory was horribly humiliating to him and the agony that he endured as he forced himself to tell it can hardly be described. The session ran late that night and I bypassed the "sharing" phase since any one else's stories at that time would trivialize both.

It was notable that there was no actual drama per se. Overt enactment was superfluous, yet the event would not have occurred in a narrative format. The drama in its nascent form was the necessary final stimulus. Miltos had to (1) feel safe enough with me, (2) feel safe enough in the group, (3) observe other psychodramas, (4) experience a milder psychodrama as a protagonist, (5) be just about to relive the crucial scene. At that moment the repression lifted.

Immediately after exposure of highly charged material there is a critical period during which a patient is exquisitely sensitive to how the revelation is received. There was the danger of Miltos' feeling mortified that others now knew what he himself had been afraid to know. At the next individual session I therefore reassured him of how moving his drama had been. He said that he had felt very dazed all the next day. At the next group I allowed him to remain silent but drew out the group members on their sharing reactions to the previous session. This seemed right since his tears welled up slowly and easily in contrast to the shameful and involuntary sobs of the previous week.

To prevent resuppression of the memory during the next weeks, I tried neither to allow the event to be ignored nor to leave Miltos with an open emotional wound. I made comments like: "That was a terrible humiliation, Tom. Is that a small sample of what you went through, Miltos, or does it sound like a different kind of thing entirely?" The memory of life in the barn was related to his ongoing experience. "I shouldn't wonder that you don't want to eat lunch with those men at work. After the three guys you grew up with, it would be strange if you liked their kind of teasing repartee at the table."

About a month after the revelation we did a short vignette using the mirror technique. Other members acted out the scenes he had described deliberately underplaying the emotions at my request. Having regained access to the material everything was done to enable him to master the experience without being overwhelmed again. Eventually he did replay the scene himself but never with full intensity. He was able to recall a host of lesser memories that occurred during that lost year.

Miltos' political ambition faded. It had functioned as a compensatory fantasy for his powerlessness and a magical connection with his natural father but it was unrealistic considering his limited social skills. He did finish his dissertation and married a woman with a large, welcoming, Italian family. While he could not share their effusive warmth he was happy just to be there. He advanced rapidly in his electronics work until he could go no further without having managerial responsibility, which still made him too uncomfortable. He commuted from a country house where he farmed several acres in his spare time. They had three children.

Some of Miltos' ego functions were jeopardized by disintegrating traumas. He has lost some capacity to feel without being overwhelmed so that his speech was strangely mechanical and he could not make eye contact. Even more crucial, what was threatened for Miltos was that which makes us unique among animals, the ability to create language with which to communicate with each other and to think. But Miltos never surrendered to his circumstances. He remained intent on returning to the struggle for his dignity and was therefore able to use the psychodrama to face the impossible in digestible doses. He had only the weapons of repression and symbolization but life after repression was limited and lonely. He doggedly returned to face his stepfather. If he could entrap the situation in words he would no longer be the prisoner entrapped in repression. The psychodramatic moves were designed to provide him with an arena where he could approach the experiences that might have negated his humanity and to try again to be a man.

12

Couples Groups

Phillip B. Reichline, M.S.W.
and Jeanette G. Targow, M.S.W.

We are psychodynamically trained therapists who, after many years of experience with individual and group therapy, concluded that the problems of couples could be more effectively treated in groups. We have added to our armamentarium theory and techniques from gestalt, transactional, family systems, and humanistic-existential approaches.

Couples who seek help with troubled relationships and are willing to work together toward developing a compatible communication system are invited to enter the group. In the initial interview we discuss both conjoint and group therapy as possible modalities, unless the couple is referred specifically for group. It usually takes several conjoint sessions including familiarizing them with the modality of the group process before the clients are ready and willing to join the group. It is important to introduce the possibility of group therapy in the early sessions to counter resistance that often occurs when the clients and therapists form deep attachments as a result of their work together.

A couples group offers maximal growth for the individual as well as the relationship. Intrapsychic and character disorders are readily translated into interpersonal problems that the couple can address with the help of the group. There are instances when additional individual work is recommended, particularly when lack of self-esteem is the core problem within the couple relationship.

Our experience with treatment of individuals, couples, and groups has resulted in the conclusion that group process has been the most effective in achieving mature communication. The confrontation and feedback from the other members make an invaluable impact. Framo has said: "One of the reasons couple group therapy is the treatment of choice for premarital, marital, and separation and divorce is that the other couples provide not only models of how marital struggles can be worked out, but also models of what to avoid" (1980, 1986). In addition, as individuals, they learn by identifying with the problems and successes of other group members and evolve as much more mature beings through the support and understanding of the group.

A significant phenomenon occurs after a couple has experienced the group process for a period of time. They become "assistant therapists" as they alternate between client, patient, and observer roles. This adds to the clients' feelings of adequacy and competence as well as helping them integrate positive changes of behavior patterns.

These are the goals that can result in a successful relationship, although we are aware that few couples would be likely to achieve all of them.

1. Enhancement of self-esteem occurs as individuals become conscious of the behavior patterns, rules, and myths of the family of origin. As they experience the process of interaction that includes the caring and maturing of group members they move from immature dependence to mature interdependence.
2. Communication skills enables couples to:
   a. Express their honest feelings without being accusatory or abusive

b. Accept each other as valuable human beings with their own uniqueness and boundaries and discard irrational expectations of marriage
c. Have the freedom to state clearly what each wants and needs without the fear of the other's disapproval
d. Negotiate decisions based on what is appropriate or fitting rather than the need for personal power

Each of the previously stated goals assists the couple to develop the ability to overcome the fear of closeness and intimacy prevalent in many couples.

We find the optimum number of couples in a group to be four, but we have begun with three, and have had as many as five. We have a strong belief that most effective leadership can be achieved by a male and female cotherapy team. Both genders then feel they have the support and identification with the same sex therapist. The groups also learn from the leaders as a model, whether they are negotiating, expressing differences of opinion, or even verbalizing angry feelings to each other. On occasions when the latter has occurred, a certain number of group members experience considerable fear. When we ask for reactions, as we always do, we discover the fear response has to do with childhood fears of parental fights. This yields important material on which to focus.

When we start a new group or add a new couple (our groups are open-ended) the first order of business is to establish a climate of trust and a feeling of safety. When we lead a workshop for conferences, as at AGPA, with couples who do not know each other and have never met us, we ask each person to introduce himself or herself, tell us what each is feeling as a participant in the group, and what he or she would want to achieve during the experience. When we introduce ourselves, we respond to the same questions. When a new couple enters our group, the same procedure is followed except that, in addition, the other group members are asked how they feel about a new couple joining them. This method has been successful in allaying the apprehension with which most individuals enter groups.

Since the case material will be selected from our ongoing current group, it will be helpful for the reader to know something about each member; the following are thumbnail sketches.

Jane and George have been part of a group for many years;
Jane has had concurrent individual therapy with Jeanette for
two years, and George has experienced family-of-origin therapy early with Virginia Satir and then with Phil. They have
been married for ten years. Jane is Eurasian, born in Hong
Kong, and moved with her mother, half-sister, and English
stepfather to England when she was 8 years old. She was emotionally deprived from infancy, never knew her birth father
and moved away from the family home at age 16. Her adolescence was stormy and defiant and she experimented with
several of the drugs prevalent in England at the time. In her
own words, "Coming from a past with no foundation, I've spent
a large portion of my life exploring different relationships and
life styles." She is still hoping to learn more of the mysterious
circumstances surrounding her origin, and through her work
in therapy "has learned that honesty and having no secrets
hidden in closets makes for a more tranquil life and for a better relationship with the important people in my world."

George is 40 years old, the second oldest male of four children, coming from a Western family characterized by a pos-
sessive and insecure mother and a father who once was a drug
and alcohol abuser. George states, "My wife and I came into
group therapy approximately ten years ago, unaware of any
serious problems between us; the intention was to enhance an
already good marriage. Little did we know, that as time went
by, our pasts would surface to create rifts and difficulties between us. Each of us came from a family in which chemical
dependency, violence, dishonesty, and secrecy were prevalent. Neither of us are chemically dependent or violent, but
we found many of the destructive behavior patterns taught to
us as children and *despised* by us as children creeping into
our relationship. Therapy helped alleviate some of the difficulties, but more importantly gave us tools for dealing with
them in positive ways that afford each of us mutual respect
and dignity, neither of which existed in our families of origin.
It is my belief that, without this help, our marriage would
have crumbled; I am equally convinced that because of it, it
never will."

Judy has had several years of individual therapy before her
arrival in California and one and a half years of group with

Jeanette. She is the third of four children in a middle-class Jewish family she describes as dysfunctional. Her parents were emotionally unavailable and withholding, and remained uninvolved during Judy's school years. In her own words, "My withholding father and competitive mother left me feeling confused, unloved, depressed, and self-destructive. Trusting the love of another person has been a struggle to this very day." Judy, through her efforts, received a degree in Fine Arts when she was 27 and moved to Los Angeles to work in the film industry. She and Doug have been living together for almost two years, and she is having difficulty committing herself to marriage.

Doug had several years of individual therapy as an adolescent and young man after his father, a physician, committed suicide when Doug was 16. He is the third child of four. He has two sisters, six and nine years older, and a brother, two years younger. His sisters were out of the home at the time of his father's death and he became the caretaker in the family. He became involved with drugs, and suffered a breakdown. However, with psychotherapy and a change in life style he recovered and is eager to marry Judy and have a family.

Inez and José had been living together for eighteen months prior to joining the group with a date set for their marriage in June of this year. Inez has had individual therapy before as a result of a depression some years ago, but until José joined her for conjoint sessions with Jeannette, he had never experienced any psychological work. Inez was married when she was 18, has two daughters, 8 and 13, and has been divorced for five years. José was married at 19 for seven years, but the marriage had never been consummated and he was convinced he was impotent. It was only after a neighbor seduced him while he was still married that he realized he could enjoy a sexual relationship. He is the eldest of eight children in a Hispanic family and received no affection or support from his parents who are rigid and very religious. His father is a fundamentalist Protestant minister. Inez is the middle child of five in a Catholic Hispanic family. Her mother is a loving, warm woman who suffered a situational depression in the early years of Inez's childhood. Her father had not been willing to marry her mother until the birth of their fourth child, and this information was held as a secret from the children until they were adults. It created havoc in the family. Inez was raped by a neighbor when she was 8 years old and reports she didn't understand what was happening to her. She told her older sister who informed their parents. They were supportive of her and went on to prosecute the neighbor who was convicted and sent to jail. The fact that her parents accepted her story and were supportive ameliorated at least part of the trauma.

Mary is 27 years old, the oldest of three children in a middle-class Jewish family. She was raised by a controlling and critical mother, and a father who, though more affectionate, was largely absent because he was a busy physician. Mary had individual therapy for two years preceding her marriage to Drew and since her arrival in Los Angeles has had individual and group therapy with Jeanette. She has stated: "Both of my parents were attuned to my material needs but neither was a good role model for expressing feelings or for helping me meet my emotional needs. Consequently, as an adult I have had to battle feelings of loneliness, undesirability, and fear of intimacy and abandonment." Mary urged Drew to come into the couples group because her most pressing problem is her sexual relationship with him; since their engagement four years ago she has frequently been resistant to sex and has lost interest in it. They joined the group "with the goals of exploring and working through Mary's lack of desire, obtaining new options for relating to another sexually, and improving the way we communicate our needs and feelings to one another."

Drew is the middle child of three, the only son in a middle-class Jewish family. He met his wife while in college and the two were married after both were graduated. He has had several years of individual therapy and about six sessions of conjoint with Jeanette before entering the group. He describes himself as follows: "I initially went into therapy because I felt incapable of giving and taking love and affection openly. The closer I got to people the more barriers I put up, leaving me lonely and alienated. I needed to relearn relationship skills because those I recorded from watching my parents fight brutally and consistently were destructive. In addition, I needed to express my intense rage at being ignored while my parents fought and refought the same battles over and over again." The following are excerpts from four different sessions.

Monday evening—June 14, 19—

We have selected this part of the session because it best demonstrates the advantage of insights feedback from couple to couple that could not take place in conjoint therapy or in individual couple therapy. In addition, this session illustrates group process as it leads to profound intrapsychic and interpersonal awarenesses and changes.

George and Jane are continually frustrated by how to end one of their many arguments. Their theme is very familiar to themselves and the group. George pushes for clear statements and expression of feelings on the part of his wife, Jane, and she constantly feels criticized, controlled, and angry. In this instance George complains about her mumbling.

Jeanette points out how important it was for Jane to express her angry feelings.

JANE: I'm not able to, at this point.

JEANETTE: He wants it straight. Wouldn't it be better to tell George how furious you are and that you don't like it?

[Jane at this point is not able to do so. We are aware of the feeling of relief that comes with "getting it off your chest," but are also aware that catharsis is not enough. We see catharsis, in itself, only as a beginning of working through interpersonal difficulties. There ensues further arguing, blaming, accusations of holding onto anger, not listening, etc.]

JANE: I might have listened before. I confess I am not doing that lately. Something stopped in me. I have not been aware of it till now. I always used to put myself in your shoes [George's], trying to understand your point of view—at my expense. Now my energy is in trying to understand myself—just focusing on me.

GEORGE: The way you and I ended was disturbing to me. I was brought up to have closure—it was very important to finish things. I still feel that. I said we each need to be more sensitive. I feel that was a very nice thing for me to say.

JANE: Fine.

GEORGE: What do you mean, fine? You don't sound like it.

JANE: Fine, stop bugging me.

JEANETTE: It seems each of you has to have the last word.

[George pushes for validation of his interest in reaching closure reasonably and Jane replies that she has to speak with him very carefully—using "right" words and hating to do that.]

GEORGE: I don't do that.

JANE: You said it would be nice to end it nicely. You have a certain expectation that goes with it.

GEORGE: I expect a response.

JANE: I gave it to you, O.K. I said, I'm finished.

GEORGE: You're saying you're fed up.

JANE: That's my response.

GEORGE: Why would you give me that response—you must still be mad at me. It must not be finished with you. In our group here, there is closure—a nice feeling to it. I am frustrated. You say you want it to end—I too. We both want the same thing. What's wrong?

[We encourage them to look into themselves, not at the other, indicating the blaming or being right doesn't and hasn't gone anywhere.]

JANE: This is amazing. What comes to my mind is my mother talking. (*Jane makes a bubbly gibberish sound imitating her deceased mother's incessant talking*). I finally would say to her, "Shut up!" Jane laughs out loud in the group.

JEANETTE: Could you say to George when he talks to you, "I hear my mother and it brings back all my terrible resentful feeling?"

JANE: I could say it if I could tie into it—I just now became aware where my feeling is coming from.

[Jane spoke of her being talked at, of how irrational her mother was; how she would try to reason (like with George) and reason would not work. Her mother kept repeating herself (like George does at times) and then Jane would finally say, "Shut up!"]

MARY: Is that where it comes from—that trying to get in George's shoes is at your expense.

JANE: It is.

MARY: So those are your two choices, like with your mother, either agreeing with the other person and sacrificing your

needs or shutting them out. You seem to have only these
two options in dealing with conflict.

JANE: I would try to listen and reason. If that didn't work I
would remove myself [as she did with George and their 9-
year-old daughter]. At other times, I would put myself in
their [others'] situation [shoes], see their points of view,
though at my expense, because my whole focus was on them.
I don't try to understand them. I try to make myself into
them, experience what they experience.

PHIL: Then there's no conflict. You're as one? If you are your
mother and your mother is you, I see this as an attempt
on your part to deal with the conflict, except you, Jane,
give yourself up in the process. I see this as an emergency
coping attempt at the time with your mentally irrational
mother—and I congratulate you—you made it. However,
these two options that Mary mentioned you still use, they
don't fit now.

[We are aware that a person's reaction to early life relationships is played out in their lives—and it impacts the
relationship destructively.

Jane states that her style is different now and that she
doesn't see herself this way or behaving this way in the
group.]

MARY: Maybe this only happens in certain circumstances, where
it gets triggered off for you. The child, Jane, gets triggered
off—like in this instance tonight. George in his own way
was trying to end a fight—and for you it triggered off that
irrational unrestrained nagging memory of your mother—
and maybe in situations like this, you switch to that.

JANE: I agree. Another thing that happens is George's need
for closure, and for me it's not that important.

GEORGE: It is important. Important for you that I *not* do it.

JANE: When I think what's happening—it is that I'm still
angry.

GEORGE: I think you are too.

JANE: Well, how in hell, if I'm still angry, am I going to say,
it's so nice to resolve this now. You're asking me to do what
is impossible to do.

DREW: You feel resolved and you get angry at Jane when she
doesn't respond to your gesture for closure. When I get

done with it, it has no necessary relation to when Mary is done with it. We had an example last night. I remember saying to Mary that I was sorry she couldn't do what I wanted her to do. I accepted that; if I kept pushing . . .

GEORGE: As you talk Drew, I can recall a feeling where I can identify with that. I grew up in a family where there was something my father always did. We'd get into a big argument and when he was ready to end it, to wrap it up, something I try to do with Jane, he would do that. No matter how I tried to continue, he insisted on wrapping it up [closure] and it would infuriate me. I felt controlled—he demanded the last word—to officially end it.

PHIL: Does your awareness of these experiences with your dad, and your insightful connection, help you understand Jane's reaction?

GEORGE: Yes, very much so.

PHIL: What could you now do differently?

GEORGE: Well, what comes to mind is—I could change my urgent need to wrap it up—but I do not want to do that out of fear—the fear would be uh-oh, you don't want to hear that.

JANE: Your talking would trigger my anger.

DREW: Because you talk at her, George, you sort of suck her in and set her up. She feels talked at so much.

MARY: You have the option of telling George you cannot continue right now because you're too angry; that you need to cool down; need some space, but as soon as you can, you will continue. In that way you will be showing George you're really done with it.

JANE: I wouldn't feel attacked.

GEORGE: Do you feel that?

JANE: All the time.

GEORGE: It doesn't come through to me—the way you talk to me.

JANE: I feel put down.

PHIL: She doesn't feel heard—feels controlled—that's like being attacked.

GEORGE: Yes, I hear that.

PHIL: You haven't heard that because Jane tunes you out and hasn't been able to be open with you.

[Jeanette and Phil encourage Jane to talk about her own

feelings—to look into herself and see what has been going on.]

JANE: (*laughs*): I think I'm being courteous letting George go on [ranting like her mother]. Inside, I am fuming—inside I'm wanting to say "Oh, shut up."

PHIL: Exactly like with your mother. When you do that, you're not courteous and you're not listening.

[Jane laughs and Inez states there is a volcano inside.

After a brief meaningful silence, Phil speaks of his excitement about Jane and George's awareness.]

GEORGE: I do too.

JANE: This opens up a lot of stuff that I've not been aware of inside.

Monday evening–July 5, 19–

All four couples are present. The following excerpt deals with anger, the communication, fulfillment of life's need for closeness, and particularly effective or destructive styles on the part of members, attention is paid to options, yearnings, longings, expectations and, naturally, the impact on the relationship and the self-esteem of the members involved.

MARY: Sometimes I think we have a real barrier. You think you are communicating with me and because I don't feel I'm being heard, I get very angry and it gets worse between us. It's how we express our feelings to each other. It's the words we use. I had a fight with Drew an hour ago and I feel very frustrated that I am butting my head with someone I love so much. No matter what I say, I am not getting through, and I am feeling very frustrated.

DREW: I guess I should tell the actual story or it's not going to be clear. We were invited to go to a reunion at Phoenix this weekend where my ex-girlfriend and her husband and child live. I asked Mary if she cared to join me there and she hesitated. I knew that Mary was not going to stay the whole time so I gave her the option. I said to her we are going to Phoenix and I would like to know whether you want me to see them after you leave, or do you want to go with me?

MARY: I don't know if that is a good idea.

[Mary explains that her hesitation was not connected with old jealous feelings. She had dealt with that in previous

therapy. It was that she might not have much time to be
with him. Drew said he wanted his parents to also meet
Laurie and her baby, and also wanted to show his old girlfriend his parents' house.]

DREW: Before I call her I would like to know so that I can
discuss alternatives with Laurie [his ex-girlfriend].

MARY: I figured we would be seeing her and then, in addition
to spending time with her and her baby and husband, we
would also be spending time visiting his mother and I didn't
like that. I have a habit of role-playing fantasies and I proceeded to do this. I said [imitating Drew's mother]: "Oh,
Laurie, it's so good to see you and the baby!" Continuing:
I was making up a dialogue in my head and this is one of
the ways for me to get in touch with my feelings.

[Drew reports that he got very upset and yelled at Mary.
"Why don't you be honest," and she replied, "I am honest,
I am getting in touch with my feelings, and Drew yelled,
"Stop it!"]

MARY: As I was doing the role-playing, I got in touch with
my feeling that I would be there as an appendage to Drew,
and I was already feeling left out, and the thought of this
additional visit to Drew's mother was upsetting me very
much. When you, Drew, said "Stop it," I found it very
offensive.

DREW: When I said why don't you be honest, I meant tell
me what you are feeling and thinking.

MARY: That's what I was trying to tell you, but you said "Stop
it," I felt pushed by you, controlled by you, and I resented
it. You said to me, "Stop it, I don't want to hear that shit,
that crap, and I felt brushed off and it pushed my buttons,
and I really forgot about talking to you about my worry about
being an appendage.

DREW: When I said "Stop it" I wanted to hear what your concern was, and instead you screamed at me.

[Both are doing some mind-reading, some projection.]

JEANETTE: You must have known, Mary, that it was disturbing
to you when you found out that in addition to visiting Laurie and the baby and her husband that you were asked to
also visit his mother with them.

MARY: It was so quick, my reaction. I now know what I was

leading up to and how I felt. Of course, whatever little bit of time we had was being taken up. When you, Drew, told me to cut out this crap and I was stupid, my focus changed. I don't like being blown off. You never said to me in an inquiring way, in a way that invited me to tell you what I was thinking or doing, you just said "cut out the crap." You didn't say it in a voice that says, "I really want to know what it is that you are feeling." Of course, one hour later you apologized to me for just saying "Stop it." I am glad you did and I accepted that, but we are still not resolved.

PHIL: Did you tell Mary the reason you were asking her to stop it was so you could hear and understand her better?

DREW: No. At the time I didn't say that or perhaps didn't fully have that in mind. As I think about it now, as she was doing her role playing, I really wanted to hear what her concern was.

PHIL: As you think about it, do you feel you got your message across?

DREW: No.

PHIL: What stopped you?

DREW: I got so angry when she started to yell at me that I just started to walk out.

PHIL: Did Mary's anger prevent you from getting your message across?

MARY: He gets freaked out when I get angry.

JEANETTE: You started to walk out because you were angry with her explosiveness?

DREW: I didn't want to hear these explosions anymore.

PHIL: Did you believe those explosions were directed at you?

DREW: Yes, of course.

PHIL: Were you exploding at him?

MARY: No, I was just angry being cut off. I was not interested in attacking you, Drew. I just resented being cut off.

JANE: I am reminded about feeling defensive, and when I find myself feeling defensive, I am not able to hear. I also feel or sense humiliation.

MARY: I was not trying to hurt you Drew.

JANE: For me, I can see where Drew would feel that your role-playing was hurtful.

MARY: If that fits, Drew, if the way I was role-playing made you feel hurt, I would have loved for you to tell me that.

JEANETTE: I was also surprised, Mary, that you were not aware that Drew might feel he was being made fun of.

MARY: What did I do?

DREW: I didn't tell you I was feeling ridiculed, I just asked you to stop it in my attempt to understand what it is that you were feeling.

[Things calmed down considerably between Drew and Mary at this time. At this point Phil encouraged Mary and Drew to process the whole thing over again, but to do it more effectively in terms of what they now knew about themselves and each other.]

GEORGE: I want to say I need to work on something.

[We encourage all members to announce if they need time to work.]

Both Mary and Drew processed this experience again before the group. Drew said to Mary, "I talked to Laurie about our impending visit to Phoenix, and I shared with her some ideas of our getting together with them. Would you like to join us?"

Mary indicated that that would be okay with her. She would actually like to see Laurie's baby. Drew at this point said he was thinking, after the visit with her, of taking Laurie and her husband and baby to visit his folks. At which point, Mary said, she was not wild about that idea, and then said to him: "I feel that our time is limited, and there won't be much time for us to be together if we, besides visiting, also take time to go to your mother's house and visit there, too." At which point Drew said: "It is not my plan for all of us to go to my mother's house to have a social event and have lunch. In fact all I was interested in was showing Laurie the house in which my parents live." Again, Mary said she was worried about the time and Drew replied "that is important to me." And then Mary suggested: "How about us visiting Laurie, and then finding out if your folks are going to be home or not, and if they are not there, do it. Perhaps, if your folks are there and the visit would be an extended one, you can go back with Laurie and her husband and child after I leave, because I won't be home the latter part of the weekend." To which Drew replied, "Yes, that's a good idea, and I will be glad to do that."

The whole group, including Mary and Drew, responded in unison, "Wow!" and laughs with relief and joy; both Mary and Drew saying "What happened to us? This is so simple."

DREW: I can't believe that this is so easy.
MARY: I still wonder why we went the other way, and how we escalated things.

This vignette reflects the way we work together in the group, with a strong emphasis on communication that includes the feelings, meanings, styles, and expectations that go on underneath the surface of these exchanges.

Whether members in a couples group look at their sex relationships is in large measure related to how comfortable, competent, open, and specific are the therapists. The following vignette is one small piece of such a session.

Monday evening–July 19, 19–

In their car, on the way home from group, Mary talked of her confusion and frustration regarding her sexual relations with Drew. This in part was triggered during the preceding session by Inez and José who had talked about their wonderful sex compared to their previous marriages.

MARY: As I cried a lot, I remember saying to Drew that I couldn't remember the last time I felt excited about having sex with him.
JEANETTE: How does that make you feel?
DREW: It makes me feel sorry for her.
JEANETTE: But what about you?
DREW: There were times I would have been crushed by that and taken it very personally. But I really don't now.
PHIL: What's happened—a metamorphosis?
DREW: I'm better at expressing what I want, and what I need regardless of what the solution is or what Mary feels.
   [It is obvious that Drew is denying his pain and anger and we talk further to each other about his need to defend himself by repressing the hurt.]
MARY: I don't look forward to sex—I don't anticipate it—that's what I meant—the anticipation, but there are times when

I am turned on by Drew, but not very frequently. That has nothing to do with him. When you approach me and say I want to make love now or I want you to touch my penis, that doesn't do anything for me—or at worst it's "ugh." (*Mary makes a face.*)

PHIL: What comes to mind?

MARY: When he talks like that I hear a child and that's not exciting. He whines a little and doesn't have a passionate look on his face, and I don't like that.

JEANETTE: Are you aware of that, Drew?

DREW: Sometimes I am.

JANE: What do you want, Mary? How about verbalizing to Drew so that he will understand what would make it easy for you to respond?

MARY: I have to preface this by saying I don't know—I could tell Drew all these things I would like—and my resistance still might not go away. I like it when he holds my face, and appears passionate and caresses me, strokes me.

[Mary recalls a planned visit to Phoenix where Drew, as she was trying on her clothes, spontaneously embraced her, kissed her passionately, and said, "I love you."

What followed was an awareness of how tentative they had become in approaching each other, except for moments of spontaneity. Each expressed fears of rejection and searched for explanations. What was very clear was the respect and turn-on, at times, they felt for each other. They kept trying, they said, because they loved each other.]

MARY: I don't need to hear any words. This is me—when I hear him say he wants to make love to me there's an expectation—a standard for me to meet. He wants me to be turned on and I don't at that minute. I get anxious and that's not his fault.

[We find that most men and women, similar to Drew and Mary, believe these expectations come from the other and then react to being controlled by the other. In this instance, each of them had his or her own internal expectation. For Drew, like most men, penile stirrings means immediate action—direct sex. Mary has the expectation that she should immediately be aroused and ready for intercourse.]

JANE: I'm interested in the history of Mary's attitudes toward sex.

MARY: My sexual development was a very healthy one. I danced all my life, was aware of my body—masturbated at a young age and wished a boy could do that for me. I was very open and had many sexual experiences at college, most of which were positive.

JANE: The reason I asked, for myself, I am very protective of my body—that's mine and I have control over it. One of the few things I have control over. But I felt a lot of times that was the guy's interest—my body. The way you talk reminds me of my past.

DOUG: You have expectations of Drew. What are you willing to do?

MARY: I told him what I'd like to do—it is that when I found myself pulling away from him, I would try not to lay it on him. I would tell him I'm finding myself retreating. I get so upset and anxious when that happens. I get hypercritical and seem irritated.

PHIL: You can do more than that. If you find yourself pulling away, you can say, I'd like you to stop, or I don't think I'm really ready to have sex with you now, or I'm not ready but don't stop—I still welcome your reaching out to me. To me these are loving messages because they are straight. Of course, there are other options.

GEORGE: For me this is a wonderful thing to be talking about. All sorts of things about our sex is going through my mind. Communication about sex is a very difficult thing and it's a sticky point for a lot of couples. I can remember a time when Jane was very nervous about my coming on to her because to her it meant we had to make love, have sex. That developed into a bigger problem—I would sense that and pull away, and for a long time we didn't have much of a sex life, finally we addressed that and worked it through.

Two sessions later, on the way home from the group, Drew recalled our asking him and Mary to look deeper into themselves for their own contributions to the dilemma. He made a sincere effort and became aware of the pain he felt as a youngster and adolescent watching helplessly as his parents continued their ugly fighting. He recalled the many occasions which he would try to rescue his mother, seeing her as the victim. His even greater pain in living this period, was that he felt deprived because he never was rewarded with love and appreciation by his mother. Consequently, he made a promise to himself to never invest so fully in a relationship with a woman again. Even though he knows he loves Mary, he is aware that since their engagement he has held back, not expressing the warmth and tenderness that he has been repressing. Mary felt great relief that the problem could no longer be attributed only to her. Important pieces of the puzzle started to come together. His mechanical, tenuous approaches to Mary were manifestations of unconscious and unfinished business with his mother.

Though we are describing mostly what goes on in our couples group, at times we believe in doing a piece of individual work, as it contributes to the couples' functioning. Doug and Judy, as compared to the other couples, have seemed tentative in expressing their open differences with each other. We believe Doug, for one, has been fearful of angry feelings. This session is a positive step from him in that direction. Also, this session features some countertransference that has been handled.

Monday—August 9, 19—
All four couples are present.

Doug begins the meeting by telling both his girlfriend Judy, and Jeanette that he felt attacked during the last group.

GEORGE: You seem very angry at Jeanette.
DOUG: I am.
JEANETTE: I remember in the last session it didn't become fully clear, till near the end about what I was reacting to and I said to myself, "Doug must be angry at me." I recalled, Doug, that you had a friend visiting in your house who was overstaying his leave and Judy was quite upset at the time. I saw you as not taking care of Judy and I realize now that Judy was not taking care of herself.
DOUG: You attacked me.
JEANETTE: At that moment, I knew my assumption was all wrong and, again, I became aware that Judy wasn't really taking care of herself.

[We would like to emphasize here that what we try to encourage in our work with couples in our groups is the freedom to comment; to say what they feel and think at all times.]

PHIL: Jeanette, as you think about it, what happened that you didn't say anything at that moment when you became aware of what you were doing?

JEANETTE: It was going on so fast and it was near the end. I didn't think fast enough, though the thought did come to my mind that Doug was probably angry. It sounded as I listened to myself as if I was accusing you.

GEORGE: I, too, felt that way; that you were accusing Doug.

We believe that part of the feeling and building of trust comes from the therapists, openly admitting their errors, sharing the process of what they believe is going on with them and not being defensive. We process our own behavior and feelings in the group and own up to them as soon as we become aware of them.

We see ourselves as models for the group members, many of whom have not experienced "mother" and "father" confronting one another, taking responsibility for our productions and ending up friends with growing trust and respect. There have been times when we have had heated exchanges with each other and like members of the group, we process these exchanges and get in touch with some unfinished business of our own. The "magic" of taking responsibility and looking into one's "own stuff" leads to trust, cohesiveness, intimacy, and growing self-esteem. Sometimes, when modeling these human interactions with each other, group members believe we are "acting" to demonstrate this model; by processing our own misunderstandings we provide another chance at identification where better modeling is made possible. Obviously, when the therapists disagree, members are stimulated to talk of their fears, their taking sides, their recollections at what they saw and experienced with their parents.

GEORGE: If I hadn't heard your voice and had just been looking at your face, Doug, I would not have known that you were angry. I was struck by your smile and "looking so sweet."

DOUG: It seemed humorous to me; I like vaudeville.

PHIL: Doug's being super reasonable, being humorous, was a defense, obviously, that he had learned to use in coping with his angry feelings or his inability to openly express his angry feelings. Doug, were you aware that you were smiling?

DOUG: Yes, I smile all the time.

JEANETTE: As you think about it, what were you covering up? Sometimes a smile disguises other feelings like anger, hurt, or distrust.

DOUG: I don't know.

GEORGE: I see you hurt or nervous.

DOUG: Nervous.

JEANETTE: That's what I mean.

PHIL: Could you tell us, Doug, something about your back and forth experiences (transactions in your family) where you learned to cover up.

DOUG: Sure. I kept getting strong messages from my parents as they would say to me, raising their voices, "don't raise your voice; don't get angry; don't question me."

PHIL: How did you cope? I mean these were very important, powerful people in your life and you had to find a way to make it in the world. How did you do that? What were your survival reactions?

DOUG: I felt frustrated and I became rebellious. I became involved with drugs and alcohol.

JEANETTE: What about being depressed?

DOUG: Yes.

JUDY: When he was 20, he had a breakdown.

[At first Jeanette and Phil had some concern about Doug's confidentiality boundaries being violated by Judy. But Doug said it was okay. Phil felt it important to quickly support Doug.

PHIL: Your breakdown, among other things, was an emergency coping. It was a way of reacting to stress and a way of coping also. It enabled you to be alive and to get out of the situation. Undoubtedly, the effect of alcohol and drugs as well affected your perception, your integrative mechanisms, and the availability of other options.

DOUG: I am not sure it was all connected with my childhood history and experiences. It is not clear to me. My father

was a physician and had committed suicide five years before, I had spent a tremendous amount of time taking care
of my mom and sister.

JANE: I don't know much regarding your father and for that
matter about your family. Did your father suicide in the
house?

DOUG: My father suicided in the house. My parents were very
loving and I had two older sisters and a younger brother.

[It is obvious that Doug's father's suicide was painful to
his whole family. There were stresses in the individuals and
in the family system, yet Doug states that his parents were
loving and presents a somewhat rosy picture. This, again
confirms for us that Doug was and is not really free to say
what he feels and thinks, in fact, this is a style or rule in
the family. It seems quite probable that there are secrets
in Doug's family for this tremendous discrepancy to exist.
We are arriving at some guidelines for his work. In our
work with Doug, we realize these denials are his current
defense and were necessary during his youth as a means of
coping.]

GEORGE: Were you the rebellious one?

DOUG: In the early years, I was not rebellious. I believe now
it was a combination of stresses in my household and too
much partying. I did not take care of myself.

[Upon inquiry he talked of his therapy, prescribed medication, ten days in the hospital, one year of outpatient
therapy three times a week, and then returning for a year
to live with his mother's sister. We also talked about his
interest in music and how that helped him a great deal.]

DOUG: Part of the reason I don't get excited now comes from
the catastrophic results I had. I had become explosive to
the extreme and I am scared of that.

JEANETTE: Are you blaming yourself? Are you saying that your
rebelliousness and anger caused you to have a breakdown?

DOUG: When I was having my breakdown, I felt hyperactive.

JEANETTE: Are you afraid that if you let go now this might
happen again?

DOUG: It's been a fear of mine.

JEANETTE: I can understand.

GEORGE: What is your picture of a nervous breakdown?

[George is inquiring about the meaning that Doug gave to having a nervous breakdown and is also trying to get his own meaning by his freedom in asking this question.]

DOUG: I became psychotic. I had hallucinations. A lot of them were visual; I was paranoid. There was a whole chain of events and perhaps some of it was drug-related. I feel real good in sharing this with the group.

[The group responded with appreciation, acknowledgment and empathy.]

JEANETTE: I want to encourage you to do all of that here, to take a chance and express yourself like you, Doug, were able to do in the beginning of the session with me.

A major part of our philosophy is to process as if we were in a nurturing functional family. There isn't anything that cannot be talked about in the group. We were very pleased that George was free in asking Doug about his picture of his psychotic breakdown and that the rest of the group was equally free. We think this candid exchange in and of itself had in it respect and trust and a vote of confidence for Doug. There weren't really any rules which in effect said "oh, no, this is to dangerous, this will upset our client." In a well-functioning family or group, the old taboos surrounding physical, sexual, substance abuse and emotional problems can be explored and surmounted.

Conclusion

We hope the reporting of these excerpts will give our readers some ideas as to what can be accomplished with the treatment of couples in a group. Perhaps this paper will be a stimulus to others to experiment with this modality.

13

Family Network Groups

Uri Rueveni, Ph.D.

One of the roles that family therapists need to engage themselves in when working with dysfunctional family systems is that of helping members of the family group to reconnect with sources of emotional support available within the nuclear or extended family network system (Rueveni 1979, 1982, 1984). Intervention approaches that can help family members become engaged and involved in a process leading toward greater mobilization of support and empowerment require the use of techniques designed to enable the dysfunctional family group to heal. Empowerment can be viewed as a process that enables members of the family group as well as the entire family system to strengthen coping skills and abilities.

Although an empowerment process can take place when one works with an individual or a couple, the focus here is on empowerment techniques that can be employed with a group, a family, and/or an extended family or community during a crisis. Encounter techniques provide group and family therapists with opportunities for maximal system empowerment, particularly when working with crisis-laden family groups (Rueveni and Speck 1969). When a family member experiences severe emotional crisis, where desperation and feelings of hopelessness and helplessness are expressed by various family members, the use of encounter techniques can and does facilitate and increase the opportunities for greater crisis resolution and empowerment.

Involving the Family Network in the Empowerment Process

One of the most powerful methods of empowering the family in crisis is via the mobilization of its network support system. The networking process can unfold its effects when a family in crisis is able to call on its extended family and friendship system for help and support. Much like a call for a familiar family reunion, family members can prepare lists of friends and relatives and invite them for a three- to four-hour meeting targeted specifically to helping resolve a difficult family crisis. To help the family prepare for such a meeting, a team consisting of two to three professional networkers, therapists, or group facilitators are usually needed. Team members can meet either at the family's home or in any convenient setting where plans can be made for the family network intervention session. The goals for the network meeting vary according to the type of family crisis at hand, but usually include attempts at reducing the magnitude of crisis and efforts at engaging family and extended family members in a dialogue focusing on the development of available alternatives for crisis resolution via the formation of temporary support groups.

The Network Intervention Empowerment Process

A fully mobilized network ideally needs to consist of between forty and fifty members who can initially meet for four to five hours and will be available to reconvene for additional meetings if the need arises. Such meetings can take place at home or any other location the family or team can agree upon. In the past, network meetings were held at homes of family or friends, in hospital or clinic settings, in schools, churches, and community recreation facilities.

In preparation for the network meeting, team members need to adequately prepare an intervention strategy that will be primarily based on data obtained from the initial discussion of the family's concerns as well as their own clinical judgment as to how to intervene and accomplish the empowerment, the strengthening of the family's ability to resolve the existing crisis and obtain support while doing so. To be able to function smoothly and effectively, team members need to select a leader who would lead the networking process while being aided and assisted by other team members. For a large network meeting two or three professionals will constitute the minimum requirements for a team.

Any large group meeting to include a networking meeting will usually proceed in predictable phases that need to be understood by team members as they become involved in the efforts of helping the network be effective in its empowerment process. The appropriate sequence of the network phases have been described elsewhere (Rueveni 1979; Speck and Attneave 1973). Basically, it includes a phase of meeting and getting to know the rest of the network, which has been termed the *retribalization phase*; the *polarization* phase, during which time disagreements among network members develop; *mobilization*, a phase where active searches for solutions are being undertaken by some network participants; *depression*, a phase where a temporary lull in activities develops; a *breakthrough* phase where active alternative proposals for crisis resolution are being considered in support groups, leading toward the last phase of *exhaustion-elation*, where a feeling of accomplishment and hopefulness is being expressed by most members, including members of the nuclear family.

Network sessions can often remain "stuck" in a polarized or depression phase without a sufficient amount of energy among its members being available for moving toward the breakthrough phase and its consequent phase of exhaustion-elation.

Themes Underlying the Intervention Strategies

Although planning for effective intervention that will help mobilize and empower a network is issue-specific and is dependent on the nature of the family conflict to be resolved, the themes of anger, loss, love, and forgiveness need to be introduced and discussed during many of the network sessions. Of particular importance are network sessions mobilized around family members who experience depression and have considered or attempted suicide. Such issues as a family member's inability to express anger in a nondestructive manner, to be able to effectively accept and deal with the loss of loved ones or one's own potential death, to be able to accept and receive love and be intimate with one's spouse or children, and to be able to accept forgiveness as a healing process in life are of immense importance to all of us, particularly to families in crisis. Such family members, more often than not, have great difficulties in working out productive solutions that can, if implemented, lead toward self- as well as family empowerment.

The skills of the network intervention team come into play as they are able to channel the energies and efforts that begin to take place as the network assembles. As people mill around and meet others, team members can often suggest that members of the nuclear family initiate a "sing-along," where all can participate in singing or humming along with a favorite family melody. As the network members settle into their chairs, members of the nuclear family can form a small inner circle where they begin to share some of their own concerns as well as needs from the invited network of friends and relatives. As the phase of polarization occurs, team members need to be able to acknowledge the different points of view that exist, and that in fact it is out of these different ideas and needs being expressed that alternatives can be explored. During the depression phase team members need to encourage an additional effort for continued communication among family members, as well as their network. Often during this phase, team members can initiate one or more experiences that can involve the participants to a greater extent with the four themes discussed earlier. For example, during a network meeting aimed at mobilizing and empowering support for a family struggling with a depressed and suicidal young woman, team members encouraged a verbal confrontation between the mother and daughter. As the exchange of angry feelings became increasingly heated, the daughter threatened to kill herself in the near future, provoking the mother to hug the daughter while sobbing intensely, expressing both anger and tenderness toward her. A dramatic exchange of feelings followed between many family members and the invited network, the main themes of which included the expression of anger and the feelings of loss and mourning. As this particular network session ended, the themes of love and forgiveness dominated the final phases of the meeting.

In another case, a network session assembled for the family of a young man who had previously attempted suicide, angry feelings were exchanged between father and son concerning the father's unfairness toward the son and his "favoring" of the oldest brother. Both son and father were expressive in their vehement anger toward each other, taking a blaming stance. Following a brief consultation with team members, the team leader suggested that the father "pretend he was dead," and requested that the son as well as others in the family network eulogize the now "dead" father. The young man approached his father, who was now lying on the floor covered up with a sheet over his body, and began to sob. Within a short time he expressed feelings of love and caring toward his father. At the conclusion of this ceremony both father and son were able to hug each other, which by their own admission they were unable to do for years. Following this experience, both continued in a dialogue with the help of many in the network, aimed toward investing additional efforts in improving their relationship.

The use of simulated loss experiences such as the one just described is a powerful intervention particularly during large network assemblies. The energies expressed in the form of the range of feelings of love, anger, loss and forgiveness being expressed by both family and network members are effective in mobilizing the network to explore further these issues with a particular focus on improving and strengthening previously dysfunctional relationships. When some of the issues that families struggle with during a network session become clear and "exposed," team members need to suggest that network members form support groups around members of the nuclear family. A support group can consist of between five and ten members who meet to discuss available options and alternatives for resolving the immediate family crisis. Such support groups may agree to reconvene without depending on the team to conduct or lead them. In fact, it is desirable that support groups form their own agenda around each of the ailing family members and utilize the team members as consultants.

It is important for team members to encourage the network participants to be available if their is a need for any future network meetings.

The effectiveness of this process can be attributed to a number of factors. The ability of team members to plan carefully and execute skilfully effective intervention strategies that can help family members mobilize the network constitutes one important factor. The availability of an "action-oriented" group of people who can become actively involved with members of the ailing family, even on a temporary basis, is another factor that contributes to effective networking. Another important factor contributing to effective empowerment is the degree of desperation as well as the ability of family members themselves to "risk" exposing their often severe dysfunctional emotional and relationship problems and concerns in front of a large group of family and friends. Networking is a process that does not and cannot encourage or promise confidentiality. The painful, often secretive nature of dysfunctional relationships is not a desirable commodity during the network process. This process requires openness, and often public exposure of difficulties, which, if not shared with the entire body of participants, may hinder at times the possibility of effective empowerment.

The main role of team members is to be able to encourage the rebuilding of self-strength and self-confidence through rebuilding one's own relationships with other family members and friends. A goal as noble as this some may argue might take a lifetime. In my experience, the networking process can allow people, particularly those who experience severe crises, to initiate steps aimed toward the accomplishment of the previously stated goals.

Case Vignettes

The vignettes presented here are intended to demonstrate the utilization of network intervention in a variety of family crisis situations.

Facilitating a Mother-Son Disengagement

At 24 Joe quit his graduate studies, following the death of his father, and returned to live at home with his 64-year-old mother and 20-year-old sister. Since his return home Joe had refused to go to work, stating that he was not going to let his mother push him to work as she had his father. Joe was determined to make life difficult for his mother. He would wait for her to prepare his meals when she returned from work, sleeping during the day and playing music all night long. Mother, on the other hand, was unassertive and unable to control her son's often irrational behavior. Joe's sister, Debra, felt helpless, finding herself drawn often to the constant conflicts and fights between her own mother and brother. The family was referred for a network intervention session by a team of family therapists, who felt that the mobilization of Joe's family system might provide additional resources for helping Joe and his mother and sister reduce the conflicts in the family. During the first network session, attended by over fifty network members, a variety of techniques were used by the intervention team. To speed up group cohesion and greater intermember familiarity, as well as to prepare the entire network toward the tasks at hand, certain warm-up rituals were utilized.

The Network Speech. The group team leader greeted the participants and outlined briefly the purpose for the meeting, challenging the entire group to become involved in the unfolding events as they were going to be described by family members and others who were familiar with the nature and scope of the family conflicts. The leader indicated the uniqueness of this effort in that he and the team were counting on the network's help in creating favorable conditions that in turn would allow members of the immediate family access to an increasing number of alternatives and options in their effort for crisis resolution. The leader briefly outlined the unfolding network phases and prepared the group for the need to later on form support groups for each of the three family members.

The Milling Ritual. The entire network group was asked to mill around the room and introduce themselves to as many members as possible. Following a brief period of time the group members were instructed to pair up with an individual standing nearby, learn their partner's first name, and on cue face each other and scream each other's first name. This activity usually creates an increase in group energy via the expenditure of a combined physical activity with the use of one's voice.

The Family Song. Members of the family were asked to lead the network in a favorite melody. The group members held hands and chose the theme song from the movie "Fiddler on the Roof." As the members sang the melody Joe's mother began sobbing and was held and comforted by her younger sister.

The rituals described above were helpful in speeding up the network's retribalization phase, preparing the group for a greater level of involvement.

The Inner-Outer Group Ritual. Members of the family were asked to form an inside circle while the rest of the network of relatives and friends sat in an outer circle. Family members were asked by the team leader to describe briefly their own perception of the problem. Joe felt "attacked" by his mother, while his mother and Debra expressed feelings of desperation in their inability to help Joe and the constant sense of frustration and conflict that existed in the family. Following a brief period, members of the outside circle were asked to sit inside the circle while the family members were instructed to take the outer circle, listening to the discussions.

This ritual frequently led the network to its needed polarization phase, since members expressed different points of view, as indeed was the case with this network. Joe's family, including his aunts and uncles, as a whole were critical of him. On the other hand, some of Joe's younger cousins and other network members were more supportive of Joe.

Whose Side Are You On? In order to facilitate greater involvement and input, network members are often confronted by the team as to whose side they would take. When this question came up, many of Joe's aunts and uncles clearly felt supportive of his mother, while some of Joe's younger cousins and other members supported Joe himself. Similar questions to be asked during this polarization phase are: Are there any secrets in this family? Who else is having a problem in this family? or What is the problem in this family? This type of inquiry by team members usually can lead to a greater amount of input and a greater variety of points of view with regard to the concerns at hand.

Men's Group/Women's Group. Another variation of getting the network members to mobilize their differences and to be able later on to come up with a more coherent and coordinated intervention strategy is for the team to suggest that two main subgroups could form temporarily and discuss the issue independently. A group of many of Joe's men friends and family formed around Joe discussing some of their concerns with him. Another group of women formed around Debra and her mother. The groups met for a while producing some constructive discussions and suggestions. However, these groups were not able to break completely the existing impasse, since the network seemed stuck in a depression phase. Under these circumstances the team strategized a series of rituals designed to break the impasse and possibly lead the network toward a breakthrough phase.

A Sculpting Ritual. Team members agreed to utilize and choreograph a sculpting ritual involving Joe, Debra and their mother. Debra was asked how she could demonstrate nonverbally her present position in her family. She immediately chose to stand in the middle between her mother and Joe. The team asked both to push with their shoulders and attempt to "squeeze" her physically as much as they felt they needed or wished to do so. Debra was asked how it felt to be pushed by both her mother on one hand and her brother on the other. She felt she wished she could get out of the bind and leave. Debra was encouraged to push Joe and get out of her current

predicament. She replied that she could not push him since
he was too strong, and if she did push him he might hurt her.
Since she was unable to push him, the three stood there, each
feeling helpless to do anything or to move anywhere. The
sculpting ritual had made it clear to all network members the
difficult bind all three family members were involved with.
The team members strategized a follow-up ritual aimed at
helping both Debra and Joe initiate a symbolic disengagement
from home.

Breaking Out of the Circle. Group members were asked to
form a tight circle first around Joe's sister, who in turn was
asked to attempt to break out of the circle. Members were
instructed to resist this breakout attempt. Included in the circle were Joe and his mother. Following a few minutes of a
fairly strong physical expenditure of energy, the sister was able
to break out of the circle, receiving much support from many
in the group. Immediately following this experience Joe was
instructed to do the same thing, which he was able to accomplish. This ritual represented for both Joe and his sister a symbolic disengagement from home. It also was discussed in the
group and acknowledged by Joe and his sister as well as welcomed by the mother, who expressed her wish and hope that
Joe indeed could leave home. This ritual increased the group
members' involvement and broke the impasse of the network's
depression phase.

The Death Ritual. Throughout the network phases team members felt that both Joe and his mother were engaged and bonded
to such extent that their relationship was mutually self-destructive and hurtful. Mother needed to initiate a process
whereby she could "let go" of her son, while being supported
in doing so by her own family and friends. Joe's ability to break
out of the circle provided the energy for mother to marshal
some additional strengths and face her feelings of fear and possible loss toward her son. The death ceremony usually can
provide a powerful experience for the expression of loss, grief,
love, and forgiveness. In order to perform this ritual, Joe was
asked to lie on the floor and was covered by a white sheet.
Mother was instructed to kneel beside her "dead" son and express any feelings she had for him. Mother began sobbing,

sharing her feelings of sorrow and misery, as well as the promise she had made to her own father prior to his death, that she would take care of Joe, his only grandson.

Mother proceeded to express feelings of anger toward Joe for giving her "torture and misery" and that she felt it was time for him to find a job and leave home. Other family members as well as friends approached Joe and expressed mostly feelings of support and willingness to help him.

Following this ritual, Joe, Debra, and mother were able to share with the network their feelings from participating in the ritual. Joe felt that a lot of people cared for him. Both mother and Debra felt that although it was difficult for them to go through the ritual, they were more encouraged following the experience.

Support Group Formation. Following the death ritual, network members formed three support groups, where Joe, Debra, and their mother had an opportunity to share as well as receive support and ideas as to what alternatives they might need to consider in the weeks to come. Mother's support group encouraged her to change the locks at home and not to let Joe sleep there any more. She was encouraged to maintain daily contact with members of her support group and not to "give in" to her son's often "irrational demands."

Joe's group members had arranged for him to sleep at a friend's home, as well as to begin a process of helping him find a job.

Debra's group was instrumental in supporting her need to return to school and resume her social life without feeling overwhelmed by guilt in leaving her mother and brother.

The follow-up of this case indicated that while for the first seven months following the network Joe had the most difficult time in adjusting to a new life style, both his mother and sister made significant progress toward leading a much less conflictual daily life. Following a short hospitalization stint and some therapy, Joe was able to live away from home and to develop a more constructive relationship with his family.

The "Stuck" Professional

Another example of how effective network intervention can be at facilitating disengagements comes from a case where a therapist who had been working with a 34-year-old single woman for a period of five years in weekly therapy sessions decided to terminate them.

During the discussions on termination, the patient claimed that she wished to continue forever with her therapist and threatened suicide if he let go of her. During the last session with her therapist she proceeded to slash her wrist and destroyed much of his office furniture. Following a brief hospitalization, the therapist was interested to explore the possibility of involving himself, his patient, and a large support system of family and friends assembled at the patient's home. The purpose of the network group was to initiate a new ritual where the therapist would publicly state his intentions to terminate therapy in front of the group consisting of his peers, the patient's family, and ex-therapists, friends of the two. The goals of this network were to separate the two as well as to provide a supportive group for the patient so that self-destructive options could be minimized.

The "Good-bye" Ritual. During the network session the team prepared the therapist to bid his farewell to his patient, to say "good-bye" and leave the meeting. The therapist was able to express his warm and affectionate feelings for his patient, indicating all the positives about her and explaining his reasons for the need for her to seek a new therapeutic relationship. When he left, the network group members remained to discuss the implications of the loss to the patient, a process that finally led to an initial exploration of constructive alternatives for this patient. In this network, as in many others, the powerful effect of the group involvement, particularly during the support group meeting with this patient, provided her with encouragement as well as new energies to be able to minimize her anger and feelings of self-destructiveness and to seek alternative courses of action.

Attempting to Prevent Self-Destructive Acts by Mobilizing the Network Support

The Case of Linda

Linda was 24-years-old and divorced when her father found her overdosed in her apartment. Following a brief hospitalization Linda's parents were interested in exploring the possibility of conducting a network intervention session in their home. During the home visit team members discussed the goals, rationale, and procedures for mobilizing a family network session with Linda, her parents, and her younger brother. The family agreed that the primary goals for the network was to mobilize the family's support system and consider alternatives that would reduce the possibilities of another suicidal attempt on Linda's part. The family was able to mobilize over fifty members from its extended family and friendship system. During the two network sessions (conducted two weeks apart) team members were able to use a number of psychodramatic techniques and rituals instrumental in helping the network mobilize and reach a breakthrough.

Early in the first session mother and daughter found themselves in conflict over Linda's recent divorce. Linda blamed her mother for meddling in her marriage, while the mother felt that Linda was too passive and did not stand up to her husband. The mother seemed dominant and controlling, while Linda was unable to stand up to her, claiming that she would rather be dead than controlled by her dominating mother. The father was passive and took his daughter's side. To allow Linda an opportunity to express her feelings toward her mother, the team utilized a series of techniques involving both mother and daughter.

Stepping On the Chair. Linda was asked to step on the chair while her mother knelt looking up toward her daughter. This ritual allowed Linda to express her feelings toward her mother, since she was in a physically dominant (higher) position than her mother, who was now looking up toward her daughter. Later on the mother was instructed to ask her daughter to help her, while the daughter was instructed to reach out to-

ward her mother only when she felt her mother expressed
genuine feelings.

Alter Ego Dialogue. In this psychodramatic technique two team
members spoke each for either mother or daughter. Linda and
her mother were instructed to confirm or deny the feelings
expressed by their alter egoes. This ritual allowed for deeper
exchange of feelings each had about the other.

During the two network sessions with this family Linda was
able to find new friends and return to psychotherapy with little need to take her own life, while her parents were able to
work out their marital problems later on in couple therapy.

The efforts of the support group members who assembled
around Linda, her father, and her mother in three separate
groups provided the initial needed support for each. The support groups met once weekly for a period of a month, enabling
Linda and her family to have a new beginning, where blame
was replaced with dialogue, and severe self-destructiveness on
Linda's part was gradually replaced by her decision to initiate
new, more productive goals for her own career as well as for
her social life.

Using Religious Rituals

When a network group session is conducted at home, or in a community facility such as a church or a synagogue, there is an opportunity for team members to utilize opening or ending of session
rituals that can bring both family and friendship network group
members closer together more rapidly.

In a network assembled to help a 22-year-old, depressed black
woman who felt extremely rejected following her breakup with
her boy friend, the team asked the family's minister to join
the network in blessing the group. The minister, whose church
was across the street from the patient's family's home, arrived
at the session with a large group of his parishioners and was
warmly welcomed by the young woman and the entire network. At the end of the session, which was effectively used
in helping the young woman, the minister delivered a farewell
blessing, serving as a moving, emotional, and productive cli-

max for members of this family, particularly since they were very religious.

Another example of a religious ritual occurred during a network assembled to help a 25-year-old drug addict. Meeting at home on Friday evening, the family practiced the traditional Jewish ritual of the lighting and blessing of two candles. The patient's brother was a rabbinical student, who agreed to perform the ceremony and welcome the Sabbath with the entire network joining in the song of blessing the Sabbath. In this particular network the nonverbal confrontation between the father and son was utilized, as well as the death ceremony, where the son eulogized his father. These rituals helped the network mobilize toward a breakthrough phase where, following two network sessions, the son joined a drug-abuse facility and made substantial progress toward his recovery.

Does Mother Love Me?

In a network assembled to help Joyce, a 45-year-old, depressed woman, the network team decided to use two rituals designed to facilitate a long-overdue encounter between Joyce and her deceased mother, who according to Joyce never loved her the way she loved Joyce's sister. In addition, Joyce's husband was passive and dependent on his own mother, creating resentment on Joyce's part.

> *The Empty Chair Ritual.* Adapted from gestalt work, this popular ritual required both Joyce and her sister to face an empty chair and to communicate their feelings toward their mother, who was listening to them but could not directly respond verbally. This ritual allowed Joyce to complete her grief work by letting her mother know how much she loved her. Her sister confirmed those feelings. In addition, the group leader asked Joyce to reverse roles and take her mother's position. Speaking for her mother, Joyce was able to confirm her mother's strong feelings of love. Many in the network supported Joyce in her struggle to reexperience what seemed like a cathartic and positive experience.

> *The Rope Ritual.* The second focus of the group was to allow Steve, Joyce's husband to acknowledge his excessive depen-

dency on his mother and create the condition that would allow him to initiate a slow disengagement process from her.

A rope was tied to both Steve's and his mother's waists. Steve was told by the team that he was too engaged and dependent on his mother. He was asked what were his plans with regard to this "umbilical cord" attached to his belly-button. Initially Steve resisted any suggestion from the group that he should remove the cord. Later on he agreed to do so, symbolically indicating a possible breakthrough in his relationship with his mother. The follow-up of this case indicated that following the network, the relationships of both Steve and Joyce improved significantly. Steve's mother seemed to welcome the change, too.

Summary

In this chapter an attempt was made to describe the family network intervention as an empowerment process designed to mobilize energies for families in severe emotional crisis. The techniques and rituals described have been used by practitioners in various group settings, using encounter, gestalt, psychodrama, and family therapy sessions.

When encounter techniques and rituals can be used to accomplish a specific therapeutic goal, they become an important tool for clinicians who are interested in promoting effective use of groups, particularly in family network intervention work.

Section 2

**Behavioral and Directive
Group Psychotherapies**

14

Behavior Therapy in Groups

George Bartzokis, M.D.;
Robert Paul Liberman, M.D.;
and Robert Hierholzer, M.D.

The work of behaviorally oriented clinicians with therapy groups is distinguishable from other approaches by its emphasis on (1) *specifying problems and goals* in concrete, behavioral terms; (2) using *principles of learning* to facilitate behavioral change; and (3) *measuring change* in behavior from the problematic to the desirable. The clinical application of behavioral and learning principles with therapy groups was stimulated by experiments with contrived laboratory groups, in which contingencies of reinforcement were shown to powerfully influence the sequencing of conversations, the contribution of group members, and the distribution of status and leadership among the group members.

The initial focus on specifically and concretely defining the clin-

This paper was prepared in part with support from NIMH research grant MH 30911 and NIMH research grant MH 14584.

ical problems of patients leads the behavior group therapist to an elaboration of therapeutic goals for each individual group member and for the group as a whole. Goal-planning is a mutual, collaborative effort between the behavior therapist and the patient and is often begun during intake sessions held before referral to the group. A thorough understanding of behavioral principles permits the therapist to make "working," clinical hypotheses about the environmental influences that maintain problem behaviors and interfere with patients' adaptive functioning. These hypotheses are usually confirmed or disconfirmed as the group experience unfolds and a plan of treatment is formulated in collaboration with the patient. Principles of learning, such as positive and negative reinforcement, modeling, shaping, extinction, punishment, satiation, time-out from reinforcement, prompting, stimulus control, fading, and counterconditioning, are then used as *treatment tactics and strategies.*

The development of a simple but reliable recording and measurement system for monitoring the target behaviors provides an opportunity to evaluate *therapeutic progress.* The therapist and patients in the group should frequently review their progress for decisions about changing goals and interventions. The single most important feature of behavior therapy is its inextricable bond with empiricism through measurement of clinical change. The clinical implication of empiricism is that a technique is used only when it has an effective, quantifiable impact on behavior, an approach that demands technical flexibility on the part of the therapist.

Advantages of Behavioral Group Therapy

If we assume that psychotherapy is a learning process, then group therapy affords some natural advantages over individual therapy for learning new behaviors and attitudes. For example, much of our learning goes on through the process of imitation, also called modeling, or identification. In the group situation, each individual has a variety of social and role models to imitate and hence the potentially assimilable repertoire is much greater than in individual therapy. It is also known that imitation occurs more rapidly and thoroughly when the models have features in common with the imitator;

thus having peers present, in addition to a therapist, facilitates observational learning.

Adaptive behavior is strengthened as it is reinforced by the social environment. There are many sources of reinforcement in the group—the group itself, the individual co-members and the therapist(s)—and some may be more effective than others. Finally, the stimulus situation in group therapy is closer to naturally occurring social situations than that in individual treatment. Generalization of what is learned in group therapy to real life situations should occur more readily. There is also the opportunity, to structure the group therapy situation so that it closely simulates the problematic situations of the patient(s), using various members of the group in role-playing or in scenes where behavioral rehearsal reenacts stressful or demanding interpersonal encounters.

Types of Behavioral Group Therapy

There are two general categories of behavioral approaches to group therapy. The earliest efforts were made by those clinicians who infused behavioral specification, recording, and technology into conventional, nondirective, or unstructured group formats. In this approach, behavioral techniques were superimposed upon the ongoing group dynamics that had unfolded without prestructuring by the leader. Many of these clinicians were themselves trained in the analytic, nondirective modes of doing therapy and developed expertise in behavioral principles at a later stage of their careers. The second type of approach, which has gained in popularity, involves the structuring of the group format in ways that maximize the directed input of behavioral techniques, with less encouragement of spontaneous group process. The approaches differ in the degree to which the leader is directive in structuring and prompting what happens in the group.

Group therapy formats in which the leader is strongly directive are structured by the leader with objectives for behavioral change planned prior to the session. Spontaneous and free-flowing group interactions may be discouraged by the leader if they do not promote progress toward predetermined clinical objectives for the group members. Invariably, group dynamics such as cohesiveness do continue to develop, even in behaviorally structured groups, and facilitate the learning that goes on at a more explicit level.

Behavior therapy groups, with varying degrees of directive structuring by the leader (see Liberman et al. 1986), have been evaluated for process and outcome in controlled research (Falloon 1981). One aim of this investigation was to elucidate the role of patients' attraction to the leader and for the group as a whole in promoting effective social functioning, enhancing self-esteem, and in reducing attrition from group therapy. The patients were randomly assigned to one of three conditions: (1) group discussion: (2) role rehearsal and modeling: and (3) role rehearsal and modeling, plus behavioral homework assignments.

It was hypothesized that the structured and directive group therapy approach that promoted positive interpersonal contact during therapy sessions, through modeling and role-playing techniques, would foster greater group cohesiveness than the spontaneous discussion approach where constructive problem-solving statements concerning social interaction were simply reinforced by the leader. Falloon reported that the attraction to the group and to the leader were significantly greater in the modeling and behavioral rehearsal groups than in the discussion group. In all groups patients were initially attracted more to the leaders than to the group, but in the role-rehearsal groups, attraction for the group caught up within three or four sessions and remained at a high level. In contrast, group cohesion in the discussion groups never approximated patients' level of attraction for the leaders. Moreover, patients in the behaviorally directed groups demonstrated greater improvement of interpersonal social functioning, greater self-esteem and lower rates of dropping out. The addition of behavioral assignments yielded improvements over and above role rehearsal and modeling.

Behavioral Methods in Unstructured Group Therapy

A variety of behavioral methods have been used in conventional group therapy settings in which there is little or no interference by the leader in the spontaneous group interaction. Verbal prompting and reinforcement have been used to increase "personal" and "group-centered" references made by a wide variety of group therapy patients. In these groups, whenever desired responses occurred, the therapist "rewarded" patients by giving verbal acknowledgment or approval. As another example of the utilization of a learning principle in conventional group therapy, silences were effectively eliminated in a group of chronic psychotics by surreptitiously introducing a noxious noise whenever the group fell silent for more than ten seconds. The noise was turned off as soon as a group member broke the silence; thus the group avoided the aversive stimulus by increasing their talk.

Shapiro and Birk (1967) showed how systematic, pre-planned use of approval and attention from the therapist can serve effectively as a therapeutic tactic in dealing with patients' problems, such as hogging the group's attention, distancing maneuvers, and lack of assertiveness. Birk (1973) has extended this approach to an intensive, five sessions-per-week model of group therapy in which each patient's targeted problem behaviors and their adaptive alternatives are given negative and positive feedback respectively by the leader and other members of the group as they emerge in the natural social interaction. This format appeared to be helpful for patients who had severe depression, social isolation, drug abuse, suicidal behavior, and depersonalization, and had not responded to other forms of psychotherapy.

In a controlled study of two matched therapy groups of nonpsychotic outpatients, Liberman (1971) found that an experimental group led by a therapist who systematically reinforced intermember expressions of cohesiveness and solidarity experienced faster improvement of symptoms than a comparison group led by a therapist in a more intuitive, psychodynamic fashion. The patients in the experimental group also showed significantly greater cohesiveness, measured sociometrically, as well as changes on personality tests that assessed dimensions of interpersonal competence and comfort. In both groups, whether or not the therapist was aware of the contingencies of reinforcement, a lawful positive relationship was evident between the group members' expression of cohesiveness and the therapist's activity in prompting and acknowledging this dimension of group dynamics.

Reinforcement methods have been applied to children's play

therapy groups (Clement, Fazzone, and Goldstein 1970). Second and third grade boys who were referred to the clinic by their teachers because of shy, withdrawn behavior were randomly placed in groups of four and met once weekly for twenty consecutive sessions. In the behavior modification group, the boys received tokens for social approach behavior with each other during spontaneous play. The giving of the tokens was paired with praise by the therapist, and the tokens were exchanged for small toys and candy after the session. A comparison group of boys was given verbal praise for socializing and playing together, but did not receive tokens. The boys in the token group improved more than the comparison group and no-treatment control groups, and they continued to be better adjusted at a one-year, post-therapy follow-up. Modeling or learning through imitation has also been effectively used to increase the social skills of withdrawn children. Withdrawn and socially isolated nursery school children who viewed a narrated film showing sociable peer models increased their level of social interaction in the school playroom to approximate that of nonisolate, normal children (O'Connor, 1969). More recently, cognitive behavior therapy techniques have been used effectively in group therapy with conduct-disordered and hyperactive children (Kazdin 1988).

Token reinforcement was also used in a clinical investigation aimed at increasing social interaction among four chronic schizophrenic women, each of whom had been hospitalized for over 15 years (Liberman 1972). Reliable, quantitative records were made of their social conversation during 50-minute meetings. During the baseline period, conversational interchanges occurred at an average rate of one per minute. Contingent reinforcement for conversation was introduced using tokens that could be exchanged for candy, cake, cigarettes, and jewelry. The tokens were distributed at the end of each session. A noncontingent reinforcement phase was next introduced with the patients receiving their tokens before the session. This was done to assess the causal influence of the contingent use of tokens. A final phase returned the patients to reinforcement contingent on their social conversation. Using the same design, another series of sessions was run using a table game that evoked conversation. Contingent token reinforcement increased participation in an open-ended conversation by ten times over the baseline and noncontingent reinforcement phases. Although the game situation alone produced a high baseline conversation, introduction of contingent reinforcement doubled the rate of the baseline conversational activity.

In custodial settings, where patients are not encouraged or reinforced for interacting with each other or with staff, staff attention is often contingent on the patients' acting in a disturbing way or expressing delusional and bizarre talk. Applying basic principles of learning to the reduction of delusional speech in chronic, paranoid schizophrenic patients, Liberman and Teigen (1979) found both task structure and token reinforcement as effective interventions for enhancing rational conversation. A combination of task structure and tokens proved to be the most powerful intervention, doubling the amount of rational talk from the baseline period. On the other hand, verbal prompting and feedback from the therapist were ineffective in improving the content of speech of these chronically psychotic patients. This study also demonstrated that individuals responded differently to the various conditions used, thus underscoring the importance of using flexible treatment strategies that can be empirically validated through ongoing measurement of behavioral improvement.

In dyads of chronic psychotic patients, it has been demonstrated that reinforcement contingencies, but not information, increase conversational behavior. Conversation was operationalized as talk between the dyads about a specified topic of general interest, with eye contact at least once every 15 seconds. Providing the two patients with information about the specified topics just prior to the sessions was ineffective in generating conversations.

In summary, controlled experiments using within-subject or group designs with a variety of patient populations have clearly demonstrated the effectiveness of systematic and contingent reinforcers, both social and tangible, in improving the amount and content of social conversation in relatively unstructured therapy groups. A further extension of these findings has been speculatively applied to the behavior of individuals in sensitivity and encounter groups (Houts and Serber 1972). The creative and stimulating techniques used by group leaders in the "humanistic" or human growth movement might be made more effective in generating longer-term and generalizable changes in members' behavior by an infusion of social learning principles without sacrificing the immediacy of the group's impact on feelings.

Behavioral Methods in Structured Group Therapy

In this section, the group therapy formats that will be described have been structured by the leader with objectives for behavioral change planned prior to the session. Spontaneous and free-flowing group process and interaction is limited and focused, and may be discouraged by the leader if it interferes with achieving the predetermined objectives. The therapist takes a task-oriented, educational role with the group, prompting interaction among group members and giving "homework" assignments. However, as in any task-oriented group, dynamics such as cohesiveness do inevitably develop and can be harnessed to enhance the learning that goes on at a more explicit level.

Systematic desensitization, one of the first of the behavioral therapies, is used for patients with avoidance problems based upon fear or anxiety, such as phobias. Desensitization has been applied in group settings for patients with various anxiety reactions. Individuals with a similar problem are taken through the steps of the desensitization program simultaneously. Patients with fears of traveling, public speaking, examinations, and socializing, have been successfully treated in group settings with a substantial economy of therapists' time. The use of desensitization in groups appears to be as effective as individual desensitization, and in several controlled studies more effective than conventional psychotherapy (Marks 1987). The group situation can be engineered so that patients with different avoidance problems can be treated at the same time. This is done by providing each person with an index card or note paper from his individualized hierarchy, e.g., "Now, picture the next scene on our list as vividly as you can while remaining deeply relaxed." Each person moves at his own pace, so that some individuals will complete their desensitization before others. In recent years, exposure *in vivo* techniques have supplanted imagery-based desensitization in group therapy of agoraphobics with high levels of efficiency and efficacy (Marks 1987).

Assertion training or social skills training are generic terms that include any structured group situation that facilitates the acquisition of emotionally expressive behaviors. Behavioral goals can include learning how to "stand up for yourself," say "no" to people who are exploiting you, obtain a variety of instrumental needs, express affection, anger, tenderness, or sadness. Other terms in use to describe this type of group are personal effectiveness training, and structured learning therapy. The behaviorist position assumes that once the appropriate overt expressions of emotions are learned, practiced and reinforced, the correlated inward or subjective feelings will be experienced.

The process of social skills training involves a series of steps:

1. Identify and specify problems
2. Target interpersonal goals involving emotional expression
3. Simulate the problem situation using roleplaying
4. Use modeling and shaping
5. Give positive feedback
6. Give assignments to practice in "real life."

While assertion training methods are used in individual and family therapy, their most efficient application lies in therapy groups. The ingredients of social skills training—problem specification, goal setting, behavioral rehearsal modeling, prompting, and feedback—can be effectively used with homogeneously or heterogeneously composed groups and in closed or open-ended groups. Structured learning groups have been developed and evaluated for hospitalized chronic psychotics, couples experiencing marital conflict, divorced and separated individuals, depressed patients, alcoholics, drug addicts, mentally retarded persons, parents learning more effective child management skills, and for anxiety disorders such as social phobics (Liberman, DeRisi, and Mueser 1989). A large amount of evidence has demonstrated the effectiveness of structured learning in groups for poor and underprivileged patients, for women's consciousness-raising, for training paraprofessionals in therapy skills, and for supervisors and managers in business enterprises (Goldstein 1973).

Social skills training in groups was introduced as a fundamental component of the clinical services offered by a comprehensive community mental health center (Liberman et al. 1975). Patients with a variety of problems were taught to improve their interpersonal communication in six-session, crisis intervention groups. Groups of adolescents practiced problem solving with peers, and adults and children underwent social skills training with the aid of video tape feedback and token reinforcement. Anxious and depressed outpatients participated in a group format utilizing both anxiety management training and personal effectiveness training. Conflicted married couples in distress received group training in communication skills, such as giving empathy, initiating requests, giving positive feedback, and expressing negative feelings directly. The married couples also learned to recognize and reinforce pleasing behaviors in their spouse and to negotiate and agree on a contingency contract.

Social skills training was the keystone of treatment for a mixed group of psychotic and marginally functioning patients at the day hospital of this typical community mental health center (Liberman et al. 1976). Patients referred to the day treatment program as an alternative to hospitalization had major deficits in their repertoires of emotional expressiveness and social functioning. Such patients had chronic and relapsing major psychiatric disorders and were passive, withdrawn and reluctant to stand up for their rights. They failed to generate reinforcers from their families and work settings, but instead allowed the world to ignore or exploit them. Some patients were deficient in expressing affection, anger, or sadness. Teaching patients to express these emotions and attain their daily living needs for community adaption was the goal of social skills training, which was held in groups of 6 to 12 three to five times each week.

An evaluation of social skills training showed that 78 percent of 50 unselected, consecutive interpersonal scenes or situations that were rehearsed in the day treatment program were reported by the patients as having been performed successfully outside the group in their natural milieus (King et al. 1977). In a second phase of the evaluation, fifty additional scenes were rehearsed in the group. Direct observation in the community by research assistants indicated that 80% of these practiced scenes were actually performed by the patients. This evaluation demonstrated that structured group therapy is effective with a broad range of psychiatric patients, enabling them to transfer the behaviors learned in the mental health center to everyday problem situations. More controlled, experimental data from several research centers indicated that the social skills training "package" on methods is causally related to improvements in behavior and symptoms of carefully diagnosed schizophrenics (Liberman and Mueser, 1989). Moreover, patients randomly assigned to social skills training experienced significantly fewer relapses and rehospitalization, suggesting that this modality exerts a protective effect in schizophrenia.

The behavioral approach to group therapy, with its more systematic and specific guidelines, makes it less likely that a therapist will adventitiously reinforce or model contradictory behavior patterns. The behavioral approach, consistently applied, offers an effective means of modifying maladaptive behavior in groups. While the technology of behavioral clinicians, based on empirical laws of learning, is important in treatment, therapists' relationship with the group members also contributes to the outcome. Therapists who do not have a positive alliance with their group do not possess reinforcing or modeling properties. Their role as educator and lever for initiating changes in the group reinforcement contingencies depends partly on their capacity to show empathy, warmth, and concern for those they work with.

A Social Skills and Problem-Solving Group for the Chronic Mentally Ill

As a concrete example of the functioning of behavioral groups, the details of a social skills training group for chronic mentally ill patients will be described in detail (Hierholzer and Liberman 1986). The success of such a group is improved if its therapists and referring physicians view structured and skill training interventions as synergistic with drug therapy for the major mental disorders. Thus, a social skills training group for mentally disabled patients with schizophrenia and mood disorders often works well in conjunction with an outpatient medication clinic where maintenance antipsychotic and antidepressant drugs are prescribed. Since 1984 a social skills training group at the Brentwood VA Medical Center in Los Angeles has promoted behavioral improvements superimposed on the symptom suppressing benefits of psychotropic medication, even in severely impaired patients.

Setting, Patients, Group Format, and Goals

The weekly social skills training group was established in an after-care medication clinic of a 500-bed VA hospital that provides 150,000 outpatient visits each year. Referrals were generated from the hospital's interdisciplinary treatment teams, and the group was open to any patient who needed improvement in conversational skills, independent living skills, or problem-solving skills. The participants were treated in an open-ended fashion for one or more sessions in a heterogeneous group in terms of diagnosis, age, and sex.

Almost all members had multiple hospitalizations, been ill for at least five years, and were on maintenance medications. The most common diagnoses were schizophrenia and chronic depression with lesser numbers of patients suffering from bipolar disorder, substance abuse, and obsessive-compulsive disorder. Virtually all participants were unemployed and relied on some form of public assistance. Most lived in small apartments or boarding houses and had little contact with their families. Each session lasted 90 minutes which was sufficient time for 6 to 10 patients to go through the sequence of problem identification, goal setting and behavioral rehearsal.

Patients were assisted in formulating and working toward goals in acquiring social and problem-solving skills. The chronic schizophrenic patient who wanted friends but who had poor eye contact, poor conversational skills, and froze from social contacts after saying an awkward hello exemplified an individual in need of skill training. Teaching problem-solving skills involved helping patients generate viable options to vexatious situations. A chronic patient might have fair social skills but was thwarted by his inability to see more than one way to tackle a problem. For example, a patient experiencing frustration in gaining cooperation from his board-and-care roommate to lower the TV or stereo volume concluded that there was nothing more that could be done. Patients were encouraged to think in terms of long- and short-term goals—the latter being interim steps to achieve the former. This was in keeping with a model of social skills training that reinforces successive approximations to ultimate functional goals.

Group Structure and Process

The group sessions were open-ended in that attendance was encouraged but was not mandatory; moreover, the group was also advertised for drop-in or crisis intervention purposes. Some participants found it convenient to come to the group whenever they had a concurrent appointment with the clinic physician for medication—usually monthly or twice monthly; however, most attended weekly. Group attendance ranged from four to ten patients.

The group sessions opened with a three-to-five-minute orientation in which experienced returning members described the group's aim and methods to new members. An educational, upbeat, but realistic tone for the session was established at the outset by this brief introduction which set favorable expectations. Most of the time in the group was spent working individually with each patient on specific problems using a sequence of techniques that is illustrated in figure 14.1.

New and returning members alike were encouraged to select specific, current interpersonal problems to work on. Selected problems that do not necessarily seem interpersonal can usually be recast as such. An example is a patient who said she needed housing. Having her talk with her social worker about finding suitable housing converted the problem into an interpersonal situation lending itself to role play.

Specifying problems in interpersonal terms is a crucial and challenging step for patient and therapist alike. While some patients want to improve and can identify areas requiring improvement, others who complain of an assortment of life burdens may have little or no insight into how to articulate specific problems and set priorities. Such patients require guidance and direction from the therapist, who can help identify problem areas by obtaining background information from the referring physician or other clinic staff or by systematically interviewing the patient about his or her life. For example, a 53-year-old man with an organic brain disorder, mystified by his diagnosis, was helped to formulate the goal of asking his doctor about his diagnosis and prognosis. A 29-year-old woman with a diagnosis of schizophrenia had a goal of saying no to unrea-

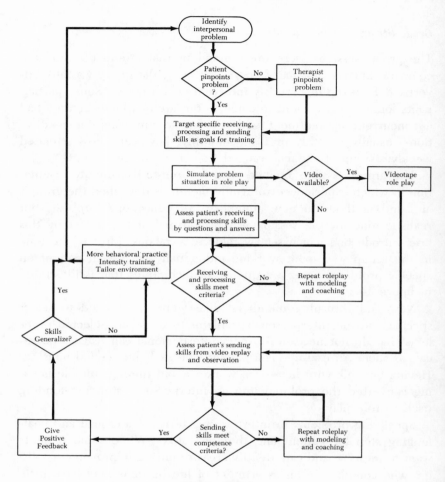

Figure 14.1
Flow chart depicting the procedures and sequence of assessment
and treatment steps used in a social skills training group.

sonable demands made of her. To aid patients in developing needed skills and working through a selected problems, several posters on the wall of the group room were used to guide the therapy process. These are depicted in tables 14.1 to 14.4.

Table 14.1
Successful Living

Pick-a-Problem Situation—Choose Your Goal
Dry Run Rehearsal
Develop Alternatives for Improvement
Positive Feedback
Homework Assignment

Table 14.2
Successful Living Through Personal Effectiveness

Eye Contact
Facial Expression
Voice Tone and Volume
Speech Fluency
Gestures and Posture
Body Language
Verbal Content and Alternatives

Table 14.3
Successful Living Through Problem Solving

Pinpoint the Problem
Generate Opinions and Alternatives
Weigh Pros and Cons
Choose a Reasonable Option
Develop and Plan to Implement
Evaluate and Reward Progress

Table 14.4
Successful Living Alternatives for Solving Problems

Terminate or Withdraw Politely
Come Back Later Ask for a Delay, or Make Later Appointment
Comply with Other's Request
Repeat Your Request Positively
Make a New Request
Explain Your Position
Highlight the Importance of Your Needs
Ask for Assistance or Help
Compromise
Ignore Criticism
Acknowledge Positives with Thanks
Give Compliments or Praise.

The Dry Run. After choosing a problem area, a dry run rehearsal that simulates the problematic interpersonal situation was used to determine the patient's skills and deficits. No coaching or prompting was offered by the leader during the dry run; thus, it served as an opportunity to carry out a behavioral assessment. Other group members participated as surrogates in this role-play of a particular patient's selected problem. Patients may select other participants to role-play significant others; alternatively, therapists may choose participants who need to be more engaged in the group or who might benefit from playing a role that is difficult for them.

The dry run offered the therapist a glimpse of how patients function in society and an opportunity for assessing which skills are needed. Patients often protested before a dry run that they knew how to do something, only to show glaring deficits during the dry run. The point of the dry run, however, was not to expose the patients' glaring deficits. Rather it was for the therapist to discover what skill can be added in a manageable quantum to the patient's repertoire to maximize success in overcoming a problem.

After completing the dry run, patients were given positive feedback on *specific* aspects of the task done well. Such social reinforcement helped to ensure that the patient will continue doing those things well and created a supportive, encouraging atmosphere in the group. It was critical to make the positive feedback contingent on concrete behavioral elements in the patient's role playing and to avoid being vague or general. For example, telling a patient that he or she did a "good job" rather than commenting on specifics such as appropriate use of gestures or eye contact may lead to confusion since the patient may assume everything about his performance was good when in fact it was not. The therapist may have to search diligently to find something a patient did well, but behavioral assets—good eye contact, a friendly manner, a nice smile, or serious tone of voice—can be found for even the most chronic patients.

Although a patient's strengths will occasionally stand out and engender spontaneous praise from other group members, the therapist must more often actively solicit feedback from the group, guiding members to comment positively on specific components of the dry run. For example, the therapist "shaped" positive feedback by asking, "Mary, what did you like about John's eye contact?" or "Jim, what did you think was good about Jane's voice volume?"

Training Phase. After the praise, corrective feedback were given, patients were instructed to add new behavioral skills to their performance to increase their likelihood of real-life success. Higher functioning patients needed only straightforward and clear instructions. They could internalize the suggestions and readily re-rehearse the scene using the suggested new skills. However, most patients needed to watch someone—either the therapist or another patient—model the improved behaviors. In addition, the therapist commented on the modeling to focus the patient's attention on the relevant behaviors being demonstrated and to increase the patient's capacity to internalize the observations. Therapists should not assume that patients will automatically learn from models without directed annotation.

The therapist must be creative when choosing areas for improvement. Sometimes the refinement needed will be obvious, such as improving eye contact, organizing a request better, or getting to a point quicker. The dry run may show that some patients will so lack the necessary skills to achieve a desired long-term goal that it will have to be approximated in a series of shorter term goals or exercises.

One such patient in the group, for example, was quite withdrawn, lacked basic conversation skills, and was understandably anxious in social situations. Yet she wanted to be able to converse comfortably so that she could make friends. At her first session she was so timid she had difficulty looking others in the eye and simply saying hello. To set a goal for her of introducing herself to someone and striking up a conversation would have been too ambitious. Instead her goal was to say hello to each person in the group. Her conversational skills were developed sequentially over a three-month period, during which time she gradually added skills such as using open-ended questions, reflecting back, and self-disclosure. By the end of this time she was initiating conversations with strangers and inviting acquaintances for social activities.

When the patient was ready to rehearse the added behaviors himself, the therapist assumed a coaching stance alongside the patient, offering either positive feedback or prompts if the patient floundered. These behavioral rehearsals had to be repeated several times before the desired incremental improvement in social skills occurred. Time constraints, however, usually prevent doing more than two reruns.

The group process of social skills training, summarized in table 14.5, included the following steps: Interpersonal goals are selected, a dry run of the interpersonal situation reveals strengths that are praised as well as behavioral deficits, and finally, needed skills are taught through instructions, modeling, and behavioral rehearsal in which the therapist takes the part of an active coach.

Homework Assignments. Homework assignments were integral to the group's aim of helping patients live better lives outside the hospital. Usually the assignments were for patients to try outside the group whatever has been practiced in the group. Patients were always asked if they were ready to try an assignment. If care had been taken in problem selection and in behavioral rehearsal, patients usually felt confident to do so. If not, it was necessary to make the assignment less ambitious, to rehearse the interpersonal situation again, or simply to express confidence that the patient is capable of carrying out the assignment.

Assignments were written down on small cards for each patient

Table 14.5
Procedures Used in Social Skills Training Groups

SPECIFY THE INTERPERSONAL PROBLEM BY ASKING:
1. What emotion, need, or communication is lacking or not being appropriately expressed?
2. With whom does the patient want and need to improve social contact?
3. What are the patient's short and long-term goals?
4. What are the patient's rights and responsibilities?
5. Where and when does the problem occur?

FORMULATE A SCENE WHICH SIMULATES OR RECAPITULATES THE FEATURES OF THE PROBLEM SITUATION. THE SCENE SHOULD BE:
1. Constructed as a positive goal
2. Functional for the patient
3. Frequently occurring in the patient's life
4. Specific
5. Consistent with the patient's rights and responsibilities
6. Attainable.

OBSERVE WHILE THE PATIENT AND SURROGATE ROLEPLAYERS REHEARSE THE SCENE. DURING THIS "DRY RUN," POSITION YOURSELF CLOSE TO THE ACTION SO YOU CAN MAKE AN ASSESSMENT

IDENTIFY THE ASSETS, DEFICITS, AND EXCESSES IN THE PATIENT'S PERFORMANCE DURING THE "DRY RUN." PRAISE ASSETS AND EFFORTS.

ASSESS AND TRAIN "RECEIVING" AND "PROCESSING" SKILLS BY ASKING THE PATIENT:
1. What did the other person say?
2. What was the other person feeling?
3. What were your short-term goals?
4. What were your long-term goals?
5. Did you obtain your goals?
6. What other alternatives could you use in this situation?
7. Would one of these alternatives help you reach your goals?

EMPLOY MODELING TO DEMONSTRATE POTENTIALLY EFFECTIVE ALTERNATIVES USING EXPRESSIVE AND ADAPTIVE "SENDING" SKILLS.

HIGHLIGHT THE DESIRED BEHAVIORS BEING MODELED AND REVIEW "RECEIVING," "PROCESSING," AND "SENDING" SKILLS.

RE-RUN THE SCENE WITH THE PATIENT, GIVING POSITIVE FEEDBACK TO REINFORCE PROGRESS AND EFFORT.

Table 14.5

(continued)

USE COACHING TO SHAPE BEHAVIORAL CHANGES AND IMPROVEMENTS IN SMALL INCREMENTS, STARTING WHERE THE PATIENT IS AT.

FOCUS ON ALL DIMENSIONS OF SOCIAL COMPETENCE IN TRAINING "SENDING" SKILLS.

1. Topical content and choice of words and phrases
2. Nonverbal components
3. Timing, reciprocity, and listening skills
4. Effective alternatives.

GENERALIZE THE IMPROVEMENTS IN COMPETENCE BY:

1. Repeat practice and overlearning
2. Selecting specific, attainable, and functional goals/scenes
3. Providing positive feedback for successful transfer of skills to "real life"
4. Prompting the patient to use self-evaluation & self-reinforcement
5. Fading the structure and frequency of the training
6. "Programming" for generalization in the natural environment.

which are depicted in figure 14.2. The card also had space for the patient's name, the therapist's name, and the date the assignment was given. As with all other stages of skills training, specificity is a must. Cues for effectively carrying out the assignment were also listed on the card. They included maintaining eye contact, using the hands, leaning toward the other person, having a pleasant facial expression, and speaking with a firm tone and at a fluent pace. Typical assignments have been (1) approaching three people (a bus driver, apartment manager, or classmate) and saying hello; (2) setting up an appointment with a vocational counselor; or (3) saying no to a relative's demand for money and explaining that one has financial obligations of one's own.

Homework assignments from the previous week were reviewed individually before new problems were selected. Detailed discussion of how the assignment was carried out helped safeguard against the therapist's readily accepting the patient's word that everything went well. Reasons why assignments were uncompleted were explored, and failed assignments often became the focus of the day's work. Generous praise was given for completed and attempted as-

PERSONAL EFFECTIVENESS
ASSIGNMENT – REPORT CARD

Name _____

Date assignment given _____

PE Assignment _____

_____

_____

Date assignment due _____ (_____)
(*check when completed*)

                              Counselor's initials _____

                                A

CUES FOR PERSONAL EFFECTIVENESS

1. Maintain **EYE CONTACT**

2. Use your **HANDS**

3. Lean **TOWARD** THE OTHER PERSON

4. Pleasant **FACIAL EXPRESSION**

5. Speak with **FIRM TONE** and **FLUENT** pace

                                B

Figure 14.2

Graphic example of (a) the front and (b) the back of a homework
assignment card used to spur generalization of skills learned in
the social skills training group.

signments, and the eventual likelihood of successful outcomes was emphasized. Repeated failure to do an assignment suggested that the task was too difficult or not relevant for the patient and should be modified.

Group Dynamics in Social Skills Training

The development of group dynamics in the context of social skills training groups is directly influenced by the group leader. Group cohesion is promoted by the direct involvement of the leader and other members in activities such as role playing, positive corrective feedback (sometimes even containing applause), the buddy system of group members helping each other to accomplish homework assignments, and encouraging helping relationships (comradery and social support) outside the group.

The constant push for independence from the leader goes hand in hand with discouraging regressive behavior from the onset. For this reason, from the moment a new member joins the group, increasing responsibility in selecting problems and goals is encouraged. In addition, the reality orientation of the group meetings and the emphasis on outside activities in the form of homework assignments work to mitigate against the development of intense, counterproductive dynamics.

Case Examples

Two case vignettes may be helpful in illustrating how the social skills training group helps patients achieve their goals.

JM was a 53-year-old, unmarried, and unemployed veteran with chronic paranoid schizophrenia. In addition, the patient had a longstanding pattern of substance abuse with cocaine and marijuana. Although the patient was moderately responsive to and compliant with antipsychotic medication, his persisting persecutory and grandiose delusions were destructive to his interpersonal, social, and work life. The patient was referred to the social skills training group by his psychiatrist who felt that medication could not further improve the patient's difficulties in socializing.

Grandiose wishes for a woman to bear him children, which he verbalized within the first few seconds of meeting most females, severely limited his interpersonal and social relationships, to the point of causing the emergence of depressive symptoms. His belief that he should only work in high-level administrative positions for which he was unqualified had kept him unemployed for years. The patient's verbalizing his delusions interfered with his social life, his ability to obtain a job, and rendered him unable to negotiate critical social interactions including critical ones with the police when apprehended for minor infractions.

Initial evaluation of the patient in the behavioral group revealed a variety of deficits in interpersonal skills; for example, he spoke in a low volume, avoided eye contact, rarely initiated conversations, and inappropriately disclosed grandiose delusions.

The patient's treatment evolved over one and a half years in behavioral group therapy with a social skills training format. The long-term goals, formulated with the patient, were to achieve a more successful and broader social life. This goal was consistently addressed throughout the length of the treatment by constant demonstration and reinforcement of appropriate social interactions. One frequent paralinguistic skill that was emphasized was speaking in a louder voice instead of mumbling.

His short-term goals varied throughout the treatment. In the beginning, goals were oriented toward having the patient develop confidence in initiating even the simplest social exchanges with other people. Later, the quality and intimacy of the interchanges became a focus of treatment. In table 14.6 is shown the sequence of goals that were developed and the situations that were rehearsed in the group. The progression reveals the patient's progress and reflects the behavioral principle of "shaping" successive approximations to long-term goals. Minute but crucial details such as posture, tone of voice, eye contact and the importance of developing a two-way exchange in a social interaction were addressed repeatedly in weekly sessions.

Throughout these sessions, verbalization of grandiose delusional material was discouraged and the patient was redirected toward goal-oriented, reality-based exchanges of infor-

Table 14.6
Goals and Interpersonal Situations Rehearsed Sequentially in
Weekly Sessions of a Social Skills Training Group by Patient JM.

INTERPERSONAL GOAL	SITUATIONS REHEARSED
To increase socializing in evenings	Phone a group member and invite him to go to a cafe.*
	Phone an acquaintance and invite him to attend a movie, have dinner, or go to a cafe.*
Engage in conversations with women without revealing grandiose ideas	Start a conversation with a woman at a social gathering and talk about neutral subjects, such as his military service.*
	Inquire of a woman her experience traveling, then express interest by asking open-ended questions.*
Enter vocational rehabilitation activity	Telephone and make appointment to meet a vocational counselor.*
	At interview with counselor, express interest in rehabilitation options.*
	At second interview with counselor, repeat request for options and gather information on requirements for participating in various rehab activities.*
	Ask for instructions on horticulture job from supervisor without sounding condescending.*
	Give horticulture supervisor positive feedback about her efforts.*

NOTE: The patient's long-term goals of improving socialization, dating, and eventually having employment were served by repeated practice of approximations to these goals and through modeling and reinforcement of appropriate content and form of his conversational interchanges.
*Patient completed the homework assignment in his real life.

mation. This reorientation of the patient's speech eventually resulted in the patient verbalizing fewer grandiose delusions. As a result, the patient was able to deal with his legal difficulties and eventually was even able to obtain and participate in sheltered work. He was able to reevaluate his grandiose plans of "getting rich quick" and began working successfully in a nursery growing vegetables and plants for local restaurants and garden shows. This transition was facilitated by his therapist's framing this activity as an acceptable and respectable activity; that is, the patient could tell his acquaintances that he was a "gentleman farmer."

This case is exemplary of the therapist's conpetencies needed for successful behavioral treatment in a group setting. These include a focused delineation of the short-term and long-term problems and goals, thorough familiarity with learning principles and methods, consistent application of those principles throughout the treatment, willingness to re-evaluate—with the help of the patient—the effectiveness of the various approaches, creativity and flexibility when choosing appropriate areas for improvement, and persevering with the approaches that prove effective. In addition, as with all therapeutic endeavors, an ability to be empathic is crucial to understand the patient's point of view and help him reframe his difficulties and his goals in ways that allow incorporation of new, helpful and effective behaviors into his repertoire.

MK was a 29-year-old, single, male college student with schizophrenia who had a good remission of his religious delusions and excellent preservation of affect and social relations. The referring physician requested assistance from the social skills training group in helping the patient to function better in his social and school life.

Although this patient was much less symptomatic and his long-term goals were clearly stated as financial independence and the development of a career, the patient had several behavioral deficits which markedly impeded his progress in achieving these goals. These deficits included unrealistically high self-expectations, overemphasis on negative consequences of actions, overconcern with the details of situations, poor time planning, and lack of assertiveness. A series of shorter-term goals were introduced to help him develop, in a stepwise fashion, the skills necessary to achieve his longer-term goals. The shorter-term goals consisted of asking the school counselor for advice in curriculum planning, obtaining feedback about study groups, and requesting that his mother discuss her opinions more openly, and thus improve family communications and reduce family stress.

Over the course of treatment, the shorter-term goals were addressed one at a time, increasing the patient's success in dealing with everyday problems.

The achievement of MK's shorter-term goals were associated with improvement in his self-esteem, reducing the high expectations and demands placed on himself, setting limits on the time used for various every day activities, and improving his communications with family and friends which increased their awareness of his needs and desires. The patient was eventually able to obtain the assistance that he needed from his friends and family and succeeded in completing college classes while maintaining part-time employment.

Summary

Behavioral methods in groups have become more structured as they have been infused by social learning principles. While more traditional forms of group therapy have been of equivocal value to patients with severe and disabling mental disorders, the more structured methods have promoted the acquisitions of social and independent living skills in patients facing the challenges of community adaptation (Liberman and Mueser 1989; Liberman et al. 1986; Liberman 1987).

A major advantage of the more active and directive behavioral interventions in groups is their adaptability to group dynamics and the personality of the therapist. Once the learning principles of reinforcement, behavioral rehearsal, shaping, prompting, generalization priming, and modeling have been mastered, the group therapist is free to draw upon his or her own personal resources, assets and style in helping patients to change.

Behavioral group techniques have recently been "packaged" in modules that provide a uniform framework for practitioners. These modules include a highly prescriptive Trainer's Manual, a Patient's

Workbook, and a professionally produced videocassette that can model or demonstrate the skills required by persons with pervasive disabilities, such as chronic schizophrenia (Liberman and Evans 1985; 1988). Because the methods of behavioral group therapy are specified and operationalized, they can be readily taught to psychiatric residents, psychology trainees, and multidisciplinary staff of inpatient and outpatient facilities. This specification of the methods also permits replication of the evaluative research that has been a cornerstone of behavior therapy that leads to evolutionary improvements in the treatment techniques as empirical data shape practitioners' interventions.

15

Rational-Emotive Therapy

Albert Ellis, Ph.D.

Although I originally designed rational-emotive therapy (RET) for individual psychotherapy, I soon discovered that it is ideally suited to group work; and since 1959 I have led five regular therapy groups every week at the Institute for Rational-Emotive Therapy in New York. My regular groups each have eight to thirteen members, who are seen weekly for 2 1/4 hours. In addition, I and other RET practitioners throughout the world do demonstration workshops, hold rational encounter marathon sessions, conduct RET intensives, give RET courses and do various other kinds of group work.

RET is especially suited to group therapy for several reasons: (1) It largely follows a teaching model, so that a number of individuals can be efficiently taught by a single therapist. (2) It encourages RET clients to teach RET to others, and thereby learn it better themselves; and they can get practice and supervision in such teaching when they join an RET group. (3) While being heavily cognitive,

RET also steadily employs many emotive-experiential and behavioral methods and these can often be best done within, as well as be reported back to, a therapy group.

RET, along with the other cognitive-behavioral therapies it inspired, has been shown to be effective in scores of controlled outcome studies; and a good many of these successful outcome studies have been done with group rather than individual psychotherapy (DiGiuseppe, Miller, and Trexler 1979; Ellis and Dryden 1987; Ellis and Whiteley 1979; McGovern and Silverman 1984). A number of studies also show its effectiveness when taught to large groups of children and adults (Ellis and Dryden 1987; Ellis, Sichel, Leaf, and Mass 1988).

What is RET?

RET is a pioneering method of cognitive-behavior therapy that I originated in 1955 after abandoning psychoanalysis because of its inefficiency and philosophic superficiality. It is always cognitive, emotive, and behavioral but instead of being merely eclectic, it integrates many different techniques within the framework of a humanistic philosophic theory (Bard 1987; Bernard 1986; Ellis 1957, 1962, 1973, 1986, 1988a, 1988b; Ellis and Dryden, 1987; Ellis and Harper, 1975; Rorer, in press).

Briefly, RET posits the ABCs of emotional disturbance (and of some important aspects of personality). It hypothesizes that humans start with Goals, purposes, and values (G) and that they often get blocked or thwarted by Activating Events (As) that they create or that are presented to them—especially, Activating Events that interfere with their desires for accomplishment, approval, and comfort. When their Goals are thwarted people have a choice of Consequences (Cs). They can consciously or unconsciously choose appropriate (self-helping) Consequences (aCs) or inappropriate Consequences (iCs). The former consist of appropriate negative feelings (such as disappointment, sorrow, and frustration) that usually help them to resort to appropriate positive behaviors (such as actions to minimize or change the thwarting Activating Events (As). Inappropriate (self-defeating) Consequences (iCs) consist of inappropriate feelings (such as panic, depression, and rage) that usually help them to bring about inappropriate behaviors (such as procrastination, alcoholism, drug-taking, overeating, and social withdrawal).

People largely (not entirely) create or construct their Goals (Gs), some of their Activating Events (As), and most of their emotional and behavioral Consequences (Cs). They do so in a variety of ways; but the most important of these, especially for purposes of psychotherapy, is the way in which they construct their Beliefs (B). The theory of RET clearly says that if they choose to think rational Beliefs (rBs), they will usually create appropriate (self-helping) Consequences (aCs), while if they choose to hold irrational Beliefs (iBs), they will usually wind up with inappropriate (self-defeating) Consequences (iCs).

RET even more precisely states that the main rational Beliefs (rBs) that people hold are flexible preferences, wants, and wishes— "I very much *want* to succeed at work, school, or love—*but* I don't *have* to. Too bad if I don't!" "I strongly *prefer* to win your approval—*but* it's not *necessary* for me to have it and I can *still* find happiness if I don't." The main irrational Beliefs (iBs) that people dogmatically hold that usually lead to individuals' exaggerated emotional disturbances consist of absolutist, rigid, unconditional shoulds, oughts, musts, demands, and commands. Such as: "Because I very much *want* to succeed at work, school, or love, I absolutely *must*! I'm *no good* if I don't!" "Because I strongly *prefer* to win your *approval*, I completely *have* to want it! I can't bear it if I don't!"

RET theorizes that when people consciously and unconsciously devoutly create and maintain absolutist *musts* and *shoulds*—or subscribe to what Karen Horney (1950) aptly called "the tyranny of the shoulds"—they frequently (unconsciously) derive from them many unrealistic misperceptions, attributions, and unrealistic conclusions. For example: "Because you did not accept my friendship—as you *must*—I surely did something wrong; you don't like me at all; I'm a real failure!" These antiempirical conclusions *could* be correct, but they rarely are.

More importantly, when people rigidly hold unconditional *shoulds*— "Under all conditions at all times I *should* do well at work!"—they frequently derive from or add to them four correlative irrational Beliefs (iBs): (1) *Awfulizing.* "Because I lost three jobs in a row (as I *must* not!) it's *awful, terrible,* and *horrible!*" (2) *I-can't-stand-it-*

itis. "Because I lost those jobs and have to look for another (as I *should* not have to) I *can't stand it! I can't tolerate it!*" (3) *Self-downing.* "Because I did badly on my last three jobs (as I *should* not have done!) I'm a *rotten worker,* and an *inadequate person!*" (4) *Allness* and *neverness.* "Because I failed on my last three jobs (as I *must* not fail!) I'll *always* fail and *never* succeed. I *can't* do well on any job!"

Once people strongly create and forcefully stick to primary musts they usually create primary symptoms about work, love, and comfort. But if they are profound musturbators—as they frequently are—they also tend to construct *musts* about their primary symptoms, such as: "I *must* not be anxious or depressed!" "I absolutely *should* never procrastinate!" "I *must* be rational and *have to* give up my *musts!*" "I completely have *got to* do better at therapy!"

Cognitive Group RET Techniques

When doing group therapy, RET uses just about all the cognitive, emotive, and behavioral techniques that it frequently uses in individual therapy (Bard 1980, 1987; Bernard 1986; Bernard and Joyce 1984; Dryden 1984; Ellis 1962, 1971, 1973a, 1988a; Ellis and Abrahms 1978; Ellis and Becker 1982; Ellis and Bernard 1985; Ellis and Dryden 1987; Ellis and Grieger 1977, 1986; Ellis and Harper 1961, 1975; Ellis and Whiteley 1979; Grieger and Boyd 1980; Walen, DiGiuseppe, and Wessler 1980; Wessler and Wessler 1980). I shall now describe some of these main RET methods as they are applied to groups. First, the main RET cognitive methods.

Disputing Irrational Beliefs (iBs)

RET group leaders teach all group members the ABCs of RET and then show them how to go on to D (Disputing) their irrational Beliefs (iBs). To do this, they frequently give minilectures; show individual members, whenever they raise a problem, what their ABCs of this problem are; explain how to Dispute their iBs; supervise other individuals in Disputing other group members' iBs; assign RET literature and cassettes; and correct RET self-help forms (Sichel and Ellis 1984) that certain members have filled out.

Members are all taught the Disputing process, which consists of scientific questioning of their own and other's iBs (Bernard 1986; Ellis 1988a, 1988b; Ellis and Dryden 1987; Ellis, McInerney, DiGiuseppe, and Yeager 1988; Ellis and Yeager, 1989). For example: "Where is the evidence that you *must* succeed in school?" "It's unfortunate if you only get poor jobs, but why is it *awful?*" "How does failing in love make *you* a failure or a *rotten person?*" "Prove that because you were rejected by several partners, you'll *never* have a good relationship." "When your friends don't invite you to dinner, how does that show that you must have done something wrong?"

Using Rational Coping Statements

Group members are shown how to get to Es (Effective New Philosophies) when they Dispute their iBs. These are checked by the RET leader and by other group members. When Es are figured out, members are often given homework assignments to say them to themselves several times during the week. Thus, they may declare—and think through—rational coping statements like these: "I do *not* have to get great marks at school—but that would be highly desirable!" "I am *not* a rotten procrastinator—only a person who foolishly delays making business calls now and who can, and will, definitely make them!" I don't *need* the immediate gratification of smoking, and *can* go through the pain of stopping!" (Ellis 1988a; Ellis and Becker 1982; Ellis and Dryden 1987).

Reframing

Group members are shown how to see the good side of unfortunate happenings. Thus, they can tell themselves that it is *good* to be quickly rejected in love, because they can then save time and go on to look for a more suitable partner. They are particularly helped to see the *challenge* of stubbornly refusing to panic, depress, or enrage themselves when quite undesired things happen to them (Ellis 1988a; Ellis and Dryden 1987).

Referenting

Group members, especially when they are addicted to smoking, drinking, drugging, overeating, or any other harmful act, are asked to make a long list of the disadvantages of their addiction and the advantages of giving it up. They are to let the group members see this list and make suitable additions to it. Then they are assigned to reviewing the revised list several times each day, to help motivate them to stop their addiction (Danysh 1974; Ellis 1978, 1988a; Ellis and Becker 1982; Ellis and Dryden 1987; Ellis and Whiteley 1979).

Psychoeducational Methods

RET stresses psychoeducational methods for clients. Thus, group participants at the Institute for Rational-Emotive Therapy in New York are given a number of pamphlets to read and are usually asked to also read *A New Guide to Rational Living* (Ellis and Harper 1975), *A Guide to Personal Happiness* (Ellis and Becker 1982) and *How to Stubbornly Refuse to Make Yourself Miserable About Anything—Yes, Anything!* (Ellis 1988a). They also frequently read RET self-help books by Hauck (1973, 1974), Young (1974) and others. They listen to RET cassettes (Ellis 1973b, 1977, 1978, 1982). They can elect to attend RET talks, workshops, and intensives (Institute for Rational-Emotive Therapy, 1989). All these psychoeducational adjuncts to RET tend to hasten and intensify the group process; and group members frequently urge other members to use them.

Proselytizing

RET encourages clients to try to use RET with others and to try to help these others change, because this has been found to help the proselytizer change his or her ways (Bard 1980, 1987; Ellis 1973a, 1988a; Ellis and Abrahms 1978; Ellis and Becker 1982; Ellis and Dryden 1987). Group members are especially encouraged to talk other participants out of their irrational Beliefs (iBs) and to suggest rational Beliefs (rBs) to replace them. They also steadily suggest

homework assignments and thereby encourage themselves to do
similar assignments.

Cognitive Homework

Group participants are frequently given cognitive homework by the
therapist and other participants, such as finding and disputing their
iBs. They are urged to keep filling out the RET self-help form (Sichel
and Ellis 1984) and to read these and have them corrected and
commented upon by the leader and other group members.

Semantic Reconstruction

Following the ideas of general semantics (Korzybski 1933), RET
challenges people's overgeneralizing and their misleading uses of
language. Thus, group members actively—and sometimes humor-
ously—correct each other's language when one of them says, "I
should perform better!" "I *need* to be loved" or "My mother *makes*
me angry."

RET Emotive Group Techniques

RET favors many emotive-evocative-dramatic techniques, especially
in group therapy, because it theorizes that most clients *forcefully*
and *vividly* promulgate their irrational Beliefs (iBs) and that they
therefore had better powerfully and dramatically uproot them (Bernard 1986; Bernard and Joyce 1984; Dryden 1984; Ellis 1969, 1973a,
1988a, 1988b; Ellis and Bernard 1983, 1985; Ellis and Dryden 1987;
Ellis and Whiteley 1979; Walen, DiGiuseppe, and Wessler 1980).
Some RET emotive techniques that are especially used with groups
are described in the following.

Shame-Attacking Exercises

Group members, both within the outside the group, are encouraged to do acts that they consider shameful or foolish and but *not*
to feel ashamed, embarrassed, humiliated, or self-downing (Ellis 1969,
1973c, 1988a; Ellis and Abrahms 1978; Ellis and Becker 1982). Group

participants sometimes go out with other members to push them to do these shame-attacking exercises and to report back how effectively they did them.

Rational-Emotive Imagery

Rational-Emotive Imagery (REI) was created by Maultsby (1975) and adapted by Ellis (Maultsby and Ellis 1974). It is done in group by having members imagine one of the worst things that could happen to them (e.g., losing a series of relationships or jobs); letting themselves feel *in*appropriately anxious, depressed, or angry about the Activating Event; then changing their *in*appropriate feeling to an *appropriate* feeling (e.g., sorrow, disappointment, or frustration), which they do by changing their absolutist *shoulds, musts,* and *demands* to unrigid *preferences* (e.g., change "I *have* to do well, else I am *no good!*" to "I'd *like* to do well but I never *have* to!"). They then *practice* REI for thirty or sixty days until they automatically feel sorry and frustrated rather than anxious and depressed when and if this worst Activating Event actually occurs.

Forceful Rational Self-Statements

Group members are rehearsed in group and given homework assignments outside of group to *forcefully* and *powerfully* tell themselves rational self-statements, such as "I *never* have to succeed at work, though I would very much like to!" "People *should* act unfairly to me, because that is often their nature!" "I hate unfortunate family conditions but I *can* stand them and *still* lead a fairly happy life!" Group members often suggest these strong coping statements to other members and check to see if they actually keep using them. (Dryden 1984; Ellis 1988a; Ellis and Abrahms 1978; Ellis and Becker 1982).

Role-playing

Group participants frequently play a role (such as job interviewer or social relator) with other participants; and then the other group members critique how effective the interviewee or would-be relator was in the role-play and how he or she could improve in his or her job or social performances. When role-players become anxious or depressed during their role-play, the leader (or other members) get them to stop and discover what they are thinking to create his or her disturbed feelings and how they can dispute and change disturbance-creating irrational Beliefs.

Recorded Disputations

Group members are given homework assignments of making three- to five-minute Disputations of their iBs on tape. The group listens to their tapes and critiques not only their rational content but also the forcefulness and rigor of their Disputing and shows them if desired, how to do better and more vigorous Disputing.

Unconditional Acceptance

RET specializes in helping all clients to accept themselves unconditionally, no matter how foolishly or badly they behave and do this by having the therapist evaluate the ineffectiveness of the clients' *acts* but never devalue their *selves* or *personhoods*. The therapist also actively *teaches* the clients how to always accept *themselves*, though not their poor *behaviors* (Ellis 1972, 1973a, 1976a, 1979, 1988a; Ellis and Becker 1982; Ellis and Harper 1975). In group clients learn to feel unconditional acceptance of themselves and to *show* it to other members, even when these others act obnoxiously, they thereby practice tolerance to others as well as nondamnation of themselves.

Warmth and Support

RET group participants often give other members warmth and support, during the sessions themselves and outside of group as well. They often befriend each other, call each other during the week, go out together, and remind each other to use RET in between sessions (Ellis and Dryden 1987).

Humor

As group leader, I often use humor to rip up members' irrational Beliefs and in RET groups, workshops, and intensives the leaders frequently use rational-humorous songs to help participants surrender their overseriousness and take a lighter view of life (Ellis 1987).

RET Behavioral Group Techniques

RET, from its start in 1956, has highly favored behavioral methods and has held that many clients will only give up their irrational Beliefs if they consistently *act* as well as *think* and *feel* against them (Bernard 1986; Bernard and Joyce 1984; Dryden 1984; Ellis 1957, 1962, 1971, 1973a, 1976b, 1979, 1988a; Ellis and Abrahms 1978; Ellis and Becker 1982; Grieger and Boyd 1980; Walen, Di-Giuseppe, and Wessler 1980; Wessler and Wessler 1980). Group members are invariably given behavioral assignments within and outside of group and they also play an active role in suggesting such assignments to other members and in checking to see whether and how they carry them out. In a recent study of RET assignments for the five groups that I lead at the Institute for Rational-Emotive Therapy in New York each week, I found that 61 percent of the group members were given verbal homework tasks, 60 percent were given activity tasks, and 5 percent were given special emotive tasks (Ellis 1988c). In addition, all the group members during the period studied were given shame-attacking exercises, which are a combination of activity and emotive tasks.

Some of the most common RET group behavioral techniques are the following: Open a conversation with a stranger. Finish writing your job resume and bring it in for the group to review. Speak up about other group members' problems at least three times this session. Join a gym and go there at least once a week. Stick to the Weight-Watcher's diet this week.

In Vivo Desensitization

Where Wolpe (1982) largely favors systematic desensitization of anxieties and phobias that clients do through imagining uncomfortable things in their heads and relaxing while they bring these things closer and closer, RET favors *in vivo* desensitization (e.g., actually walking a feared dog instead of only imagining oneself walking it). Clients do such live activities during group sessions (e.g., speak up no matter how anxious they are about doing so) or agree to do them as homework assignments. They also suggest and later check up on and discuss other members' in vivo desensitization asssignments.

Implosive Desensitization

Where most behavior and cognitive-behavior therapists favor gradual desensitization homework, RET often uses such assignments but also favors implosive desensitization, which frequently is quicker and more effective. Thus, group members will give other members, and carry out themselves, assignments like "Since you are irrationally afraid of elevators, why don't you try getting on twenty elevators every day this week? If you die in the process, we promise to give you a very lovely funeral!" "Because you never approach suitable members of the other sex to ask them for a date, we suggest that you find ten attractive ones this week, approach all of them and ask every one for a date."

Bearing Discomfort

RET group associates often work on the low frustration tolerance of themselves and other members by encouraging those with low frustration tolerance to stay temporarily in uncomfortable situations—such as poor jobs or marital situations—until they learn that they *can* bear discomfort, and *then* (if they still wish to do so) leave these situations for better ones. They also give moral and philosophic support to addicts who are going through uncomfortable withdrawal periods, and show them how to convince themselves that they *can* bear the pains of withdrawal and *can* accept the challenge of working through to future gains. Discomfort-bearing homework assignments are frequently given and monitored by RET therapy groups.

Skill Training

RET frequently involves skill training (Ellis 1962, 1973a, 1975, 1976b, 1979, 1988a; Ellis and Abrahms 1978; Ellis and Dryden 1987; Ellis and Grieger 1977; Ellis, Sichel, DiGiuseppe). The therapist and other members often show group participants how to be more assertive, how to communicate better, how to socialize, how to have better sexual, marital, and family relationships and how to improve their other living skills.

Reinforcement Penalties

In RET group therapy, reinforcements and penalties are often employed when members have trouble doing their homework or keep refusing to do it. Using the principles of B. F. Skinner (1971), they are encouraged by the therapist and their group participants to make enjoyable pursuits contingent on their doing difficult ones; and when they keep avoiding their agreed-upon homework, they often contract with the group to penalize themselves (e.g., by burning money or performing an obnoxious task) until they actually do it (Ellis 1988a; Ellis and Abrahms 1978; Ellis and Becker 1982).

Excerpt From Group Therapy Protocol

Protocols of RET group and marital therapy have been published elsewhere (Ellis 1962, 1971; Ellis and Dryden 1987; Ellis and Harper 1961). Here is an excerpt from a recent session, in which the main presenter to the group is Joel, a 40-year-old programmer who procrastinates on many tasks and who is afraid to encounter new females after having been divorced for a year.

> THERAPIST: Your homework assignment, Joel, was to refrain from viewing television every day this week until after you had spent at least half an hour working on your overdue tax return. Did you do that?
> JOEL: Yes, for the most part.
> ROB (a 25-year-old marijuana addict) *(hostilely)*: What do you mean for the most part?

HELEN (a 55-year-old homemaker): Rob, you sound hostile!

ROB: Me?

THERAPIST: Yes, you do. What are you telling yourself to make yourself hostile to Joel?

ROB: Nothing!

JOHN (a 33-year-old lab technician): Shit, nothing!

THERAPIST: I agree with John. What did you tell yourself just before you zapped Joel?

ROB: Uh . . . "Joel's copping out again. He never *really* does his homework!"

MARIANNE (a 19-year-old student): "As he *should!*"

ROB: Yes, dammit! As he damned well *should!*

THERAPIST: Why is that a nutty statement?

JOHN: Because Joel is a fallible, fucked-up human!

THERAPIST: Yes. And why else, Rob? Why *must* Joel do his homework perfectly?

ROB: I suppose you want me to say, "There's no reason why he must, though it would be nice if he did."

THERAPIST: That's a good answer, but why are you resisting saying it?

ROB: Because . . . I guess I really think that I *should*, I *must* give up pot—and so Joel, too, *must* do his homework. Not sometimes—but *both* of us, *always*.

TED (a 59-year-old accountant): See your dogmatism! At least you're consistent!

THERAPIST: Yes, dogmatic for yourself, for Joel, and everyone in the world! Great consistency! *(Group laughs.)*

THERAPIST: Well, we'll get to you and your hostility later, Rob. Now back to Joel. How many days this week did you skip your homework?

JOEL: To be honest, four out of seven days. Rob was really right about my goofing.

THERAPIST: And what did you tell yourself every time you didn't work on your tax return—and, I imagine, nonetheless did watch the television?

ROB *(nonhostilely)*: I can guess!

JOEL: O.K.—guess.

ROB: "It's too goddamned hard to do! It *shouldn't* be so hard!"

THERAPIST: Right, Joel?

JOEL: Yes, right on. "I *shouldn't* have to do the boring taxes!" And "I *deserve* nevertheless, to watch my favorite TV shows."

THERAPIST: O.K.—dispute that *should* and that *deserve*.

JOEL: Yes, I see. I *should* have to do the boring taxes. Because no one else will do them for me. And I'll get a stiff penalty if I don't finish them soon.

THERAPIST: And you *deserve* to do them because?

JOEL: Because I got myself into this hole, so *I* deserve to do the work to get out of it.

THERAPIST: Yes, and the universe—and specifically the IRS— *deserve* to be the harsh way they are. Because?

JOEL: Because they *are* the way they are!

GEORGIA (a 34-year-old teacher): And will *continue* to be the harsh way they are!

JOEL: Right. You're right. I'd better really see that.

THERAPIST: Yes, and *accept* it. *Seeing* is far from accepting!

ROB: You can say that again! I see that steadily smoking pot is no good for me. But I still don't accept it.

MARIANNE: Nor *won't*, I would say, till you *force* yourself, many times, to refrain.

HELEN: Yes! What did you tell yourself, Joel, after you *didn't* do the homework. The four days you didn't do it. Did you put yourself down for goofing?

JOEL: I certainly did! After I watched television without working on my taxes, I told myself I was a no-good slacker, and that the group would hate me and that would prove what a shmuck I am.

THERAPIST: What good did this self-downing do you?

JOEL: No good! It helped me goof more!

GEORGIA: It usually does! What could you tell yourself instead, to give up your self-loathing?

JOEL: I *did* badly. But I'm only a person *who* did badly, never a *bad person!"*

JOHN: Right

THERAPIST: Yes, right. Now how could you *believe* what you just said!

JOEL: By going over it many times, strongly.

THERAPIST: Correct. And by *proving* to yourself that no human, including you, is rotten or subhuman. Just fallible and human!

JOHN: Right!

ROB: And by doing the homework this week!

THERAPIST: No, doing the homework is a good idea, Rob. But

it won't make him *un*conditionally accept himself, as we'd like to see him do. Do you see why?

ROB: Uh—yes. Yes, I see. It might even hurt if he just did the homework. Because he then would probably accept himself conditionally—*because* he did it. And we would like to see him accept himself *unconditionally*—*whether or not* he does his homework.

THERAPIST: Very good, Rob. That goes for you too. We want you to accept yourself *whether or not* you stay off the pot. If you do, you'll then have a better chance of staying off it. But you're right about reassigning the homework. Will you take that assignment again, Joel?

JOEL: Yes, I think I should!

HELEN: Watch that *should*. Unless you mean *preferably* and not *absolutely* should.

JOEL: Right! I *preferably* should take it again.

THERAPIST: Good. Now what else bothers you this week, Joel?

JOEL: I am very anxious about the date I'll be having Saturday night. I've only talked to her on the phone and never seen her yet.

TED: "And when I see her, I *must*"—what?

JOEL: Of course, "I must totally impress her!"

HELEN: *That* will make you anxious!

MARIANNE: It certainly will!

THERAPIST: Not necessarily, but most probably.

HELEN: Why not necessarily?

MARIANNE: Yes, why not? I thought that . . .

THERAPIST: No, we almost always, but not necessarily, end "I must totally impress her" with "Or else it's *awful,* I'm *no good,* and I'll *never* get a woman I really want."

HELEN: We certainly do!

THERAPIST: Yes, but Joel theoretically *could* tell himself, "I must totally impress her or else I'm deficient at impressing women. Too bad. I'd better get more practice and overcome my deficiency."

MARIANNE: But he practically never *would* mean that once he put in "I *must* impress women."

THERAPIST: Right. He must almost always imply that if he didn't do as he absolutely *has to* do, it is awful, he *is* no good, and he *will* never get a woman he really wants. Is that so, Joel?

JOEL: Definitely! Especially, "I *must* win this woman, or I'll *never* get a good one!" That's what I *really* told myself to make myself anxious.

JOHN: Where'd you get that *never?*

GEORGIA: Or even *hardly* ever?

THERAPIST: Yes, Georgia is right. If you totally screw up with your date on Saturday, it doesn't even prove that you'll *hardly ever* or *rarely* impress a woman you desire. It only proves that *this time,* under *these conditions,* you failed.

JOEL: Yes, I know.

THERAPIST: You mean you know *lightly. Very* lightly. Now how can you get yourself to *strongly* believe that if you fail with *this* woman *this* time, you may *well* succeed with women you really want—including even this one!—in the future?

JOEL: I'm not sure. I really often feel eternal doom if I fail.

THERAPIST: O.K., group. Give Joel some ideas on how to *forcefully* give up his irrational belief that he *has* to succeed with this date right now or else he will *never* deserve and get a good woman?

ROB: Look, Joel, why not try doing rational-emotive imagery? Vividly imagine that you fail several times with this woman, let yourself feel very anxious and depressed, then work on your feeling until you feel only sorry and disappointed, and then go on to make yourself feel *determined* that ultimately you will succeed with her or some other desirable woman.

JOHN: Yes, that's good. I would also suggest that you do your best to find several very attractive and desirable women to date, even though you're sure you could never impress them. Then show yourself that you actually *can* do well with at least a few of them and that even if you don't you can persist at trying.

GEORGIA: Sounds good to me. But I'd really like to see you take that sentence, "If I fail this time, I'll *never* be able to succeed the way I want to, put it on a tape cassette, and then for several minutes powerfully dispute it, and bring us the tape so we can see how strong your disputations are."

THERAPIST: Any more suggestions for Joel to work at? (After no one responds further): O.K., which of these suggestions, Joel, would you like to work on this week?

JOEL: I think I'll take Georgia's suggestion of doing the tape. Today is Monday, so if I do the tape and work on it till

Saturday, I think I may reduce my anxiety about failing on the date before I have it on Saturday night. So let me try this assignment.

THERAPIST: Fine. And if you do make the tape tomorrow and work on it and listen to it every day this week, what goody will you use to reinforce yourself?

JOEL: I really like swimming every night, so I won't let myself swim unless I work on the tape before swimming time.

THERAPIST: Good. And, to be on the safe side, what penalty can you give yourself every day that you don't work on the tape?

JOEL: How about burning a ten dollar bill?

JOHN: Make it twenty.

ROB: Fifty!

JOEL: O.K.—I'll even accept the penalty of burning fifty.

THERAPIST: Fine. We'll write that down and check you on it next week.

Discussion of Group Protocol

The foregoing excerpt from one of my RET group sessions shows several things:

1. The therapist is quite active-directive and has no hesitation in conducting and leading the group.
2. Several group members besides the therapist question and challenge the presenter, make specific suggestions to him, and point out homework assignments he may take.
3. One member, Rob, becomes hostile to the presenter, Joel, and his angry feelings are actively pointed out to him and discussed. Later in the session, after the discussion of Joel's problems has ended, Rob's anger (and his other problems) are dealt with in more detail.
4. Joel's homework from the previous week is checked upon; his irrational beliefs interfering with his doing it explored; and the same homework reassigned.
5. Joel's secondary symptoms—his downing himself for not doing the homework—are brought out and tackled by the therapist and the group.
6. Joel's irrational beliefs about the homework and about his failure to do it are revealed and actively disputed.

7. General principles and philosophies of RET—such as that of *un*conditional self-acceptance—are raised and taught.
8. The semantics of *preferably should* and *absolutely should* are differentiated.
9. Joel's *musts* as well as some of the inferences he derives from these *musts* are brought out and disputed. The therapist shows how *musts* do not have to lead to overgeneralized and antiempirical inferences but that they usually do.
10. Joel is shown that he *lightly* believes various rational statements but that he still *strongly* believes contradictory irrational ones.
11. The therapist and the group try to help Joel to *forcefully* challenge some of his main irrational beliefs. Emotive and behavioral, as well as cognitive, techniques are suggested.
12. Joel agrees to take another homework assignment and to use reinforcements and penalties to encourage him to carry it out.

Summary and Conclusion

Rational-emotive therapy (RET) is an integrative theory of emotional-behavioral disturbance and what can be efficiently done to alleviate it. Although it focuses on clients' irrational and unrealistic philosophies, which they largely construct and by which they mainly disturb themselves, it sees them as strongly and habitually maintaining these ideas and requiring a number of powerful cognitive, emotive, and behavioral techniques to change them. It holds that small and large group processes are often more effective than individual therapy in helping people tackle and minimize their dysfunctional feelings and activities.

16

Transactional Analysis and Redecision Therapy

Robert L. Goulding, M.D.

Transactional Analysis (hereafter usually referred to as TA) is a theory of personality and a systematic psychotherapy, first developed by Eric Berne, M.S. in the mid-1950s. The basic concept is that each of us is made up of three parts, Parent, Adult, and Child. The Parent is a set of ego states borrowed from real and surrogate parents; the Adult is our reality testing part, and the Child ego state is a repetition of feelings and behavior from our past. The classical Bernian school primarily identifies Ego States, analyzes transactions between ones own ego states and those of others, analyzes games, and life scripts. A game is a series of transactions between one's own ego states and/or those of others, that end up in personal misfortune and/or unhappy feelings. The script is a life plan formed in childhood and lived on in adult years.

Dr. Eric Berne first became aware of some of the phenomenological pieces of behavior that furnished the basis for Transactional

Analysis in his own practice. He noticed that people behaved differently at different times in an organized way; for example, sometimes a person would seem to behave as if he were a small child, while other times the same individual would seem to be behaving like a nurturing, or perhaps a critical, parent. Still other times the same person would be very straight, nonemotive, information giving or receiving, as when he gives directions to someone about finding his house.

As stated previously these different phenomenological states of being Berne called ego states, and differentiated the three as Child ego state, Parent ego state, Adult ego state. (In this paper we will use the capital "C," "P" or "A" to represent these ego states, as Child, Adult, Parent.)

Berne first wrote about these ego states in a book entitled *Transactional Analysis in Psychotherapy* (Berne 1981). Because the theory of TA is now so much a part of the popular domain, I do not intend in this article to do more than review some of the major points, and then go on to the theory of Redecision Therapy as an example of one way that TA is used today.

Berne (1961) described various kinds of transactions as direct, indirect, complementary, crossed, ulterior. A direct transaction is an overt one between an ego state of one person and an ego state of another—so that a direct transaction may be from the Adult of one: "How do I get to Carmel?" to the Adult of the other, and the response, also direct, might be "follow Highway 1 south from San Francisco until you reach the Monterey Peninsula, and then watch for the signs." Another direct transaction might be between two Child ego states: "Let's go play some baseball, man," and "wow, yeah, groovy." It might be between the Parent of one and the Child of another, as: "That man told you how to find Carmel; don't you ever listen?" from the critical Parent, and "You're always picking on me" from the adaptive Child of the other.

An ulterior transaction is one that has a "secret message"—which is covert. The message might sound straight and overt, but there is an ulterior message. Mother says, "I work so hard for you" and that sounds factual, and clear. However, the secret or ulterior message is "Feel guilty." The child knows that whenever Mother says she works hard, she is asking the child to think that he is responsible for his existence, and to feel guilty. If the child doesn't hear the secret message, or doesn't respond to it, either by feeling guilty or verbally responding to the secret message, and instead crosses the transaction by saying, for instance "Yes, you do work hard. Thank you," then the transactions become complementary, Adult to Adult and back to Adult.

An indirect transaction is one that occurs frequently in groups, in which patients talk about one another to other patients or to the therapist. A direct transaction is "I–Thou" whereas indirect is "I–he, she, they." For example, Joe says to the therapist about his wife, who is sitting next to him, "She is never satisfied with how much I do." Gossiping is an indirect transaction.

As mentioned above, Berne and other classical transactional analysts base much of their work on the analysis of ego states (structural analysis), analysis of transactions, analysis of games, and analysis of scripts. Berne saw TA as a method of "social control" (Berne 1961), in which the primary focus was cognitive; by confronting people with their ego state structure, and what they did transactionally, what games they played, and where they were headed in their script, he thought they could change their behavior. He states:

> Structural Analysis proper deals with the mastery . . . of internal conflicts through diagnosis of ego states, decontamination, boundary work, and stabilization, so that the Adult can maintain control of the personality in stressful situations. After maximum benefit has been obtained through structural analysis alone, there are three choices open: trial or permanent termination, psychoanalysis, or transactional analysis. . . . The objective of transactional analysis in group therapy is to carry each patient through the progressive stages of structural analysis, transactional analysis proper, game analysis, and script analysis, until he obtains social control. . . . In more intensive therapeutic situations, it is also a useful preparation for and concomitant of psychoanalytic therapy. (Berne 1961:86,176)

Thus Berne did not see TA as an end-all to therapy, but as a tool to obtain social control. Neither did he see it as an alleviation of symptoms, except that which comes as a natural result of giving up games. Some of the classic TA therapists still remaining follow the same general objective. Another model of TA uses reparenting as a method of treatment, and thinks that the primary problem often is: (1) the torture of the Child by a sadistic, or a noncaring Parent ego state, or (2) a wishy-washy set of parents who seldom have clear messages. These therapists use their own or other surrogates to "reparent" the patient, sometimes treating the patient as an infant, and feeding, bathing, training, teaching so as to "replace" the Parent in their head with a new, different parent. (Schiff et al. 1975; Goulding 1976).

The Redecision model takes a different approach. We believe that the focus of therapy is to facilitate the patient making new decisions for himself or herself, not depending on us to give a new parenting experience. The remainder of this paper will discuss and demonstrate our theory and our methods, based upon the theory of TA, and techniques of gestalt, psychodrama, desensitization, family therapy, other models, and some of our own techniques.

Injunctions and Decisions

The basic theory of redecision therapy is that the child makes decisions as a youngster that are appropriate for that time and that place with those people. For instance, Jane's mother and father are isolates. They had one child because they thought they ought to, not because they really wanted one. The treated the child in a distant way: feeding her, changing her, clothing her, but seldom holding her, cuddling her. They taught her, as she grew into a little girl, what behavior they expected: to be polite, say "yes ma'am" and "no sir," sit quietly at the table, eat all her food, not make any undue noise, not get excited and boisterous, and not to bother them. They seldom held each other in her presence, and they seldom seemed to be having fun, enjoying life with others. They worked, they took care of the house, they read, they were quiet. She thus learned not to be very close with them or with anyone else, and not to have much childlike fun. She behaved as if they had given her clear messages: "Don't be close" and "don't be childlike," and when she grew up she behaved in the same way, not allowing physical closeness from anyone. Even after she married, she behaved as she had seen her parents behave, not being demonstrative with her husband.

Thus she had made decisions as she developed not to be close, not to be openly sexual, not to have much fun. She didn't decide this just one time, she decided it over and over, as she sensed what her parents wanted from her. At some point in her life she recognized how much she was missing, but when she tried to change she had great difficulties, felt uncomfortable with her new role as a warmer, more loving, more enjoying and enjoyable human being. She had made what we call "early childhood decisions," in response to messages that we, Berne, and other TA therapists call *injunctions:* Messages from the parents that were clearly irrational for most people, but for this family were ordinary ways of raising a child that didn't interfere with their lives.

The body of TA theory believes that all parents give messages to their children. Those that come from the Child ego state of the parents, such as "Don't be close," are, again, called injunctions. Other injunctions include the following:

Don't
Don't be
Don't be a child
Don't grow up
Don't make it
Don't be the sex you are
Don't be important
Don't be sane
Don't be well
Don't belong
Don't think
Don't feel
Don't want

There are others, of course, but these are the basic general injunctions that cover most messages parents (and others) give from their Child ego state. Older siblings, and other parental figures, such as teachers, scout leaders, ministers, and other people important to a child, also give these messages. The child interprets and responds to the injunctions with decisions, and with specific ways of being, thinking, feeling, depending upon the nature of the message. (Goulding 1972; Goulding and Goulding 1976).

Parents give other kinds of messages also, of course. From their Parent ego state, they teach such things as "work hard," "study," "obey," "try hard," "be strong," "hurry up," "please me," "be careful." These seem to be rational, and are, but the problem is that when the child accepts them, he will then, as an adult, continue doing some of these things even when it is no longer appropriate to do so. Some of the most difficult patients are retirees who have a hard time not working hard when there is no longer a job to do, and who received the message "work hard."

Other parental messages, from the Adult ego state, are rational, helpful, and aid the child in facing and handling the problems of life. Adult messages are almost never a problem. Injunctions and counterinjunctions usually are. A historical note: Berne called the messages from the Parent counterinjunctions because he thought they were counter to the injunctions, and that the therapeutic intervention was to get the patient to follow counterinjunctions rather than injunctions. It was his theory that people *had* to obey their parents, and that the only way to change was by recognizing the patterns cognitively, and making a deliberate choice, a decision (not *redecision*) to change and to obey the parent's Parent ego state message. We teach autonomy, that everyone is capable of making not only social change but significant other changes, in feeling, thinking, behaving, and even in one's body, as giving up a headache.

Autonomy

Autonomy is absolutely essential to redecisions. By definition a redecision is a new decision, a change in an old decision, that is made by the Free Child ego state. The Free child is one that at that moment is not responding in any way to internal or external parental messages, that is not adapting. Unless the Child feels autonomous, he is really not free, but is adapting. If he or she is adapting, then whatever the decision might be, it is made while the person is still a victim, and therefore is not made from the Free Child. We learned this early in our development of the redecision theory. We noticed that when we did straight TA, being primarily cognitive, and confronted and educated the patient, explaining about ego states, transactions, games and scripts, the patient might easily change his behavior, but he didn't feel any better, and usually would backslide. Or, he might not still being playing games, might make new decisions to get out of his script, but he would develop new symptoms. Eric used to say that he noticed that when people made important decisions for themselves, they would often end up despondent, or depressed.

It is now obvious to me why that is so. The client, when a child, made a decision that in some way got him goodies, or at least avoided trauma. Jane, for instance, remembered that whenever she, as a child, would try to climb on Daddy's lap, she would be told to leave him alone, that he was busy (reading the paper or a book, listening to classical music). Or if she tried to get close to Mommy in the kitchen when she was cooking, or canning, she would be told "later," when mommy wasn't busy. She soon learned not to get close. Now, as a grownup, she experiences anxiety whenever she is embraced by her husband, and pushes him away. This was the main reason they came into therapy; although both were therapists, and both were here ostensibly to learn our methods, his therapeutic contract was to establish a different, more intimate relationship with her, and he wanted her to change, and be more intimate with him.

So the child learns how to behave, feel, think, and whenever he or she tries to change by Adult decision, the process is either very difficult or in some way painful. The adapted Child is not wanting to change (even though the little kid originally loved closeness, even though the Adult does, and therefore the Child sabatoges in some way. Thus the therapeutic method is to do something so that the Child is willing to give up the old position, and start a new one, and thus it is most important to confront the patient, over and over again, whenever he gives up autonomy, and coax and stroke for autonomous behavior, thinking, and feeling.

Part of our therapeutic process, then, is to listen carefully to the words, to the inflections, to watch the expressions, body movements, and gestures, and to let the patient know what he or she is doing. For instance, Jane is talking about wanting to be closer physically to Jack, her husband. As she says so, a frown flits over her face, and one corner of her mouth turns down. I replay this on the video, stopping the action at the point of the frown, the corner turning down. I ask her what she sees. She gasps. "That's my mother when she is displeased!" "Say this to her," I say. She looks at the video and says, "Mother, you frown when I talk about being closer to Jack. I want you to stay out of my life now." (She has been around several days now, and knows what I am referring to when I say "Tell this to her.") "Now be her, your mother." She moves to a chair by the video, and responds as mother: "Now Jane, you know I don't like gooiness." She changes to her own chair and says "I don't care anymore what you like. To be close to Jack is not gooiness, and it can be fun. So stop laying your fear of closeness on me. I'll be as close as I want." And thus she starts to reclaim her autonomy, and makes the beginning of a redecision with a gestalt technique.

We usually are also very careful not to permit much story-telling, and to encourage all I–Thou transactions—direct transactions, rather than indirect ones. Most patients are inclined to talk about, rather than talk to, especially when the one talked about is not in the room, but also when he or she is. Part of the culture of psychotherapy is to give a history, and the history is usually a series of indirect transactions. Then, instead of activity and intimacy, the work turns into pastimes and rituals. People, according to TA theory, have only six ways of structuring time: withdrawal, rituals, pastimes, activities, games, and intimacy. Many groups start out with rituals: How are you? I am fine, how are you? How is your wife (husband, father, mother, child)? Not so good, she (he) has been angry all week. And so on. If asked what the wife, husband, parent is angry about, then the story is told, as if it were a movie, and it becomes pastimes, and no work, and no activity, occurs, and there is no intimacy. However, if I say "be your wife, and be angry," and the patient acts out the wife's part, then we get into direct, I–Thou transactions, and things begin to happen. Feelings begin to be experienced, and then the "story about" turns into a fascinating play, in which the patient becomes the author, and the actor, and I become the stage director. I often talk about the role of the therapist being, frequently, that of a stage director at a play, promoting and skillfully directing the speaking of the lines with power, emotionally.

In summary, two of our most important techniques are to keep as many transactions as possible direct, I–Thou, and to confort all words and all comments that give away the patient's autonomy, and all gestures and movements that are not congruent. Another technique is to keep as much as possible in the present, so that instead of telling stories, patients are asked to write plays and act them out, so that a childhood scene, instead of being told about, is acted out, with the patient taking all parts. This way he then has better access to his Parent and his Child. Telling a story, he may not remember what his parents said and did, but when he is taking the role of his parent, he automatically goes into his Parent ego state, and taps into material that is not as easily available when he is in his Adult.

I start off every morning session with brags, in which people are encouraged to brag about their changes since the last session, brag about what they have done to fulfill their therapeutic contract, brag about their developing relationships with each other. I encourage applauding, positive stroking. I applaud, myself, and I also brag when appropriate. Why brags? They maintain contact; they improve contact with each other; they positively stroke for positive change (behavior therapy).

Brags also start the patient off defying parental message. Almost all parents tell their children not to brag; most little kids love to brag, but they stop when it displeases Mommy and Daddy, so they become adapted. Brags help to free up the free kid.

When I first see a patient, I look for differences from the norm; what do I see about this person that it is appropriate to work with, to facilitate change. Often the patient ignores obvious problems, such as being 200 pounds overweight, with a red face and clear signs of high blood pressure; or they don't mention a chronic limp, or other evidence of some physical disability. There may not be anything to do, but it is important to check out everything the patient presents. There was a wonderful cartoon in the paper the other day—either Bizzaro or The Far Side—in this cartoon, the man in front of the computer is giving the other guy a computereese spiel about his (the other's) health. All this time, there is an arrow sticking in the "patient's" back. No mention of the arrow. I look carefully at people when they arrive, and all during the time of their residence with me, so that I don't miss the arrow.

I listen carefully to what people say as they work—not just to the content, but to the semantics. Another way in which the Child sabatoges is by the choice of words; for instance, the use of the word "try." That sounds like an O.K. word. However, one of our ways of getting parents off our back when we are children is to answer the question "Will you cut the grass this afternoon after school?" with "I'll try." Everyone is satisfied. Then when we don't get to it, and Dad says "You didn't cut the grass," we answer "Well, I tried, but . . ." add anything you used—"I had to stay after school," or "the lawnmower wasn't sharpened," or "I had football practice." As I wrote in *Changing Lives* (Goulding and Goulding 1979), I have a large cowbell, and whenever people say "try" I ring the cowbell. This is a humorous way of confronting the "try." After the first time, people watch their language much more carefully, and although at first the change in language is probably adapted, after a while people begin to learn that they give up their autonomy with their semantics, and as they take more care in what they say, they automatically begin to shed their victim position.

Another example: We were all trained as children that we were responsible for our parents' feelings. They said things like "You make me so mad when you come home late from a date." We then feel like we were responsible for their anger, whereas they could have been amused or scared or anxious or whatever their way of feeling was. So when we grow up, we believe that our spouses make us angry or that President Bush makes us angry. It is most important that in claiming their autonomy people stop blaming others for their feelings, or their behavior or their thinking. How can you redecide anything if you play victim, believing that people can make you feel what you feel? Thus our theoretical position that we are truly responsible for our own thinking, feeling, and behaving has a practical aspect. Little Johnny says "Janie made me do it" when he does something naughty, hoping that he can get out of punishment if he blames his sister, and when he grows up, he still uses that tactic— Dan White, murderer, said "twinkies made me do it!"

Along with the "try" bell, I use a code. Whenever I hear "he (she) made me feel angry (sad, anxious)" I say "Tilt." When the pinball machine reads "tilt" the game is over; when I say "tilt" I mean that unless they give up this untenable position the therapy is over, and nothing more can be done.

Contracts

Now we come to contracts. Berne often said that when we reached a good contract, the hard part was done, and I have stressed the importance of the contract in all my previous writings (Goulding and Goulding 1978, 1979). A contract is what the patient says he will change. The contract must be specific, reasonable, measurable, possible, and not just exploratory. The question I ask is "What do *you* want to *change* about yourself *today (this week, this month)*. I do *not* ask such questions as "What is your problem" or "what can I do for you," but stress first that the client is involved in the process, that change is possible, and that it is possible in the foreseeable future. I do not ask "what do you want to *work on*," because if I do they will work on and on and on and not change. Thus the question about "you changing today" avoids most of the possible ways in which the adapted Child may sabotage. Also I do not accept what we call parental contracts—which are what someone thinks the patient *should* do, rather than what he or she wants to do. For example, a patient who states that he wants to quit drinking while smelling as if he has been drinking is probably there because a spouse, child, parent, or boss wants him to change. There is a part of everyone who wants to change, but there is also a part of everyone who doesn't (the adapted Child), and this is the part that will try to sabotage self and the therapy.

It is frequently helpful to ask how the patients will be different in the future if they change according to the offered contract. This is one of the tests of the validity of the contract: is it reasonable? If it won't lead to any particular change, then it probably isn't reasonable, and is probably "parental." I don't buy parental contracts, for then I am in constant struggle with the adapted Child. For instance, the patient Pearl says she wants to stop drinking. I am always suspicious of a contract to give up an addiction—food, liquor, drugs—because usually, at first, it is a parent contract, and someone else is lurking behind the scene. So, when I ask how she will be different, I am asking what other changes whe will make besides sobriety. There are a lot of dry alcoholics in the world, who are no longer drinking but who still exhibit the same behavior as they did when they were drinking. Is she going to stop beating her husband? Spanking her kids? Is she going to stay with her position, instead of getting fired for being careless on the job? Is she going to start paying her bills, or will she continue to play the debtor even though sober? Many alcoholics do (Goulding 1966).

Chronic Bad Feelings

Most people who come to see a therapist have a principal set of feelings that TA therapists have called "rackets." I don't like the use of that word, although it is part of the "cowboy" talk that Berne liked so much. These feelings, as well as thoughts, behavior, and psychosomatic symptoms will be demonstrated, of course, in the working through of the contact, the contract, and the therapist's awareness of differences. I want to know specifically what the feelings are that the patient intends to change—specifically. I am not interested in "I want to know myself better," or "I want a peak experience!" or "I want my spouse to change." Still other individuals present physical symptoms, as headaches, backaches, or abdominal pains which may be psychosomatic, and we are willing to work with whatever part of these aches and pains may be psychological. Now these symptoms, these bad feelings (anger, depression, anxiety), obsessive thoughts, compulsive behavior, or even these body changes, are supported in their pathology by one or more of a series of events: chronic repeated games, belief systems, fantasies, and remembering or story-telling.

Games

As mentioned early in this paper, a game in TA talk is a series of transactions between one's own ego states and/or those of others, that end up in personal misfortune and/or unhappy feelings. For example, I have specifically told participants in an opening letter that they receive on arrival that the picnic table by the swimming pool is for the use of the staff, particularly at meal times. To quote: "Also, the picnic table by the pool is for the use of the staff; please respect all our rights to privacy too. The tables on the patio are for you, at any time." We need some breaks, and sometimes I sit at that table after a session is over, while waiting for the next meal.

Occasionally someone (as Paul did recently) comes up to me to ask a question, or simply to talk. I say, very frankly, "I am now resting. Ask your question in front of the whole group at the next session in the morning." Paul may take this very easily, in which case a game is probably not being played. Paul may get mad, or sad, or embarrassed (he became angry), in which case a game was being played. Our definition of a game is that it contains first an apparently straight transaction. In this case the straight transaction was "I want to ask you a question." Now that appears straight, and it may well be. It also may be the opening move in the game. The second feature of the game is that there is an ulterior transaction, a secret message. If this is a game, the message could be interpreted as "Please reject me." It is actually given at this time because part of the person already knows that the rule is "Don't disturb the staff when we are sitting at this particular table," and they have broken that rule. The third part of the game is that the playee responds to the secret message, and rejects the player, or the player *experiences the response as rejection* even when the playee was not rejecting, but merely enforcing the rule.

I have two main choices to this opening gambit. I could say (and with someone I have already experienced as being a hard player I will say) "Damn it, don't bother me now." Or I could play it cool, and respond to the straight message rather than the ulterior transaction, and say "I am resting, ask me tomorrow at the morning session." If the player feels O.K. with that, again, I don't think it is a game. However, if the player shows any negative feelings, then he experiences me as rejecting even when I am not. Thus, the fourth "rule" of the game is that the player feels badly after the response of the playee. As part of the fourth rule, and this we have added recently, the player usually says something (out loud or in his head) about self and about the other. For instance, in this case he might say about self "I am always sticking my nose in where it doesn't belong" and about me "The son of a bitch is always rejecting me." The latter is what Paul did, in his head.

The fifth feature of the game is that the whole series of transactions that end up in bad feelings is secret from the Adult. If you would rather use psychoanalytic terms, it is unconscious. In short, the player (Paul) is not aware, when he makes the first move, that he is about to play a game in which he will end up feeling bad. He sets it up, outside of his immediate awareness, in order to maintain his chronic bad feelings, his "racket." Why does he do this? Berne (1961:99) answers that question fully: in short, games structure time, the process is familiar and usually predictable, the player gets strokes to satisfy his stroke hunger (even if they are negative), the games support the familiar bad feelings (in Paul's case, he is a very angry man) and they forward the script. (Paul was a hero in Vietnam, used his anger appropriately for a war situation, to kill people.) His script was that of a hero vindicating injustices.

Fantasies

Another way that people have of maintaining bad feelings is to fantasize. Paul, for instance, in addition to playing games to stay angry, also fantasizes. He is driving his car from home to work. On the way he sees a state patrolman, going in the opposite direction. Often he starts fantasizing that the patrolman turned around and pulled him over for speeding. Of course he wasn't speeding, but he fantasizes that the cop stopped him because he was driving a Porsche, and that all Porsches drivers speed. In his fantasy, the cop tickets him for 70, when he was doing about 57. He angrily defends himself—he never speeds on the highway, he was still in fourth gear rather than going into fifth, the cop didn't follow him but simply turned around and stopped him—and so on.

Others more paranoid than Paul fantasize that his or her spouse or lover is unfaithful. Although there may not be any evidence of unfaithful behavior, the fantasizer makes it up, and then looks for any evidence that will support the fantasy. One participant here several years ago saw people pushing other people in the swimming pool. Now we don't allow such behavior, but this happened anyhow. Johann saw this happening, and immediately became fearful (his chronic bad feeling). He couldn't swim, fantasized that the participants were going to throw him in the pool, and he would drown. He didn't show up for the next session, and I asked his wife where he was. She said that he was packing to go home. When I went down to his cottage and asked him why he was planning to leave, he told me that he was afraid that the others were planning on drowning him. Paranoid? Of course, but he had convinced himself that his fantasy was factual. It took a great deal of persuasion on my part to get him to come back to the "barn" (our seminar room used to be a barn) where I asked him to ask each person individually if they would contract not to throw him in the pool. All agreed, of course, and then he was satisfied and turned off his fantasy machine.

Belief Systems

A third common method of maintaining bad feelings is to hold onto belief systems. There are some general belief systems, as the one held by the peoples living around the Mediterranean and elsewhere. In Israel, the belief system is "Don't feel too good, or something bad will happen." In Italy, the saying is "A bird that sings before breakfast gets eaten for dinner." In any case, those who believe this have a great deal of difficulty in maintaining good feelings, and as soon as they are aware that they are feeling good, they switch, so as to, in Arab terms, ward off the "evil eye." The interesting thing about belief systems is the tenacity with which people hold on to them, because they really believe they are true. This is so whether the system is a general one, as the evil eye, or a specific one, for this particular patient and the patient's family. Many of them are "grandma" tales. "If you don't wear your rubbers, you'll catch cold." "If you play with yourself, you'll go crazy (or grow hair on the palms of your hands!)." "If you don't finish your spinach your hair won't curl."

Of course, the blamers of the world blame others for their feelings, as mentioned above. If they really believe that others, or events, can make them sad, for instance, they can find all kinds of events, all kinds of people, to support their belief system. Listen to the cowboy laments, or some of the rock songs, for the theme. Often, the theme is that someone went away, or died, or rejected them, and the song is about how they were made to feel so bad. Read our literature, see how often our authors use this belief system to support the tragic ending. Start with Shakespeare!

People also believe that others make them think bad thoughts, do bad things (or good things!). Yesterday at the Monterey Jazz

Festival one of the singers sang a song entitled "He was born to feel sad." A typical blues music script! Another sang a song "Darling, you made me change my mind"—a typical way in which even an artform supports the belief system that we are not responsible for our thinking, feeling, behavior. Another song: "You made me love you, I didn't want to do it!" It is *very* important to confront every one of these attempts to forsake autonomy.

In summary, one of the presenting symptoms of people looking for psychotherapy is the chronic bad feeling; anger, sadness or depression, anxiety or fear, confusion, guilt. People support these bad feelings by their games, their fantasies, their belief systems, and remembering and story-telling.

Why do people maintain bad feelings? Usually there are several reasons. One of them is familiarity, starting with childhood. If father or mother or both are chronically angry, the child believes that the way to get along is to be angry; or conversely, the child may decide as a little kid "When I grow up I'll never be like that" and then is not angry, but may be sad to cover up the anger. Secondly, the bad feeling supports the script. If one makes an early childhood decision to kill himself some day if things get too bad (and we believe that people do make that decision, often) then one has to be sad or depressed in order to make that decision, and thus that script, come true (Goulding and Goulding 1979).

Story-Telling and Remembering

People also keep themselves feeling bad with story-telling or remembering. AA meetings are full of drunkalogues, which are stories told about terrible hangovers, weekend losses, job and spouse losses, and other painful memories. Here with an audience the teller not only is able to relive his bad feelings, he even gets his audience to "gallows laugh" at him and his tale of woe, thus getting a double benefit by obtaining positive strokes for his pain. In all fairness, the AA member then feels good having quit that behavior, but there is always a little bad feeling first as he recounts his adventures.

In common-day living, just story-telling often supports the racket. It is not uncommon for older people to tell the same story over and over again, and to weep as they tell it.

Early Childhood Decisions

Little kids make many decisions for themselves, about how they will shape their lives, how they feel, think, and behave. They respond to the stresses of the day, the injunctions, counterinjunctions, and the stroke patterns. These decisions are made over and over again, not just once, as the stresses are repeated by the parents, and by life in general. In *Changing Lives* (Goulding and Goulding 1979) we listed the decisions often made in response to the parental messages, and the reader is advised to read that chapter. As an example, with the injunction "Don't be" children might make one of these decisions: "I'll die, and then you'll love me"; "someday if things get too bad I'll run away or kill myself," "I'll get you even if it kills me"; etc. In the case of nonclose Jane described above, she made several decisions. Two of them were: "I'll never try to get close again" and "I'll never have any fun." It is important to get to a scene where those decisions were made, for that is a leverage to get to redecisions. One of the easiest ways of getting to the redecision is to get into the scene of the early decision, encourage the patient to take both sides, and then as himself or herself, fight back.

Script

The script is the life plan formed in early childhood and lived out in adult years. Many of the early TA therapists, including Berne, were very interested in working out the minute details of the script: "Some of the scripts which it has been possible to study adequately so far had awesome prototypes in Greek literature; while the common script known as "Little Red Riding Hood" is a modern real-life adaptation which follows implicitly certain versions of the folktale" (1961:117–129). Berne took great delight and great pains to nail down all the characters in the patient's life that fit the original story, after he decided which story the script was taken from. We are more interested in the general move of the script: is it heroic or tragic; does it end in joy or depression, success or suiside? Berne looked for positive scripts; we try to help people become script-free.

Impasses

I first wrote about impasses in *Voices* (Goulding 1974), describing the three different types. Simply, type 1 relates to the impasse as a result of the individual's desire to change from obeying a counterinjunction, such as, "Work hard." The Parent ego state of the parent gave the original message, and the child obeyed. There is nothing wrong with such behavior, but to lock one's self into working hard when one wants to retire makes for the impasse.

Type 2 relates to the impasse of the individual's desire to change from obeying an injunction. The serious hard-working executive has been working hard and has not been having fun, has not been childlike, now wants to play more, enjoy the lighter side of life more, and finds it difficult to do so, because he is still obeying the injunction "Don't be a child, don't have fun."

Type 3 impasse is related to what the patient experiences as having been born with. In one family, the first child is the hard working one, the second is the "natural athlete," the third child is always late (born late!) and the fourth child is the bright one. These are usually attributes; the patient doesn't recognize that a message was ever actually given, it was just "the way he (or she) was." These impasses are different in the working through; because the patient doesn't remember a parental message in type 3, we can't set up dialogues between patient and parent as we do in type 1 or type 2.

Redecision

I use the information about type of impasse carefully because the work is different. One of the ways of getting a redecision is to facilitate the patient getting into the Child ego state by setting up an early scene. This is usually done in some way to use the patient's energy; for instance, earlier I had the patient Jane see herself as mother on the TV screen. Then I had her talk to mother, and she said, "Mother, you frown when I talk about being closer to Jack. I want you to stay out of my life now." This is a good start, but she is not yet in her Child ego state, is speaking from her Adult. "Be mother," I said. She sat in the other (parent, mother) chair. "Now Jane, you know I don't like gooiness." She responded to that with the quote mentioned earlier—ending with "I'll be as close as I want." I still did not feel satisfied that she was in her Child. "Be mother again." She moved again. "How old are you, Mother, when Jane is a little girl." "Twenty to twenty-five," she says. "How come you were so much against being close to people?" "Well, no one was ever close in my family either. My Mother was always depressed, never had the time or energy for us kids." She starts getting teary. "Are you crying as Mother, or as Jane?" "Jane." "Then move to the other chair and talk to Mother." She moved, looked toward the TV set, and said, crying, "I'm sorry that you were like you were, but I don't want to be like that anymore. I wanted to be closer to you, and that wasn't possible. Now I'm not going to lose out anymore." She wiped her eyes, then grinned. "So there." I was satisfied, and so was the group, which applauded.

Here, in a type 2 impasse, dealing with the injunctions, it is usually necessary to bring in the Parent ego state, represented by Mother in this case. I did not simply set up a dialogue—I used the patient's frown when in her Parent to start the work, so that I was using her energy, not mine. Sometimes I will simply say "be a little girl and talk to Mommy," but this is harder to get into. In type 1 impasses, we may bring in the Parent, but it is usually not necessary to get into Parent affect as we did here. The rebellion against the overt counterinjunction is more easy for most people, who have been in some way rebelling all their lives against Parent messages. To simply tap into the strength of the rebellious Child, and allow them to rebel for their own sake, rather than for the sake of rebellion, is usually enough.

The type 3 impasse is different. Here there is no one to talk to, as the patient usually does not remember any messages—to be the industrious one is just the way it is, and they are living up to their attributes. Now we ask the client to be the adapted Child in one chair, and be the hard worker. In the other chair, he or she is the Free Child, and a double monologue ensues: "I am a hard worker, I was born a hard worker, I will always be a hard worker" from that side, and from the other "I didn't have to work to get born, my mother worked. I am tired of being the model oldest kid. I'm starting to have fun, take time off to play golf, go to jazz festivals, enjoy myself. I've made enough money." This usually starts off with Adult involvement, but as the monologue progresses a little humor can be elicited by a funny therapist, and the work gets done in Child ego state. Here I had said at the beginning when the patient said "I was born working hard," "yeah, you swam like mad out of the birth canal." The patient started to laugh at that, and the rest of the work was easy.

By the time we come to the Redecision phase of the work, most of the hard work has been done. We have made good contact, and have a workable contract. We have facilitated the patient to get into first-person singular, in the present, and active rather than passive. Instead of saying "It happened to me," for instance, the patient says "I did it"; instead of "I'll try to . . ." she says "I'll do it." She has learned to stop giving up her power, and instead claiming her autonomy. Thus when the redecision is made, she is already feeling tough, not a victim but a winner, and the redecision is the frosting on the cake.

Redecisions are made in many ways. Our most often used way is that of facilitating the patient getting into a childhood scene, fighting back, and making a new decision while in the Child ego state. We also use humor a great deal. a laughing Child is a Free Child, and thus decisions made with humor are usually Free Child, exciting ones. Doing phobia desensitization (Goulding 1975, 1976) we use a great deal of humor, rather than the relaxation techniques of Wolpe (1969). For example, when Mary Goulding does "little animal phobias," as those of cockroaches, mice, or other small animals or insects, she has the participant dress up their feared object in ridiculous clothes, such as a spider dressed in purple tights and jump boots(!) or a cockroach in high-heels.

We use many gestalt techniques. The two-chair dialogue, of course, is one of the most common, when people are fighting back. We also use exaggeration: if a person claims a dumb or ridiculous symptom hard enough, they reach a point of what Jim Simkin called "organismic disgust," and gives up the symptom.

References

Abelin, E. 1971. "The Role of the Father in the Separation-Individuation Process." In J. B. McDevitt and C. F. Settlage, eds., *Separation Individuation*. New York: International Universities Press.

Abelin, E. 1975. "Some Further Observations and Comments on the Earliest Role of the Father." *The International Journal of Psychoanalysis* 56:292–302.

Agazarian, Y. and R. Peters. 1981. *The Visible and Invisible Group*. Boston: Routledge & Kegan Paul.

Ahlin, G. 1988. "Reaching for the Group Matrix?" *Group Analysis 1988* 21:3, 211–226.

Alexander, F. 1929. "Psychoanalysis of the Total Personality." New York: Nervous and Mental Disease Publishing Co.

Anthony, E. J. 1972. "The History of Group Psychotherapy." In H. Kaplan, and B. Sadock, eds., *The Evolution of Group Therapy*, vol 2. New York: Jason Aronson.

Arensberg, F. 1973. "The Encounter Group as the Quest for the Nurturant Mother." *Group Process* 5:161–172.

Arensberg, F. 1985. "The Application of Self Psychology in Group Therapy." Paper presented at the Annual Three Day Group Therapy Conference of the Postgraduate Center for Mental Health, New York, April 1985.

Bacal, H. 1985. "Object Relations in the Group from the Perspective of Self Psychology." *International Journal of Group Psychotherapy* 35(4):483–501.

Bard, J. 1980. *Rational-Emotive Therapy in Practice.* Champaign, Il: Research Press.

Bard, J. 1987. *I Don't Like Asparagus.* Cleveland: Psychology Department, Cleveland State University.

Beck, A. T. 1972. *Depression: Causes and Treatment.* Philidelphia University of Pennsylvania.

Beck, A. T. 1983. *Cognitive Therapy of Depression: New Perspectives* (P. Crayton, ed.) New York: Raven Press.

Beisser, A. 1970. "The Paradoxical Theory of Change." In J. Fagan and I. Shepherd, eds., *Gestalt Therapy Now,* pp. 77–80. New York: Harper & Row.

Bennis, W. G. and H. A. Shepard. 1956. "A Theory of Group Development." *Human Relations* 9:415–37.

Bergler, E. 1949. *The Basic Neurosis.* New York: Grune & Stratton.

Berman, L. 1949. "Countertransference and Attitudes of the Analyst in the Therapeutic Process." *Psychiatry* 12:159–166.

Berman, L. 1950. "Psychoanalysis and Group Psychotherapy." *Psychoanalysis Review* 37:156–163.

Berman, L. 1954. "Psychoanalysis and the Group." *American Journal of Orthopsychiatry* 24:241–245.

Berman, W. G. and H. A. Shepard. 1949. "A Theory of Group Development." *Human Relations* 9:414–37.

Bernard, M. E. 1986. *Staying Alive in an Irrational World: Albert Ellis and Rational-Emotive Therapy.* South Melbourne, Australia: Carlson/Macmillan.

Bernard, M. E. and M. R. Joyce. 1984. *Rational-Emotive Therapy with Children and Adolescents.* New York: Wiley.

Berne, Eric. 1961. *Transactional Analysis in Psychotherapy.* New York: Grove Press.

Bertalanffy, L. von. 1968. *General Systems Theory.* New York: George Braziller.

Bieber, T. B. 1971. "Combined Individual and Group Psychotherapy." In H. I. Kaplan and B. J. Sadock, eds., *Comprehensive Group Psychotherapy.* Baltimore: Williams & Wilkins.

Binswanger, L. 1932. "Uber Indgnflucht." *Swiss Archives for Neurology and Psychiatry* 30:94–102.

Binswanger, L. 1942. *Grundformen und Erkenntnis menschlichen Daseins.* Zurich: Max Niehaus.

References   339

Binswanger, L. 1956. *Erinnerungen an Sigmund Freud*. Bern: Franke Verlag.
Binswanger, L. 1963. *Being-in-the-World*. New York: Basic Books.
Bion, W. 1955. "Group dynamics: A Re-View." In M. Klein, P. Heilmann, and R. E. Money-Kyrle, eds., *New Directions in Psychoanalysis*. London: Tavistock.
Bion, W. 1959. *Experiences in Groups*. New York: Basic Books.
Bion, W. 1961. *Experiences in Groups*. New York: Basic Books.
Bion, W. 1962. *Learning from Experience*. New York: Basic Books.
Birk, L. 1976. *Task Force Report*, no. 15. Washington, D.C.: American Psychiatric Association.
Blanck, G. and R. Blanck. 1979. *Ego Psychology II: Psychoanalytic Development Object Relations Theory*. New York: Columbia University Press.
Blanck, R. and G. Blanck. 1986. *Beyond Ego Psychology: Development Object Relations Theory*. New York: Columbia University Press.
Borriello, J. F. 1976. "Leadership in the Therapist-Centered Group-as-a Whole Psychotherapy Approach." *International Journal of Group Psychotherapy* 23(2):149–162.
Borriello, J. F. 1976. "Group Psychotherapy in Hospital Systems." In L. R. Wolberg and M. L. Aronson, eds., *Group Therapy 1976*. New York: Stratton Intercontinental Medical Book Corp.
Borriello, J. F. "Group Psychotherapy with Acting-Out Patients: Specific Problems and Technique." *American Journal of Psychotherapy* 23(4):521–530.
Borriello, J. F. "Intervention Foci in Group Psychotherapy." In L. R. Wolberg and M. L. Aronson, eds., *Group Therapy 1979*. New York: Stratton Intercontinental Medical Book Corp.
Boss, M. 1963. *Psychoanalysis and Daseinanalysis*. New York: Basic Books.
Bowlby, J. 1975. *Attachment and Loss* 7:236, 238–9. London: Pelican Books.
Brentano, F. 1974. *Psychology from an Empirical Point of View*. Leipzig: Meiner.
Brodsky, B. 1967. "Working Through: It's Widening Scope and Some Aspects of its Metapsychology." *Psychoanalytic Quarterly* 36:485–495.
Buber, M. 1965. *The Knowledge of Man*. New York: Macmillan.
Burrow, T. 1927. "The Group Method of Analysis." *Psychoanalysis Review* 14:268–280.
Cartwright, D. and A. Zander. 1968. *Group Dynamics*. New York: Harper and Row.
Clement, P. W., R. A. Fazzone, and B. Goldstein. 1970. "Tangible Reinforcers and Child Group Therapy." *Journal of the American Academy of Child Psychiatry* 9:409–427.
Cooley, C. H. 1902. *Human Nature and the Social Order*. Glencoe, Il.: Free Press.
Danysh, J. 1974. *Stop Without Quitting*. San Francisco: International Society for General Semantics.

Darwin, C. 1871. *The Descent of Man and Selection in Relation to Sex.* 2d ed. New York: D. Appleton, 1899.

Davis, M. and D. Wallbridge. 1981. *Boundary and Space: An Introduction to the Work of D. W. Winnicott.* London: Karnac Books.

De Mare, P. B. 1972. *Perspectives in Group Psychotherapy: A Theoretical Background.* London: Allen & Unicorn.

Dicks, H. V. 1970. *Fifty Years of the Tavistock Clinic.* London: Routledge & Kegan Paul.

DiGiuseppe, R. A., N. J. Miller, and L. D. Trexler. 1979. "A Review of Rational-Emotive Psychotherapy Outcome Studies." In A. Ellis and J. M. Whiteley, eds., *Theoretical and Empirical Foundations of Rational-Emotive Therapy,* pp. 218–235. Monterey: Brooks/Cole.

Dryden, W. 1984. *Rational-Emotive Therapy: Fundamentals and Innovations.* Beckenham, Kent: Croomhelm.

Durkin, H. E. 1964. *The Group in Depth.* New York: International Universities Press.

Durkin, H. E. 1974. "Theoretical Foundations of Group Psychotherapy—1." In S. DeSchill, ed., *The Challenge for Group Psychotherapy: Present and Future.* New York: International Universities Press.

Durkin, H. E. 1975. "The Development of Systems Theory and its Implications for the Theory and Practice of Group Therapy." In L. Wolberg and M. Aronson, eds., *Group Therapy: An Overview.* New York: Stratton Intercontinental Books.

Durkin, H. E. 1983. "Developmental Levels: Their Therapeutic Implications for Analytic Group Psychotherapy." *Group* 7:3–10.

Durkin, H. E., H. T. Glatzter, A. L. Kadis, A. Wolf, and W. C. Hulse. 1958. "Acting Out in Group Psychotherapy: A Panel Discussion." *American Journal of Psychotherapy* 12:87–105.

Ellis, A. 1957. *How to Live with a Neurotic: At Home and At Work.* New York: Crown. Rev. ed., Hollywood: Wilshire Books.

Ellis, A. 1962. *Reason and Emotion in Psychotherapy.* Secaucus, N.J.: Citadel.

Ellis, A. 1969. "A Weekend of Rational Encounter." *Rational Living* 4(2):1–8.

Ellis, A. 1971. *Growth Through Reason.* North Hollywood: Wilshire Books.

Ellis, A. 1972. Psychotherapy and The Value of a Human Being. New York Institute for Rational Emotive Therapy

Ellis, A. 1973a. *Humanistic Psychotherapy: The Rational-Emotive Approach.* New York: McGraw-Hill.

Ellis, A. 1973b. *Twenty-one Ways to Stop Worrying.* Cassette recording. New York: Institute for Rational-Emotive Therapy.

Ellis, A. 1973c. *How to Stubbornly Refuse to be Ashamed of Anything.* Cassette recording. New York: Institute for Rational-Emotive Therapy.

Ellis, A. 1975. *RET and Assertiveness Training.* Cassette recording. New York: Institute for Rational-Emotive therapy.

Ellis, A. 1976a. *Sex and the Liberated Man*. Secaucus, N.J.: Lyle Stuart.

Ellis, A. 1976b. "RET abolishes most the human ego." *Psychotherapy* 13:343–348. Reprinted: New York: Institute for Rational-Emotive Therapy.

Ellis, A. 1977. *Conquering the Dire Need for Love*. Cassette recording. New York: Institute for Rational-Emotive Therapy.

Ellis, A. 1978. *I'd Like to Stop but . . . Dealing with Addictions*. Cassette recording. New York: Institute for Rational-Emotive Therapy.

Ellis, A. 1978. *Brief Psychotherapy in Medical and Health Practice*. New York: Springer.

Ellis, A. 1979. *The Intelligent Woman's Guide to Dating and Mating*. Secaucus, N.J.: Lyle Stuart.

Ellis, A. 1982. *Solving Emotional Problems*. Cassette recording. New York: Institute for Rational-Emotive Therapy.

Ellis, A. 1986. "Rational-Emotive Therapy." In I. L. Kutash and A. Wolf, eds., *Psychotherapist's Casebook*. San Francisco: Jossey-Bass.

Ellis, A. 1987. "The Use of Rational Humorous Songs in Psychotherapy. In W. R. Fry, Jr., and W. A. Salameh, eds., *Handbook of Humor and Psychotherapy*, pp. 265–286. Sarasota, Fla: Professional Resource Exchange.

Ellis, A. 1988a. *How to Stubbornly Refuse to Make Yourself Miserable About Anything—Yes, Anything!*. Secaucus, N.J.: Lyle Stuart.

Ellis, A. 1988b. "The Philosophical Basis of Rational-Emotive Therapy (RET)." Paper presented at the American Psychological Association Convention, Atlanta, August 15.

Ellis, A. 1988c. "Study of Verbal and Behavioral Homework Assignments in Group Therapy." Unpublished study, Institute for Rational-Emotive Therapy, New York City.

Ellis, A. and E. Abrahms. 1978. *Brief Psychotherapy in Medical and Health Practice*. New York: Springer.

Ellis, A. and I. Becker. 1982. *A Guide to Personal Happiness*. North Hollywood: Wilshire Books.

Ellis, A. and M. E. Bernard, eds. 1983. *Rational-Emotive Approaches to the Problems. Childhood* New York. Plenum.

Ellis, A. and M. E. Bernard, eds. 1985. *Clinical Applications of Rational-Emotive Therapy*. New York: Plenum.

Ellis, A. and W. Dryden. 1987. *The Practice of Rational-Emotive Therapy*, vol. 1. New York: Springer.

Ellis, A. and R. Grieger, eds. 1977. *Handbook of Rational-Emotive Therapy*, vol 1. New York: Springer.

Ellis, A. and R. Grieger. 1988. *Handbook of Rational-Emotive Therapy*, vol. 2. New York: Springer.

Ellis, A. and R. A. Harper. 1961. *A Guide to Successful Marriage*. North Hollywood: Wilshire Books.

Ellis, A. and R. A. Harper. 1975. *A New Guide to Rational Living*. North Hollywood: Wilshire Books.

Ellis, A., J. F. McInerney, R. DiGiuseppe, and R. J. Yeager. 1988. *Rational-Emotive Therapy with Alcoholics and Substance Abusers*. New York: Pergamon.

Ellis, A., J. Sichel, R. A. DiGiuseppe, and D. J. DiMattia. (in press). *Rational-Emotive Couples Counseling*. New York: Pergamon.

Ellis, A., J. Sichel, R. C. Leaf, and R. Mass. 1988. "Countering Perfectionism in Research on Clinical Practice. 1: A Survey of Changes after a Single Intensive RET intervention." Unpublished paper. New York City: Institute for Rational-Emotive Therapy.

Ellis, A. and J. M. Whiteley. 1979. *Theoretical and Empirical Foundations of Rational-Emotive Therapy*. Monterey: Brooks/Cole.

Ellis, A. and R. Yeager. 1989. *Cult Psychology: The Dangers of Transpersonal Therapy*. Buffalo, N.Y.: Prometheus.

Ezriel, H. 1950. "A Psychoanalytic Approach to Group Treatment." *British Journal of Medical Psychology* 23:59–74.

Ezriel H. 1957. "The Role of Transference in Psychoanalytical and Other Approaches to Group Treatment." *Acta Psychotherapeutica* 7: 101–116.

Ezriel H. 1973. "Psychoanalytic Group Therapy." In L. R. Wolberg and E. K. Schwartz, eds., *Group Therapy 1973*. New York: Intercontinental Medical Books.

Falloon, I. R. H. 1981. "Interpersonal Variables in Behavioral Group Therapy." *British Journal of Medical Psychology* 54:133–141.

Foulkes, S. H. 1951. "Concerning Leadership in Group-Analytic Psychotherapy." *Introduction to Journal of Group Psychotherapy* 1:319–329.

Foulkes, S. H. 1964. *Therapeutic Group Analysis*. New York: International Universities Press.

Foulkes, S. H. 1983. *Introduction to Group Analytic Psychotherapy*. London: Maresfield Reprints. (Originally published 1948).

Foulkes, S. H. 1984. *Group Psychotherapy: The Psychoanalytic Approach*. London: Maresfield Reprints. (Originally published 1957.)

Foulkes, S. H. 1984. *Therapeutic Group Analysis*. London: Maresfield Reprints. (Originally published 1964.)

Foulkes, S. H. and E. J. Anthony. 1957. *Group Psychotherapy: The Psychoanalytic Approach*. London: Penguin Books.

Foulkes, S. H. and E. J. Anthony. 1965. *Group Psychotherapy*, 2d ed. London: Pelican Books.

Framo, J. 1980. "Couples Group Therapy." In Andolfi and Zwerling, eds., *Dimensions of Family Therapy*. New York: Guilford Press.

Framo, J. 1986. "Couples Group Therapy with Family-of-Origin Sessions." In I. L. Kutash and A. Wolf, eds., *Psychotherapist's Casebook*. San Francisco: Jossey-Bass.

References   343

Frankl, Viktor E. 1978. *The Unheard Cry for Meaning*. New York: Simon & Schuster.

Fried, E. 1954. "The Effect of Combined Therapy on the Productivity of Patients." *International Journal of Group Psychotherapy* 4:42–55.

Fried, E. 1961. "Techniques of Psychotherapy Going Beyond Insight." *International Journal of Group Psychotherapy* 11:297–304.

French, T. M. 1952. *The Integration of Behavior*. Chicago: University of Chicago Press.

Freud, S. 1914. "Recollection, Repetition and Working Through." *Collected Papers II*, pp. 366–376. London: Hogarth Press.

Freud, S. 1921. *Group Psychology and the Analysis of the Ego*. Standard Edition, vol. 18. London: Hogarth, 1955.

Freud, S. 1938. *The General Introduction to Psychoanalysis*. Garden City: Garden City Publishing.

Frew, J. 1988. The practice of Gestalt therapy in groups. *The Gestalt Journal* 11(1):77–96.

Ganzarain, R. 1959. "Study of the Effectiveness of Group therapy in the Training of Medical Students." *International Journal of Group Psychotherapy* 9:475–487.

Gay, P. 1988. *Freud, A Life for Our Times*. New York: Norton.

Gendron, J. M. 1980. *Moreno: The Roots and Branches and Bibliography of Psychodrama, 1972–80 and Sociometry, 1970–80*. Beacon, N.Y.: Beacon House.

Glatzer, H. T. 1959. "Analysis of Masochism in Group Psychotherapy." *International Journal of Group Psychotherapy* 9:158–166.

Glatzer, H. T. 1960. "Discussion of symposium on Combined Individual and Group Psychotherapy. *American Journal of Orthopsychiatry* 30:243–246.

Glatzer, H. T. 1962. "Narcissistic Problems in Group Psychotherapy." *International Journal of Group Psychotherapy* 12:448–455.

Glatzer, H. T. 1965. "Aspects of Transference in Group Psychotherapy." *International Journal of Group Psychotherapy*. 15:167–176.

Glatzer, H. T. 1969. "Analytic Group Psychotherapy: Working Through the Working Alliance." *International Journal of Group Psychotherapy* 19(3).

Glatzer, H. T. 1975. "The Leader as Supervisor and Supervisee." In Z. A. Liff, ed., *The Leader in the Group*, pp. 138–145. New York: Jason Aronson.

Glatzer, H. T. 1978. The Working Alliance in Analytic Group Psychotherapy. *Journal of Group Psychotherapy* 28(2).

Goldstein, A. P. 1973. *Structured Learning Therapy: Toward a Psychotherapy for the Poor*. Elmsford, N.Y.: Pergamon Press.

Goulding, R. L. 1966. "T. A. and Alcoholism." *T. A. Bulletin* 5(20):177. (October 1966.)

Goulding, R. L. 1972. "New Directions in Transactional Analysis: Creating an Environment for Change." In C. J. Sager, H. S. and Kaplan, eds., *Progress in Group and Family Therapy*, pp. 105–134. New York: Bruner/Mazel.

Goulding, R. L. 1974. "Thinking and Feeling in Psychotherapy: Three Impasses." *Voices* 10(1):11–13.

Goulding, R. L. 1975. "Curing Phobias." *Voices* 11(1):30–31.

Goulding, R. L. 1976. "Four Models of Transactional Analysis." *International Journal of Group Psychotherapy July 1976* 26(3):385–392.

Goulding, R. L. 1976. "Gestalt Therapy and Transactional Analysis." In C. Hatcher and P. Himmelstein, eds., *Handbook of Gestalt Therapy*. New York: Jason Aronson.

Goulding, R. L. and M. C. Goulding. 1978. In P. McCormick, ed., *The Power is in the Patient*. San Francisco: TA Press. (Collection of Goulding's articles)

Goulding, R. L. and M. C. Goulding. 1976. "Injunctions, Decisions and Redecisions," *Transactional Analysis Journal* 6(1):41–48 (January).

Goulding, R. L. and M. C. Goulding. 1979. *Changing Lives Through Redecision Therapy*. New York: Bruner/Mazell.

Greenson, R. 1965. "The Problem of Working Through." In M. Schur, ed., *Drives, Affects and Behavior*, vol. 2. New York: International Universities Press.

Greenwald, A. G., A. R. Pratkanis, M. R. Leippe, and M. H. Baumgardner. 1986. "Under What Conditions Does Theory Obstruct Research Progress?" *Psychological Review* 93:216–229.

Greer, V. J. and J. M. Sacks. 1973. *Bibliography of Psychodrama*. Privately published.

Grieger, R. and J. Boyd. 1980. *Rational-Emotive Therapy: A Skills-Based Approach*. New York: Van Nostrand Reinhold.

Grinberg, L. 1973. "Projective Identification and Projective Counter-Identification in the Dynamics of Groups." In L. R. Wolberg and E. K. Schwartz, eds., *Group Therapy 1973*. New York: Intercontinental Medical Books.

Guntrip, H. J. S. 1974. "Psychoanalytic Object-Relations Theory." In S. Arieti, ed., *American Handbook of Psychiatry*. 2d ed. Vol. 1. New York: Basic Books.

Guralnik, D. B., ed. 1982. *Webster's New World Dictionary of the American Language*, 2d college ed. New York: Simon & Schuster.

Gurwitsch, A. 1966. "Edmund Husserl's Conceptions of Phenomenological Psychology." *Review of Metaphysics* 19:689–727.

Harman, R. 1984. "Recent Developments in Gestalt Group Therapy." *International Journal of Group Psychotherapy* 34(3):473–483.

Hartman, H. 1958. *Ego Psychology and the Problem of Adaptation*. New York: International Universities Press. (Originally published in 1939.)

Harwood. I. 1986. "Group Psychotherapy with Disorders of the Self from a Self Psychological Perspective." Paper presented at the meeting of the Society for the Study of the Self, Los Angeles, Summer 1986.

Hauck, P. A. 1973. *Overcoming Depression*. Philadelphia: Westminster.

Hauck, P. A. 1974. *Overcoming Frustration and Anger*. Philadelphia: Westminster.

Heath, E. S. and H. A. Bacal. "A Method of Group Psychotherapy at the Tavistock Clinic." *International Journal of Group Psychotherapy* 18:21–30.

Heidbreder, E. 1933. *Seven Psychologies*. New York: Appleton-Century.

Heidegger, M. 1949. *Sein und Zeit*. Tübingen: Neomarius.

Hierholzer, R. W. and R. P. Liberman. 1986. "Successful Living: A Social Skill, and Problem-Solving Group for the Chronic Mentally Ill." *Hospital and Community Psychiatry* 37:913–918.

Houts, P. S. and M. Serber, eds. 1972. *After the Turn-On, What? Learning Perspectives on Humanistic Groups*. Champaign, Il.: Research Press.

Holt, H. 1959. "States of Being, An Existential Approach." *Transactions of the New York Institute of Existential Analysis* 1:86–95.

Holt, H. 1965. "Existential Group Analysis." In J. L. Moreno and A. Friedman, eds., *International Handbook of Group Psychotherapy*. New York: Philosophical Library.

Holt, H. 1968. "The Problem of Interpretation from the Point of View of Existential Psychoanalysis." In E. Hammer. ed., *The Use of Interpretation in Treatment*. New York: Grune & Stratton.

Holt, H. 1969. "Schizophrenia: A Contribution from Existential Psychiatry." *The American Journal of Psychoanalysis* 31:138–145.

Holt, H. 1970a. "Is Psychoanalytic Language Obsolete?" *Journal of Contemporary Psychotherapy* 3:53–59.

Holt, H. 1970b. "The Psychiatrist in a Technological Age." *The Journal of Psychoanalysis in Groups* 3:16–21.

Holt, H. 1975. "Existential Psychoanalysis." In A. M. Freedman, ed., *Comprehensive Textbook of Psychiatry, II*. Baltimore: Williams & Wilkins.

Holt, H. 1976. *Free to be Good or Bad*. New York: M. Evans.

Holt, H. 1978. "A Theory of the Life-World of Existential Group Therapy." *Modern Psychotherapy* 1:35–42.

Holt, H. 1979a. "An Existential View of Neurotic Conflicts." *Modern Psychotherapy* 2:20–26.

Holt, H. 1979b. "The Case of Father M." In D. Hedding and R. Corsini, eds., *Great Cases in Psychotherapy*. Itasca: Peacock.

Holt, H. 1980. "Existential Analysis with the Aging and Terminally Ill. *Journal of Pastoral Counseling* 15:32–39.

Holt, H. 1981. "Some Fundamental Ideas in Existential Analysis." *Modern Psychotherapy* 3:17–23.

Holt, H. 1985a. "Existential Psychoanalysis and Modern Psychoanalysis." *Modern Psychoanalysis* 9:21–27.

References

Holt, H. 1985b. "The Subjective Experience of the Self." *Modern Psychotherapy* 1:32–39.

Holt, H. 1985c. "Existential Attitudes Towards Terminally Ill Patients." Paper presented at the annual meeting of the International Existential Society, Zurich, Switzerland, July 1985.

Holt, H. 1986. "Existential Psychoanalysis." In I. L. Kutash and A. Wolf, eds., *Psychotherapist's Casebook*. San Francisco: Jossey-Bass.

Horney, K. 1950. *Neurosis and Human Growth*. New York: Norton.

Horwitz, L. 1971. "Group Centered Interventions in Therapy Groups." *Comprehensive Group Studies* 2:311–331.

Horwitz, L. 1977. "Group-Centered Approach to Group Psychotherapy." *International Journal of Group Psychotherapy* 27:424–439.

Horwitz, L. 1986. "An Integrated Group Centered Approach." In I. L. Kutash and A. Wolf, eds., *Psychotherapist's Casebook*. San Francisco: Jossey-Bass.

Horwitz, L. 1989. "The Evolution of a Group Centered Approach. In S. Tuttman, ed., *The Expanding World of Group Psychotherapy*. Madison, Conn. International Universities Press.

Hubel, D. 1984. "The Brian." *Scientific American*.

Institute for Rational-Emotive Therapy 1989. *Catalogue*. New York: Institute for Rational-Emotive Therapy.

Jacobs, L. (in press.) Dialogue in Gestalt theory and therapy. *The Gestalt Journal*.

Jacobson, E. 1964. *The Self and the Object World*. New York: International Universities Press.

Jaspers, K. 1963. *General Psychopathology*. Chicago: University of Chicago Press.

Jones, E. 1955. *The Life and Work of Sigmund Freud*. New York: Basic Books.

Kaplan, H. I. and B. T. Sadock. 1971. *Comprehensive Group Psychotherapy*. Baltimore: Williams & Wilkins.

Karush, A. 1967. "Working Through." *Psychoanalytic Quarterly* 36:497–531.

Kaslow, F. and E. J. Lieberman. 1981. "Couples Group Therapy, Rational, Dynamics and Process." In G. P. Sholivar, ed., *Handbook of Marriage and Marital Therapy*. New York: S. P. Medical and Scientific Books.

Kaslow, F. and E. J. Lieberman. 1981. "Group Therapy with Couples in Conflict." *Psychotherapy and Theoretical Research and Practice*, pp. 516–524.

Kauff, P. 1989. "The Unique Contributions of Analytic Group Therapy to the Treatment of Pre-Oedipal Character Pathology. In S. Tuttman, ed., *The Expanding World of Group Psychotherapy*. Madison, Conn.: International Universities Press.

Kazdin, A. F. 1988. *Child Psychotherapy*. Elmsford, N.Y.: Pergamon Press.

Kernberg, O. 1975. *Borderline Conditions and Pathological Narcissism*. Jason Aronson, New York.

Kibel, H. 1989. "The Therapeutic Use of Splitting: The Role of the "Mother-Group" in Therapeutic Differentiation and Practicing." In S. Tuttman, ed., *The Expanding World of Group Psychotherapy*. Madison, Conn.: International Universities Press.

King, L. W., R. P. Liberman, J. Roberts, and E. Bryan. 1977. "Personal Effectiveness: A Structural Therapy for Improving Social and Emotional Skills." *European Journal of Behavioral Analysis and Modification* 2: 82–91.

Kohon, G., ed. 1986. *The British School of Psychoanalysis*. London: Free Association.

Kohut, H. 1966. "Forms and Transformations of Narcissism." *Journal of the American Psychoanalytic Association* 14:243–272.

Kohut, H. 1971. *The Analysis of the Self*. New York: International Universities Press.

Kohut, H. 1977. *The Restoration of the Self*. New York: International Universities Press.

Kohut, H. 1978. "Creativeness, Charisma, Group Psychology: Reflections on the Self-Analysis of Freud." In P. Ornstein, ed., *The Search for the Self*. Vol 2. New York: International Universities Press.

Kohut, H. 1979. "The Two Analyses of Mr. Z." *International Journal of Psychoanalysis* 60:3–27.

Kohut, H. 1984. *How Does Analysis Cure*. Chicago: University of Chicago Press.

Kohut, H. and E. S. Wolf. 1978. "The Disorders of the Self and Their Treatment." *International Journal of Psychoanalysis* 59:413–425.

Korzybski, A. 1933. *Science and Sanity*. San Francisco: International Society of General Semantics.

Kosseff, J. W. 1975. "The Leader Using Object-Relations Theory." In Z. A. Liff, ed., *The Leader and the Group*, pp. 212–242. New York: Jason Aronson.

Kosseff, J. W. 1989. "The Group as Paradox." In S. Tuttman, ed., *The Expanding World of Group Psychotherapy*. Madison, Conn. International Universities Press.

Kubie, L. S. 1958. "Theoretical Concepts Underlying the Relationship of the Individual and the Group." *Psychotherapy* 8:3–19.

Kubie, L. S. 1968. "Unsolved Problems in the Resolution of the Transference." *Psychoanalytic Quarterly* 37:331–352.

Kubler-Ross, E. 1969. *On Death and Dying*. New York: Macmillan Publishing.

Kutash, I. L. 1984. "Anxiety" In R. A. Corsini, ed. *Encyclopedia of Psychology*. New York: John Wiley and Sons.

Kutash, I. L. 1984. "Victimology" In R. A. Corsini, ed. *Encyclopedia of Psychology*. New York: John Wiley and Sons.

Kutash, I. L. 1984. "Comments on Psychoanalysis in Groups: Creativity in Di-Egophrenia and Treatment Methods with Case Material." *Group* 8(1):23–26. New York: Bruner/Mazel.

Kutash, I. L. 1988. "Group Composition." *The Group Psychotherapist* 1(1).

Kutash, I. L. 1988. "A Mini Article on "A Mini Group." *The Group Psychotherapist* 1(2).

Kutash, I. L. and J. C. Greenberg. 1986. "Psychoanalytic Psychotherapy." In I. L. Kutash and A. Wolf, eds., *Psychotherapist's Casebook.* San Francisco: Jossey-Bass.

Kutash, I. L. and J. C. Greenberg. 1989. "The Remote Patient as a Symptom of Personality Disorder." *The Psychotherapy Patient.* Volume 6 Nos 1/2.

Kutash, I. L. and J. C. Greenberg. 1990. The Remote Patient as a Symptom of Personality Disorder in J. Travers, ed., *Psychotherapy and the Remote Patient.* New York: Haworth Press.

Kutash, I. L., S. B. Kutash, and L. B. Schlesinger. 1978. *Violence, Perspectives on Murder and Agression.* San Francisco: Jossey-Bass.

Kutash, I. L. and L. B. Schlesinger. 1980. *Handbook on Stress Anxiety.* San Francisco: Jossey-Bass.

Kutash, I. L. and A. Wolf. 1983. "Recent Advances in Psychoanalysis in Groups." In H. I. Kaplan and B. J. Sadock, eds., *Comprehensive Group Psychotherapy.* Baltimore: Williams & Wilkins.

Kutash, I. L. and A. Wolf. 1984. "Psychoanalysis in Groups: The Primacy of the Individual." In H. S. Strean, ed., *Inhibitions in Work and Love: Psychoanalytic Approaches to Problems in Creativity.* New York: Haworth Press.

Kutash, I. L. and A. Wolf. 1986. *Psychotherapist's Casebook.* San Francisco: Jossey-Bass.

Kutash, I. L. and A. Wolf. 1989. "Equilibrium, Disequilibrium and Malequilibrium in Groups" in *The Group Psychotherapist* 2(2).

Lacan, J. 1968. *The Language of the Self.* Baltimore: Johns Hopkins University Press.

LeBon, G. 1895, 1920. *The Crowd: Study of the Popular Mind.* London: Fisher, Unwin.

Lebovici, S. 1974. "A Combination of Psychodrama and Group Psychotherapy." In S. DeSchill, ed., *The Challenge for Group Psychotherapy: Present and Future.* New York: International Universities Press.

Lewin, K., R. Lippitt, and R. K. White. 1939. "Patterns of Aggressive Behavior in Experimentally Created 'social climates.' " *Journal of Social Psychology* 10:271–299.

Lewin, K. 1947. "Group Decision and Social Change." In T. Newcomb and E. Hartley, eds., *Readings in Social Psychology,* pp. 330–344. New York: Holt.

Lewin, K. 1951. *Field Theory in Social Science.* New York: Harper.

Liberman, R. P. 1970. "A Behavioral Approach to Group Dynamics." *Behavior Therapy* 1:140–175.

Liberman, R. P. 1971. "Reinforcement of Cohesiveness in Group Therapy: Behavioral and Personality Changes." *Archives of General Psychiatry* 25:168–177.

Liberman, R. P. 1972. "Reinforcement of Social Interaction in a Group of Chronic Mental Patients." In R. Rubin et al., eds., *Advances in Behavior Therapy* 3:151–160. New York: Academic Press.

Liberman, R. P. 1987. *Psychiatric Rehabilitation of Chronic Mental Patients.* Washington, D.C.: American Psychiatric Press.

Liberman, R. P., W. J. DeRisi, and K. T. Mueser. 1989. *Social Skills Training for Psychiatric Patients.* Elmsford, N.Y.: Pergamon Press.

Liberman, R. P. and C. Evans. 1985. "Behavioral Rehabilitation of Chronic Mental Patients." *Journal of Clinical Psychopharmacology* 5:8S–14S.

Liberman, R. P., H. E. Jacobs, S. Boone, D. Foy, C. P. Donahoe, I. R. H. Fallon, G. Blackwell, and C. J. Wallace. 1986. "New Methods for Rehabilitating Chronic Mental Patients." In J. A. Talbott, ed., *Our Patient's Future in a Changing World*, pp. 99–129. Washington, D.C.: American Psychiatric Press.

Liberman, R. P., L. W. King, and W. J. DeRisi. 1976. "Behavior Analysis and Modification in Community Mental Health." In H. Leiterberg, ed., *Handbook of Behavior Therapy and Modification.* Englewood Cliffs, N.J.: Prentice-Hall.

Liberman, R. P., L. W. King, W. J. DeRisi, and M. McCann. 1975. "Personal Effectiveness: A Manual for Teaching Social and Emotional Skills." Champaign, Ill. Research Press.

Liberman, R. P. and K. Muesser. 1989. "Psychosocial Treatment of Schizophrenia." In H. I. Kaplan and B. Sadock, eds., *Comprehensive Textbook of Psychiatry*, vol. 5. Baltimore: Williams & Wilkins.

Liberman, R. P., K. T. Mueser, and C. J. Wallace. 1986. "Social Skills Training for Schizophrenic Individuals at Risk for Relapse." *American Journal of Psychiatry* 143:523–526.

Liberman, R. P. and J. Teigen. 1979. "Behavioral Group Therapy." In P. O. Sjoden, S. Bates, and W. S. Dockens, eds., *Trends in Behavior Therapy.* New York: Academic Press.

Lichtenberg, J. D. 1983. *Psychoanalysis and Infant Research.* New Jersey Analytic Press.

Liff, Z. A. 1975. *The Leader in the Group.* New York: Jason Aronson.

Loewald, H. 1960. "On the Therapeutic Action of Psychoanalysis." *International Journal of Psychoanalysis*, p. 41.

MacLean, P. D. 1952. "Some Psychiatric Implications of Physiological Studies on Frontotemporal Portion of Limbic System." *Electroencephalography and Clinical Neurophysiology* 4:407–418.

MacLean, P. D. 1969. *A Triune Concept of the Brain and Behavior.* Toronto: Toronto University Press.

MacLean, P. D. 1970. *The Triune Brain, Emotions and Scientific Bias.* New York: Rockefeller University Press.

Mahler, M. 1971. "A Study of the Separation-Individuation Process and Its Possible Application to Borderliine Phenomena in the Psychoanalytic Situation." *The Psychoanalytic Study of the Child.* Vol. 26. New York: Quadrangle Books.

Mahrer, A. R. 1988. "Discovery Oriented Psychotherapy Research." *American Psychologist* 43:694–702.

Main, M. et al. "Security in Infancy, Childhood and Adulthood: A Move to the Level of Representation." In I. Breterton and E. Waters, eds., *Growing Points in Attachment Theory and Research 5*, Serial No. 209, 66–104.

Malan, D. H., H. G. F. Balfour, V. G. Hood, and A. M. N. Shooter. 1976. "Group Psychotherapy: A Long Term Follow-Up Study." Archives of General Psychiatry 33:1303–1315.

Marks, M. 1985. "Normal and Pathological Narcissism in Relation to the Vicissitudes of Identity Formation: A Clinical Application of the Work of Edith Jacobson." *Current Issues in Psychoanalytic Practice* 2(1).

Marks, M. 1986. "Ego Psychology." In I. L. Kutash and A. Wolf, eds., *Psychotherapist's Casebook.* San Francisco: Jossey-Bass.

Marks, I. M. 1987. *Fears, Phobias, and Rituals.* New York: Oxford University Press.

Marrone, M. 1984. "Aspects of Transference in Group Analysis." *Group Analysis* 17(3):179–90.

Maultsby, M. C., Jr. 1975. *Help Yourself to Happiness; Through Rational Self-Counseling.* New York: Institute for Rational-Emotive Therapy.

Maultsby, M. C. and A. Ellis. 1974. *Technique for Using Rational-Emotive Imagery.* New York: Institute for Rational-Emotive Therapy.

McDougall, W. 1920. *The Group Mind.* Cambridge: Cambridge University Press.

McGovern, T. E. and M. S. Silverman. 1984. "A Review of Outcome Studies of Rational-Emotive Therapy from 1977 to 1982." *Journal of Rational-Emotive Therapy* 2(1):7–18.

Mead, G. H. 1934. *Mind, Self, and Society.* Chicago: University of Chicago Press.

Meehl, P. E. 1978. "Theoretical Risks and Tabular Asterisks: Sir Karl, Sir Ronald and the Slow Progress of Soft Psychology." *Journal of Consulting and Clinical Psychology* 46:806–834.

Meichenbaum, D. 1977. Cognitive-Behavior Modification, New York: Plenum.

Moreno, J. L. 1914. *Einladung zu einer Begegnung* (Invitation to an Encounter). Vienna: Anzengruber Verlag.

Moreno, J. L. 1946. "Psychodrama and Group Therapy." *Sociometry* 9:249, 253.

Moreno, J. L. 1964. *Psychodrama*, vol. 1. 3rd ed. Beacon, N.Y.: Beacon House.

Moreno, J. L. 1947. *The Theater of Spontaneity*. Beacon, N.Y.: Beacon House.

Moreno, J. L. 1964. *Who Shall Survive?* Beacon, N.Y.: Beacon House.

Moreno, Z. T. 1965. "Psychodramatic Rules, Techniques and Adjunctive Methods." *Group Psychotherapy* 18:73–86.

Moreno, Z. T. 1967. "The Seminal Mind of J. L. Moreno." *Group Psychotherapy* 22(3–4):218–229.

Moreno, Z. T. 1979. "Beyond Aristotle, Breuer and Freud: Moreno's Contribution to the Concept of Catharsis." *Integrative Therapie* 5:135–37.

Nicholas, M. 1981. *Changes in the Context of Group Psychotherapy*. New York: S. P. Medical and Scientific Books.

Nichols, M. P. and M. Zax. 1977. *Catharsis in Psychotherapy*. New York: Gardner.

O'Connor, R. D. 1969. "Modification of Social Withdrawal Through Symbolic Modeling." *Journal of Applied Behavior Analysis* 2:15–22.

Perls, F., R. Hefferline, and P. Goodman. 1951. *Gestalt Therapy*. New York: Dell.

Pines, M. 1970. *Bion and Group Psychotherapy*. London: Routledge & Kegan Paul.

Pines, M. 1981. "The Frame of Reference of Group Psychotherapy." *International Journal of Group Psychotherapy* 31(3):275–285.

Pines, M. 1983. "On Mirroring in Group Psychotherapy." *Group Therapy Monograph 9*. New York: Washington Square Institute for Psychotherapy and Mental Health.

Pines, M. 1983. "The Fundamentals of Group Analytic Therapy." In M. Pines, eds., *The Evolution of Group Analysis*. London: Routledge & Kegan Paul.

Pines, M. 1984. "Reflections on Mirroring." *International Review of Psychoanalysis*.

Pines, M., L. E. Hearst, and H. L. Behr. 1982. "Group Analysis (Group Analytic Psychotherapy)." In G. M. Gasda, ed., *Basic Approaches to Group Psychotherapy and Group Counselling*, 3d ed. Springfield, Ill.: Charles C. Thomas.

Pratt, J. H. 1907. "The Class Method of Treating Consumption in the Homes of the Poor." *Journal of the American Medical Association* 49:755–759.

PRC (Psychiatric Rehabilitation Consultants). 1988. "Modules for Training Social and Independent Living Skills." Available from Camarillo-UCLA Research Center, Box A, Camarillo, Calif. 93011.

Rapaport, D. 1959. "The Structure of Psychoanalytic Theory: A Systematizing Attempt." *Psychological Issues Monograph 6.* New York: International Universities Press.

Reik, T. 1948. *Listening with the Third Ear: The Inner Experience of a Psychoanalyst.* New York: Farrar, Straus.

Rice, A. K. 1965. *Learning for Leadership.* London: Tavistock.

Rorer, L. G. (in press). "Rational-Emotive Therapy: 1. An Integrated Psychological and Philosophical Basis." *Cognitive Therapy and Research.*

Rosenbaum, M. 1971. "Co-therapy." In H. I. Kaplan and B. J. Sadock, eds., *Comprehensive Group Psychotherapy.* Baltimore: Williams & Wilkins.

Rosenbaum, M. and M. Berger. 1963. *Group Psychotherapy and Group Function.* New York: Basic Books.

Rueveni, U. 1979. *Networking Families in Crisis,* New York, Human Sciences Press.

Rueveni, U. 1982. *Therapeutic Interventions: Healing Human Systems,* New York: Human Sciences Press.

Rueveni, U. ed. 1984. "Application of Networking in Family and Community," *International Journal of Family Therapy* 6(2).

Rueveni, U. and R. V. Speck. 1969. "Using Encounter Group Techniques in the Treatment of Social Network of the Schizophrenic Family." *International Journal of Group Psychotherapy* 12(4).

Sacks, J. M. 1974. "The Letter." *Group Psychotherapy* 27:184–190.

Sager, C. 1959. "The Effects of Group Psychotherapy on Individual Psychoanalysis." *International Journal of Group Psychotherapy* 9.

Sager, C. 1960. "Concurrent Individual and Group Analytic Psychotherapy." *American Journal of Orthopsychiatry* 30.

Sartre, J. P. 1957. *Existential Psychoanalysis.* New York: Philosophical Library.

Satir, Virginia. 1976. *Making Contact.* California: Celestial Arts.

Satyanarayan, R. 1987. "Developmental Aspects of Role Reversal." Unpublished doctoral dissertation, Pacific University.

Scheidlinger, S. 1960. "Group Process in Group Psychotherapy, Parts I and II." *American Journal of Psychotherapy* 14:104–120, 346–363.

Scheidlinger, S. 1964. "Identification, the Sense of Identity and of Belonging in Small Groups." *International Journal of Group Psychotherapy* 9:661–672.

Scheidlinger, S. 1974. "On the Concept of the "Mother-Group." *International Journal of Group Psychotherapy* 24:417–428.

Scheidlinger, S. 1980. *Psychoanalytic Group Dynamics.* New York: International Universities Press.

Scheidlinger, S. 1982. *Focus on Group Psychotherapy: Clinical Essays.* New York: International Universities Press.

Scheidlinger, S. 1982. "On the Concept of the "Mother-Group." In S. Scheidlinger, ed., *Focus on Group Psychotherapy: Clinical Essays,* pp. 75–88.

Schiff, J. L. et al. 1975. "The Cathexis Reader." New York: Harper & Row.

Schilder, P. 1939. "Results and Problems of Group Psychotherapy in Severe Neurosis." *Mental Health* 23:87–98.

Schwartz, E. K. and A. Wolf. 1959. "The Quest for Certainty." *Archives of Neurological Psychiatry* 81:69–84.

Segal, H. 1973. *Introduction to the Work of Melanie Klein.* New York: Basic Books.

Shapiro, D. and L. Birk. 1967. "Group Therapy in Experimental Perspective." *International Journal of Group Psychotherapy* 17:211–224.

Sichel, J. and A. Ellis. 1984. *RET Self-Help Form.* New York: Institute for Rational-Emotive Therapy.

Slavson, S. R. 1950. *Analytic Group Psychotherapy.* New York: Columbia University Press.

Slavson, S. R. 1964. *An Introduction to Group Therapy.* New York: Commonwealth Fund.

Slavson, S. R. 1964. *A Textbook in Analytic Group Psychotherapy.* New York: International Universities Press.

Skinner, B. F. 1971. *Beyond Freedom and Dignity.* New York: Knopf.

Socher, Manderscherd, Flatten, and Silbergeld. "A Controlled Study of Quantitative Feedback in Married Couples' Brief Psychotherapy." *Psychotherapy Theoretical Research and Practice* 18:204–216.

Speck, R. V. and C. L. Attneave. 1973. *Family Network.* New York: Pantheon.

Spitz, R. 1965. *The First Year of Life.* New York: International Universities Press.

Stein, A. 1963. "Indications for Group Psychotherapy and the Selection of Patients." *Journal of Hillside Hospital* 12:145–155.

Stein, A. 1964. "The Nature of Transference in Combined Therapy." *International Journal of Psychotherapy* 14:413.

Stein, A. and H. D. Kibel. 1984. "A Group Dynamic Peer Interaction Approach to Group Psychotherapy." *International Journal of Psychotherapy* 34:315–334.

Stone, W. N. and R. M. Whitman. 1977. "Contributions of the Psychology of the Self to Group Process and Group Therapy." *International Journal of Group Psychotherapy* 27:343–359.

Strauss, E. W. et al. 1969. *Psychiatry and Philosophy.* New York: Springer-Verlag.

Strupp, H., R. Fox, and K. Lessler. 1969. *Patients View Their Psychotherapy.* Baltimore: Johns Hopkins University Press.

Sutherland, J. D. 1980. "The British Object Relations Theorists: Balint, Winnicott, Fairbairn, Guntrip." *Journal American Psychoanalytic Association* 28(4):829–860.

Sutherland, J. D. 1985. "Bion Revisited: Group Dynamics and Group

Psychotherapy." In M. Pines, ed., *Bion and Group Psychotherapy*. London: Routledge & Kegan Paul.

Toeman, Z. 1948. "The Double Situation in Psychodrama." *Sociatry* 1:463–448.

Trist, E. 1985. "Working with Bion in the 1940s: The Group Decade." In M. Pines, ed., *Bion and Group Psychotherapy*. London: Routledge & Kegan Paul.

Trotter, W. 1916. *Instincts of the Herd in Peace and War*. London: Fisher, Unwin.

Truax, C. and R. Carkhuff. 1967. *Toward Effective Counseling and Psychotherapy*. Chicago: Aldine Press.

Tuttman, S. 1984. "Application of Object Relations Theory and Self-Psychology in Current Group Therapy." *Group* 8:41–48.

Tuttman, S. 1986. "Theoretical and Technical Elements which Characterize the American Approaches to Psychoanalytic Group Psychotherapy." *International Journal of Group Psychotherapy* 36:499–515.

Tuttman, S., ed. 1990. *Psychoanalytic Group Theory and Therapy*. Madison, Conn.: International Universities Press.

Walen, S. R., R. DiGiuseppe, and R. L. Wessler. 1980. *A Practitioner's Guide to Rational-Emotive Therapy*. New York: Oxford.

Weiner, M. 1984. *Group Psychotherapy Techniques*. Washington, D.C.: American Psychiatric Press.

Weisman, Avery. 1965. *The Existential Core of Psychoanalysis*. Boston: Little, Brown.

Wender, L. 1936. "The Dynamics of Group Psychotherapy and its Applications." *Journal of Nervous Mental Disorders* 84:54–60.

Wertheimer, M. 1959. *Productive Thinking*. New York: Harper & Row.

Wessler, R. A. and R. L. Wessler. 1980. *The Principles and Practice of Rational-Emotive Therapy*. San Francisco: Jossey-Bass.

Whitaker, D. S. and M. A. Lieberman. 1964. *Psychotherapy Through the Group Process*. New York: Atherton Press.

Winnicott, D. W. 1965. "The Theory of the Parent-Infant Relationship." Originally published in 1960. In *Maturational Processes and the Facilitating Environment*. New York: International Universities Press.

Winnicott, D. W. 1965. *The Maturational Processes and the Facilitating Environment*. New York: International Universities Press.

Winnicott, D. W. 1976. "Egodistortions in Terms of True and False Self." In *The Maturational Processes and the Facilitating Environment*. London: Hogarth Press.

Wolberg, L. R. and M. L. Aronson, eds. 1975. *Group Therapy 1975: An Overview*. New York: Stratton Intercontinental Medical Book Corporation.

Wolf, A. 1949. "The Psychoanalysis of Groups." *American Journal of Psychotherapy* 3:525–55.

Wolf, A. 1950. "The Psychoanalysis of Groups." *American Journal of Psychotherapy* 4:16–50.

Wolf, A. 1967. "Group Psychotherapy." In A. M. Freedman and H. I. Kaplan, eds., *Comprehensive Textbook of Psychiatry*, pp. 1234–1241. Baltimore: Williams & Wilkins.

Wolf, A. 1974. "Psychoanalysis in Groups." In S. DeSchill, ed., *The Challenge for Group Psychotherapy: Present and Future*. New York: International Universities Press.

Wolf, A. 1983. "Psychoanalysis in Groups." In H. L. Kaplan and B. J. Sadock, eds., *Comprehensive Group Psychotherapy*. Baltimore: Williams & Wilkins.

Wolf, A. and I. L. Kutash. 1980. "Psychoanalysis in Groups: Dealing with the Roots of Aggression." *International Journal of Group Tensions* 10:1–4.

Wolf, A. and I. L. Kutash. 1982. Book Review on "Psychoanalytic Group Dynamics." S. Scheidlinger, ed., *Journal of the American Academy of Psychoanalysis* 10(4)632–635.

Wolf, A. and I. L. Kutash. 1984. "Psychoanalysis in Groups: Creativity in Di-Egophrenia." *Group* 1(1):12–22. New York: Bruner/Mazel.

Wolf, A. and I. L. Kutash. 1984. "Psychoanalysis in Groups: Dealing with the Difficult Patients." In H. Strean, ed., *Psychoanalytic Approaches to the Resistant and Difficult Patient*, pp. 107–127. New York: Haworth Press.

Wolf, A. and I. L. Kutash. 1985. "Di-Egophrenia and Its Treatment Through Psychoanalysis in Groups." *International Journal of Group Psychotherapy* 35(4).

Wolf, A. and I. L. Kutash. 1988. "Treating Creative Di-Egophrenics in Psychoanalysis in Groups." In N. Slavinska-Holy, ed., *Borderline and Narcissistic Patients in Therapy*. New York: International Universities Press.

Wolf, A. and I. L. Kutash. 1989. "Psychoanalysis in Groups: Dealing with Resistance." *The Group Psychotherapist* 2(1).

Wolf, A. and E. K. Schwartz. 1959. "Psychoanalysis In Groups: Clinical and Theoretic Implications of the Alternate Meeting." *Acta Psychotherapy* 7(Suppl.):540–573.

Wolf, A. and E. K. Schwartz. 1960. "Psychoanalysis in Groups: The Alternate Session." *American Imago* 17:101–108.

Wolf, A. and E. K. Schwartz. 1962. *Psychoanalysis in Groups*. New York: Grune & Stratton.

Wolf, A. and E. K. Schwartz. 1971. "Psychoanalysis in Group." In H. I. Kaplan and B. J. Sadock, eds., *Comprehensive Group Psychotherapy*. Baltimore: Williams & Wilkins.

Wolf, A. et al. 1970. *Beyond the Couch: Dialogues in Teaching and Learning Psychoanalysis in Groups*. New York. Science House.

Wolfe, J. L. 1974. *Rational-Emotive Therapy and Women's Assertiveness Training*. Cassette recording. New York: Institute for Rational-Emotive Therapy.

Wolpe, J. 1969. *The Practice of Behavior Therapy*. London: Pergamon Press.

Wolpe, J. 1982. *The Practice of Behavior Therapy*. 3d ed. New York: Pergamon Press.

Yalom, I. 1970. *The Theory and Practice of Group Psychotherapy*. New York Basic Books.

Yalom, I. 1975. *The Theory and Practice of Group Psychotherapy*. 2d ed. New York: Basic Books.

Yalom, I. 1980. *Existential Psychotherapy*. New York: Basic Books.

Yalom, I. 1985. *The Theory and Technique of Group Psychotherapy*. 3d ed. New York: Basic Books.

Young, H. S. 1974. *A Rational Counseling Primer*. New York: Institute for Rational-Emotive Therapy.

Index